C.G. Jung and Nikolai Berdyaev: Individuation and the Person

This book explores C. G. Jung's psychology through the perspective of the existential philosopher Nikolai Berdyaev, drawing striking parallels between Jung's theory of individuation and Berdyaev's understanding of the person.

Placing Jung and Berdyaev firmly within the context of secular humanism, Nicolaus draws on their personal experiences of individuation to show how both writers seek to enable a renewal of our self-understanding as persons in a post-religious society.

Topics of discussion include:

- the foundations of Berdyaev's personalism
- Jung's psychological interpretation of the Christian God-image
- individuation and the ethics of creativity.

C.G. Jung and Nikolai Berdyaev: Individuation and the Person offers a fresh perspective on the ethical implications of Jung's theory and serves also as an introduction to Berdyaev's thought. As such this book will appeal to analytical psychologists, scholars engaged with Jungian thought and all those interested in the interface between spirituality and depth psychology.

Georg Nicolaus is a UKCP registered psychotherapist in private practice. He has studied philosophy in Munich and has a PhD in Psychoanalytic Studies from the Centre for Psychoanalytic Studies at the University of Essex.

C.G. Jung and Nikolai Berdyaev: Individuation and the Person

A critical comparison

Georg Nicolaus

Routledge
Taylor & Francis Group
LONDON AND NEW YORK

First published 2011
by Routledge
27 Church Road, Hove, East Sussex BN3 2FA

Simultaneously published in the USA and Canada
by Routledge
711 Third Avenue, New York NY 10017 (8th Floor)

Routledge is an imprint of the Taylor & Francis Group, an Informa business

Typeset in Times by
RefineCatch Limited, Bungay, Suffolk

Paperback cover design by Design Deluxe, Bath, UK

Front cover images: Carl Gustav Jung © Bettmann/CORBIS;
Nikolai Berdyaev © Hulton-Deutsch/CORBIS

British Library Cataloguing in Publication Data
A catalogue record for this book is available from the British Library

Library of Congress Cataloging-in-Publication Data
Nicolaus, Georg, 1962–
C.G. Jung and Nikolai Berdyaev : individuation and the person : a critical comparison / Georg Nicolaus.
p. cm.
Includes bibliographical references.
ISBN: 978–0–415–49315–4 (hbk)—ISBN: 978–0–415–49316–1 (pbk) 1. Individuation (Psychology) 2. Individuation (Philosophy) 3. Jung, C.G. (Carl Gustav), 1875–1961. 4. Berdiaev, Nikolai, 1874–1948. I. Title.
BF175.5.153N53 2010
150.19'54092—dc22

2010002190

ISBN: 978–0–415–49315–4 (hbk)
ISBN: 978–0–415–49316–1 (pbk)

For Zenobie

Contents

Figures

Preface

This book has grown in stages. Initially it took shape in the course of my personal journey in my Jungian analysis. This eventually led to the writing of a PhD thesis that was accepted by the Centre for Psychoanalytic Studies at the University of Essex in 2008. The initial focus was on exploring the correspondences between Jung's psychology and the kind of understanding of the person that has taken shape within the relatively unknown world of eastern Orthodoxy as it finds expression in Nikolai Berydaev's thought. It became increasingly clear that more and more of the broader context of Christianity and its relationship to our contemporary secular mentality had to be included. The end result of this process remains a fragment, an essay. Considering the vastness of the subject it cannot be otherwise.

Acknowledgements

I would like to thank the following people for contributing in one way or another to the writing of this book: Zenobie, for her loving support and her infinite patience. Renos Papadopoulos for his continued encouragement, generous support and valuable advice. Eric Hutchison, who sadly passed away recently. Dagmar, for introducing me to Berdyaev long ago and for so much else. Roger, for his invaluable friendship and support. Nikolai Sakharov, Andrew Samuels, Roderick Main and Andrew Louth for their valuable feedback; Chris Robertson, Robert Sardello, Michael Whan and Mikhail Epstein for their input, both direct and indirect. My thanks also to Kate Hawes, Jane Harris and Sarah Gibson for their editorial support.

Permissions acknowledgements

Grateful acknowledgement for permission to reprint is made to Taylor & Francis Books and Princeton University Press, excerpts from *Collected Works of C.G. Jung*; Murray Stein; and Inner City books. Excerpts from *Eye to Eye*, by Ken Wilber, © 1983 by Ken Wilber, were reprinted by arrangement with Shambhala Publications Inc., Boston, MA., Texas A&M University Press. Excerpts from *Ego and Archetype*, by Edward F. Edinger, © 1972 by the C. G. Jung Foundation for Analytical Psychology, were reprinted by arrangement with Shambhala Publications Inc., Boston, MA. Excerpts from *Jung in Context* by Peter Homans were reprinted by arrangement with University of Chicago Press. Excerpts from *Elements of Faith* by C. Yannaras were reprinted by arrangement with T&T Clark/Continuum Books. Excerpts from *Paths to the Heart* were reprinted by arrangement with World Wisdom books. Excerpts from *Saving the Appearances*, © 1988 by Owen Barfield, were reprinted by permission of Wesleyan University Press. Excerpts from E. Edinger, © 1985, *Anatomy of the Psyche*, were reprinted by permission of Open Court Publishing Company, a division of Carus Publishing Company, Peru, IL. *Historischer Worterbuch der Philosophie* © 1971, Spalte 365; Felix Meiner Verlag Gmbh; *Psychologie der Weltanschauungen*. Jaspers, Karl 6. Aufl. © 1971. Nachdruck, 1989, Springer Verlag; Frommann-Holzboog

Verlag; Ann Conrad Lammers, *In God's Shadow*, published by Paulist Press, Mahwah, NJ 1994. Used with permission; *The Golden Game* © 1988 Thames and Hudson Ltd; Charles Taylor, *Hegel* © 1975 Cambridge University Press; Charles Taylor © 1989 Cambridge University Press; Spring Publications; Lindisfarne Press; SUNY Press; Guetersloher Verlagshaus; Gnosis des Christentums, Koepgen, G. © Spee-Buchverlag Gmbh Trier; Die Russische Idee, Th. Spidlik © 2002 Verlag 'Der Christliche Osten'; St. Vladimir's Seminary Press; V. Turner, J. P. Hall; Wissenschaftliche Verlagsgesellschaft Darmstadt; Novalis Verlag.

Foreword

At the outset, I wish to say clearly that this is an exceptionally important book and I feel privileged to have been asked to write this foreword. The book dares to address the notion of the person, a subject matter that is both thorny and trite, but it does so with freshness, clarity and remarkably new insights in a way that, without undue justification, could be characterized as groundbreaking.

The way we understand the human subject as a person has undergone tumultuous transformations in our postmodern world, with personhood being subjected to all kinds of theorizations, trivializations, jibes and dismissive attacks. In this book Dr Nicolaus has the courage to return to seemingly old-fashioned themes about the person, arguing, with humble conviction, that the person remains central to our understanding of our humanity today. The book focuses on an exploration of the spiritual dimension from a unique perspective, away from current trendy positions, and with a sound grasp of relevant facets of psychology, philosophy, psychoanalysis and theology. This treatise develops an original line of enquiry that investigates the interrelationship between the person and the soul within the context of lived experience. It is within this framework that the innovative comparison between the ideas of Berdyaev and Jung are located. In doing this, the book also redefines the way Jungian psychology is connected with the spiritual dimension and the way Berdyaev's approach connects with the psychological dimension. More specifically, it brings out the relevance of Berdyaev's ethics of creativity in providing a new understanding of the ethical dimensions of Jung's psychology of individuation. In effect, despite the author's modest claims, this book succeeds in articulating a fairly radical re-reading of the Jungian approach to the spiritual, away from the well-trodden paths.

It is difficult to fit the work of Nikolai Berdyaev into any neat category. The label that was used most frequently to characterize him was that of an 'existential Christian philosopher' but, as this book suggests, his voice is equally relevant to psychology and psychoanalysis and it also constitutes a uniquely original commentary on the very nature of the person in our postmodern world, especially in relation to spirituality.

Comparing and contrasting Jung and Berdyaev represents an unusual and a rather bold undertaking. It succeeds because of the author's thorough knowledge of his field, the specific type of hermeneutical methodology he chooses to employ, the explicit rationale he develops for such a comparison and, ultimately, because of his own sensitivity and respect for the two thinkers he studies. The depth of Dr Nicolaus' understanding of both Jung and Berdyaev gives the reader the feeling that he can anticipate their reactions to every nuance of any debate.

This book is a product of outstanding scholarship and is exemplary in its use of comparative methodology, relating psychoanalysis to spirituality without subsuming either one under the other. It has the potential of becoming a classic and it will be invaluable not only to academics and students but also to all serious readers who wish to delve into the mysteries of the person in our time.

Finally, a special commendation needs to be made about the unusually fine language of this book. Despite the complexity of the topics covered and arguments advanced, the book is well written, with clarity, simplicity and precision.

Renos K. Papadopoulos
Professor of Analytical Psychology at the Centre for
Psychoanalytic Studies,
University of Essex.

Chapter 1

Introduction

This book explores the relationship between C.G. Jung's psychology of individuation and Nikolai Berdyaev's philosophy of the person, which takes shape as an existential–philosophical interpretation of Christian spirituality. The notion of the person is both central to modern identity and at the same time subjected to a process of dissolution in our postmodern present.

One of the basic assumptions of this book, which some readers might find contentious, is that it is the decline of Christianity as a living spirituality that inevitably leads to a dissolution of personal identity. Jung's notion of individuation, i.e. of becoming a person, is placed in these pages within a perspective in which it is seen as intimately linked with this dimension of western spirituality and its destinies. This linkage implies that I will not be offering a contribution to analytical psychology inasmuch as it understands itself primarily as a neutral, scientific discipline, but to analytical psychology inasmuch as it is concerned with the soul, which cannot be abstracted from its spiritual concerns.

The notion of the person as it will be explored here represents the 'place of interaction' between the psychological and the spiritual dimension. The way in which the spiritual operates in the depths of the western soul is still shaped significantly by its Christian heritage, despite its decline, a fact that Jung recognized clearly. It is for this reason that he devoted so many of his writings to Christianity. My attempt, then, will not be to offer a contribution to contemporary scientific psychological theories of personality but rather to explore this boundary line between psychology and spirituality, which is constitutive for analytical psychology as a psychology with soul.

I have received valuable impulses from Evangelos Christou's essay *The Logos of the Soul* (1976) for the way in which I have conceptualized this interface of the psychological and the spiritual. Christou seeks to develop an epistemological basis for psychology beyond the Cartesian paradigm. Psychology, he argues, cannot proceed by dissecting the psyche into 'faculties' or psychical states. It has to start from the notion of *psychological experience*. Psychological experience designates a realm beyond the Cartesian split of abstract spirit (which in philosophy leads to abstract metaphysics) and an equally abstract empiricism of sense data in science. It constitutes a sphere all of its own, the sphere proper to psychology. We can, he argues

> never get away from the soul. Hence the notion of objectivity, impersonality or abstraction so dear to science is impossible when we introduce the experiencing soul into our picture of the cosmos since every abstraction is also the source of psychological experience.
>
> (Christou 1976: 37)

We will be primarily concerned with the experiencing soul. Our approach will not be scientific in the narrow sense but in a broad hermeneutical sense. Within this hermeneutical approach theology and philosophy will be the subject of this book insofar as they themselves are concerns of the soul as sources of psychological experience. In this sense this book, even though it will contain much theology and philosophy, nevertheless remains primarily psychological. But what will interest us are not the biological, but the spiritual preconditions of the psychological.

Soul as the subject of experience is neither the 'mind' of philosophy nor the 'body' of science. The *subject* of psychological experience itself can be more accurately defined as personality[1]. Using traditional language we could say that personality 'hypostatizes' soul as the originating source of the meaning of psychological experience. It does so not as a 'metaphysical substance' but as a 'unity of acts' (Scheler 1973). It constitutes the unifying, organizing centre of psychological experience by synthesizing it into a meaningful *gestalt*. It is through this activity that human spirituality becomes manifest in the psychological sphere. Interpreted this way, human spirituality is not just a matter of religion. It pervades all aspects of human life.

We ought to carefully distinguish the notion of personality that Christou proposes from a narrow 'Cartesian' subjectivity (and thus also from the 'ego' of depth psychology) on which most modern notions of personality are based:

> The problem of personality only makes sense if we place it into its meaningful context, namely, the meaningful wholeness of the soul. An understanding of the problems of personality therefore will depend on the possibility of formulating psychological experiences, and conversely the possibilities of formulating and interpreting psychological experience are themselves a product of the action of personality.
>
> (ibid.: 77)

In this action of personality human spirituality finds its expression. Christou presents us here with an interesting 'figure-ground' phenomenon. Just as a psychology that is based on a phenomenology of psychological experience needs personality as its 'logos' so personality needs this kind of psychology in order to come into view in a non-reductive fashion. If we can call the Cartesian ego 'literalized' spirit, personality in this deeper sense is deliteralized, and yet nevertheless still personal spirit. We will see that this is precisely the notion of the person, which Berdyaev develops. On these grounds therefore, an interesting complementarity between Jung and Berdyaev may be uncovered. Without soul, spirit remains literal, abstract and lifeless; without spirit, soul remains shapeless and dissolved in unconsciousness. It is this intricate dialectic of the spiritual and the psychological dimensions within the human person with which we will be concerned. I want to suggest that this figure-ground phenomenon could be formulated more clearly by complementing Christou's notion of psychological experience with that of *spiritual experience* and interpreting both as two dimensions of existential experience, which have to be distinguished while nevertheless remaining inseparably united within the actual totality of existential experience. The concrete totality of human experience always includes both of these dimensions.

This experiential totality will be considered in the pages of this book from a Christian perspective because there is not only an accidental but also an essential link between the notion of the *person* and Christian spirituality. It is of course equally possible to opt for a spirituality of depersonalisation, and tendencies in this direction are to be found even within parts of the Christian tradition itself, but if one opts for a spirituality of personalisation, it will tend more or less towards the shape of a Christian spirituality, if the latter is understood in a very universal and broad, non-confessional sense.[2]

How much this type of spirituality is 'programmed' into the spiritual 'DNA' of western man, which is the reason why Jung gives it so much attention, can be demonstrated by one example: the general declaration of human rights by the General Assembly of the United Nations affirms in its preamble its 'faith in the dignity and worth of the person' (cited from Kobusch 1997: 11, trans.). This goes to show how the whole trajectory of secularization is still implicitly shaped by this spirituality. The German philosopher Theo Kobusch has put forward on these grounds the thesis that we are not actually living in an age that is hostile to metaphysics but only to a specific type of metaphysics 'which is different from the metaphysics of the person, which can also be called a metaphysics of freedom' (ibid.: 12). This metaphysics of freedom is identified by Berdyaev very clearly as originating within Christianity and coming to full unfoldment only in modern thought, especially in Kant.

I will want to both reconnect the notion of the person to its origins within Christian spirituality and also examine how this notion of the person and the spirituality belonging to it are 're-visioned' in Jung's and Berdyaev's thought in line with our new post-religious predicament. So what exactly is meant here by 'Christian spirituality' and how does it relate to the notion of personality? In this introduction I will want to pick out just one central element that will be important to us. Berdyaev's particular understanding of Christianity is both specifically modern (perhaps in some ways even postmodern) and at the same time deeply rooted in the mystical tradition of eastern Christianity and Jacob Boehme's theosophy. All forms of more mystically oriented Christian spirituality have always been centred on the theme of a spiritual rebirth. I initially was intending to use the biblical expression 'the inner man of the heart' (taken from 1 Pet.: 3, 4 and Rom. 7: 22) as a title because it alludes to the distinction of the inner and outer man common to the mystical tradition. The inner man, or the true person, is initially hidden, unconscious. It does not manifest automatically in the developmental process. Only by passing through a process of spiritual rebirth do we truly become a person in the full sense of the word. This birth of the new man/woman implies the death of the old. We will follow this process of death and rebirth on both the personal and the collective level. Jung interprets Christianity as a form of the myth of the dying and resurrecting, i.e. the *transforming*, God. This allows him to link up his interpretation of Christianity closely with the contemporary predicament, a stratagem equally employed in recent postmodern thinking.

This process of death and rebirth has also found symbolic expression in the alchemical imagination that flourished in the early Renaissance. Especially (but by no means only) in Jacob Boehme's Christian theosophy does this classical theme of the Christian mystical tradition become enriched with the alchemical imagination. Alchemy introduces a volatile ferment into Christian symbolism, enriching it with new complexities for modern souls. And Jung's own psychological–alchemical interpretation of Christianity seek a renewal of the meaning of Christian symbols by offering a psychological interpretation of this alchemical imagination in the light of the process of individuation through which one becomes a person in the full sense. If we make the attempt to understand Jung's psychology as a psychology of the person it will therefore appear primarily within the following developmental line: Christian mysticism, alchemy, its psychological interpretation, which latter in turn enables a new, specifically psychological appropriation of Christian symbols with the aim of the renewal of the central concern of Christian spirituality – the 'second birth'. Jung offers a psychological perspective, which puts the whole of Christianity in a new light, a *psychological* light.

Berdyaev's thought, on the other hand, gives expression to the shape that such a renewed Christian spirituality *as spirituality* could take. While we will soon see that there are therefore significant tensions between Jung's *psychological* and Berdyaev's *spiritual* perspectives, a wealth of striking resonances and correspondences can nevertheless be found between their views. These resonances stem from the shared focus of both writers on the *experiential* dimension of the process of the 'second birth' as a starting point for their reinterpretation of Christian symbols in the light of the changed psychological/spiritual situation of contemporary man/woman.

What Jung and Berdyaev share is that they present us with a reinterpretation of Christianity which has passed through the dissolution of the Christian God-image in modernity. Both of them have studied Nietzsche with an equally acute awareness of his importance. Neither of them writes for those who still possess an intact traditional, confessionally bound ecclesiastic faith, which has (apparently) managed to remain unaffected by these historical processes.

Michel Foucault famously declared the Death of Man after the Death of God had already been declared by Friedrich Nietzsche. There is an inevitability about this development. Jung alludes to this inevitability when he writes in *Aion*: 'The destruction of the God-image is followed by the annulment of the human personality' (Jung 1951: para. 170). But unlike contemporary postmodern philosophers and a growing number of post-Jungians who are unhappy with concepts like 'Self' and 'individuation' and prefer a 'polytheism of the psyche' to the (supposedly) rigid 'monotheism of the Self', I want to interpret Jung on the basis of the assumption that he himself was essentially trying to restore the lost integrity to the human personality by restoring psychological vitality to the Christian symbols through developing them further.

I do not want to deny that other equally valid interpretations of Jung's psychology are possible. But, granted the relative validity of this basic hermeneutic starting point, I want to suggest that these Christian symbols can then be seen in Jungian terms, as the 'archetypal matrix of human personhood'. Jung, in this perspective, does not simply want to restore them but rather attempts their further development in the direction of a heightened emphasis on the feminine archetype of the *sapientia dei* or *Sophia* as it appears in the alchemical imagination. This shift in emphasis indicates a shift from abstract 'patriarchal' spirituality towards a grounding and appropriation of spirituality in and through psychological consciousness. It seeks to formulate a new understanding of spirituality for contemporary man. His late conception of the *unus mundus* offers a powerful corrective to modern individualism based on a defunct Cartesian paradigm. Thus Jung's psychology both dissolves modern individualism and also reconstitutes something analogous to Christian personalism within the changed framework of his psychology of individuation. We will see, though, that this changed framework implies an 'appreciative transcendence' (Dourley 2001) of Christianity, which shows itself to be the living enactment of the myth of the transforming God.

Jung may in this way have anticipated contemporary trends. The growing interest at the present time in the archetypal figure of *Sophia* and the emergence of an emphasis on feminine wisdom and its ecological vision of interdependence and a compassionate concern for the neglected minorities may be indicative of a move beyond the more caustic relativism of postmodernism. There is an emerging awareness that we need a more feminine, flowing, tolerant, open and ecologically minded sense of spiritual values. Deconstruction for its own sake has reached a dead end, however useful it may have been. More recently even postmodern philosophers themselves have shown a renewed interest in Christianity[3]. Perhaps this shows that we are slowly moving towards a new openness and humility in considering anew the classical themes of spirituality, which, according to the philosopher of culture Mikhail Epstein, was already anticipated by Berdyaev in his essay The New Middle Ages (1933: 67–119)[4].

Berdyaev attempts a development of Christian symbols that is parallel to Jung's in order to give a place to human freedom and creativity in the sphere of Christian spirituality. Much of free creative self-expression, which ought to have been given a spiritual–religious meaning, had to emigrate out of the domain of ecclesiastic Christianity into the secular sphere, even though it had its origin within it. Both of these elements which Jung and Berdyaev address, that of *soul* and that of *human freedom and creative self-expression*, could not be fully accommodated within traditional Christianity and as a consequence found a home in the 'pagan' rebellion since the Renaissance and its progressive push towards secularisation. The spirituality that had initially been shaped by ecclesiastic Christianity has burst its container and has in turn given shape to the underlying meaning-structures of modern secular society. Jung and Berdyaev share an awareness of these underlying historical dynamics.

We have learned and are still learning very bitter lessons about the link between claims of absolute truth and violence. For good reasons contemporary thinkers are more or less unanimous in their suspicion towards all 'meta-narratives' which end up justifying the violation of individual freedoms. Any return to a serious consideration of spirituality will have to remain mindful of this persistent danger. Jung's psychology offers an abundant wealth of insights about the need for remaining consistently mindful of the ways in which the shadow operates most forcefully where the light shines most strongly. But a convincing argument could be made for claiming that at present we are paying the price for the repression of religion and spirituality that occurred as a reaction to their destructive sides. In the absence of a spiritual culture the return of repressed spirituality takes destructive forms. Spirituality, by being repressed, does not disappear but mutates into more atavistic forms. This shadow side of spirituality should not make us shy away from it but on the contrary motivate us to find a way to give it a new place in our contemporary culture, a way which does not jettison the liberating gains of secular modernity.

There is no doubt that Jung's psychology has a significant role to play in this process. But in order to play this role effectively, the debate on its problematic relationship to Christian spirituality (and indeed spirituality in general) has to be sustained and refined in a constructive way. Berdyaev in particular and the representatives of Russian religious thought in general can perhaps serve as bridge-builders to carry further the failed collaborative attempt which Jung made with Victor White (see Lammers 1994, and Lammers and Cunningham 2007).

It was Henry Corbin, to my knowledge, who was the first one to notice a deep resonance between the Russian personalist thinkers and Jung with reference to what he calls Jung's 'sophiology'. In his deeply sympathetic review of Jung's *Answer to Job* (1952/1967) he interprets this work of Jung as an 'extraordinary phenomenology of the sophianic religion' (Corbin 1984: 266, trans.). This book, he continues, is an extraordinary testimony of a 'single individual' proclaiming a prophetic vision and its strange appeal will be truly understood only by those 'single ones' who followed Kierkegaard's invitation to the 'adventure of subjectivity as truth' (ibid.: 267). Those 'single ones' are essentially modern people who have irretrievably fallen out of the safety net of collective religion and traditional value systems and cannot see a way back but only forward to recover a lasting sense of values. Next to Kierkegaard

> there was the voice of Father Sergius Bulgakov, herald of Sophia and of sophianic thought, which, together with that of Nicolas Berdyaev, rediscovered the secrets of a tradition which had been unjustly neglected . . . Those which have . . . heard this voice will, without doubt be most receptive to Jung's message which will not become for them . . . a cause for scandal.
>
> (ibid.: 267)

There is, Corbin believes, a 'symphonic relation which we can perceive between Father Bulgakov's sophiology and what we might call Jung's sophiology' (ibid.: 287) and this applies, I believe, possibly even more to Berdyaev's thought.

My approach will be, in a broad sense, hermeneutical. This means that I will want to place Jung's psychology within a broad historical context and interpret it primarily as a form of 'culture-making', as Peter Homans (1995) called it. More strongly put, I will want to read Jung's psychology, following Corbin's lead, *as if* it were a religious philosophy akin to that of Berdyaev. Clearly this is not the case. At least Jung wanted his psychology to be understood as a science. But the way it has taken effect as a very successful form of culture-making highlights the fact that it certainly also contains this dimension. The '*as if*' then is the device needed to bring out this dimension forcefully, to place it under a magnifying glass, so to speak, and to explore Jung's implicit 'philosophical–religious' assumptions in the light of Berdyaev's thought. Jung's psychology is propelled by an inner logic towards becoming a 'psychological religion'. Berdyaev's philosophy allows a critical and yet sympathetic analysis and assessment of this tendency inherent in Jung's thought as it unfolds.

Two themes that Homans identifies as highly significant for Jung's work can be mentioned here. Both thinkers, so I will want to claim, want to provide a solution to the characteristic modern predicament: the depersonalization and atomization of modern man, his dissolution into mass society. The second related theme, which provides the most important context for the explorations in this book, has already been mentioned. It concerns the end of traditional religion, the 'death of God' in modern society. Homans interprets depth psychology in this context as 'a creative response to "the past that we have lost" ' (Homans 1995: xiiv). He posits that this creative response can be seen to have the following general pattern: 'Symbolic loss→mourning→redefinition of self→creation of meaning (individuation)'(ibid.: xiix).

Depth psychology as a specific form of creation of meaning – this is what I understand by the 'existential–philosophical' dimension of Jung's psychology. In some form or other, so Homans claims, 'all the originative psychologists believed that their theories reinterpreted western religion or even replaced it entirely' (ibid.: 15). But, as is easily evident, this applies especially to Jung's writings:

> Jung's writings, both autobiographical and formal, provide the most detailed sympathetic account I have found in modern history of the struggle of an individual who was unable to accept the Christianity in which he was reared but at the same time unwilling to let it completely pass him by.
>
> (ibid.: 196)

From the cauldron of this struggle emerges Jung's own creative response to 'the past we have lost', which can be understood as a religious vision for contemporary 'psychological man' (ibid.: 3).

We see Berdyaev struggling with very similar issues. His philosophy presents itself as a creative reinterpretation of Christianity in much the same way as Jung's psychology. For both thinkers what is at stake concerns the existential core of modern man. The concern is far from abstract. It is vitally existential. Unwilling to abandon Christianity Berdyaev cannot accept it in its traditional form:

> I have come to Christ through liberty and through intimate experience of the paths of freedom. My Christian faith is not a faith based on habit or tradition. It was born through the experience of the inner life of a most painful character . . . Freedom has brought me to Christ and I know of no other path leading to Him. Nor am I the only one who has passed through this experience. No one who has left Christianity based on authority can return to anything but a Christianity which is free . . . Those who have come to Christianity through freedom bring to it that same spirit of liberty . . . Those whose religion is authoritarian and hereditary will never understand properly those who have come to religion through freedom.
>
> (Berdyaev 1935a: x)

For Berdyaev, Christianity is above all the religion of love, and that means the religion of freedom and personality, because love presupposes freedom and personality. Freedom and personality are at the same time key themes of modernity. Berdyaev's thought attempts a *coniunctio oppositorum* of a radically understood modernity with an equally radically understood Christianity. Not a compromise, but a more radical form of humanism than modernity dared to give expression to, is his aim.

This centrality of freedom stands in a certain tension to the 'sophianic' focus on interdependence, the deflation of the ego's heroic claims and the recognition of our deep connectedness to the cosmos and the *anima mundi*. Confronting Jung's psychology with Berdyaev's thought means exploring this tension. Due to Berdyaev's close relationship to Russian sophiological thought, these tensions are nevertheless tempered by many points of resonance to Jung. And in the end Berdyaev is closer to Jung than any of the other sophiological thinkers due to his resolute 'modernism', which nevertheless comes with a distinctly Russian flavour. One reason for taking such a broad hermeneutic approach is its usefulness for making sense of this tension within a broad historical perspective, a tension that, I would propose, inherently belongs to the existential experience of personhood.

Jung's focus on soul leads him to want to steer his psychology away from a 'personalistic' understanding of psychology. Taking into account that for Berdyaev, just as for other existential thinkers, freedom and spirit are most intimately linked we can sum up an important aspect of Jung's uneasiness with a 'personalistic' psychology by saying that he finds it too one-sidedly spiritualistic. It leads to a spirituality of the heroic ego, which lacks soul. This becomes evident from a passage in his letter to John Trinick about his book *The Fire-Tried Stone* (1967), which Trinick sent to Jung in manuscript form.

Trinick's book points in the direction that the 'personalistic' interpretation of Jung's psychology attempted here will take. My intention will not be to inject into Jung's psychology a good dose of Rogerian 'person-centeredness' or for that matter Sartrean existentialist sombreness. Trinick is an alchemist of sorts. He conceived this book as a sort of 'companion volume' to Jung's *Mysterium Coniunctionis* (1955/56) for which he has the highest praise: 'Dr Jung's study *Mysterium Coniunctionis* must take rank as one of the great spiritual documents of this age' (Trinick 1967: 132). Jung for his part thought of Trinick as 'one of the rare alchemists of our time' (letter to Trinick from A. Jaffé, ibid.: 12). About his book, Jung wrote to Trinick: 'Your opus ought to be published, as it is a link in the Aurea Catena reaching through twenty centuries down to our benighted present' (ibid.: 11).

Trinick establishes in his book a very close link between Berdyaev's thought and Jung's psychology, in particular his magnum opus *Mysterium Coniunctionis*. In another letter to Trinick Jung comments in passing on Berdyaev. The relevant passage deserves to be quoted in full as it is to my knowledge Jung's only reference to Berdyaev:

> The 'way' is not an upward going straight line f.i. from Earth to Heaven or from matter to Spirit, but rather a circumambulatio of and an approximation to the Centrum. We are not liberated by leaving something behind, but only by fulfilling our task as mixta composita i.e. human beings between the opposites. The spiritualism of a Berdjajew and others is only the contrary of materialism, one half of the truth. There is not God alone, but also his creation. Materialism denies God, and spiritualism denies creation, i.e. the will of God in Christian terminology. 'Homo Sapiens' has to envisage both. That was the great discovery of 'Mater Alchimia'.
>
> (Jung 1976: 396)

In other words, a psychology of the person easily turns out to be 'one-sidedly spiritualistic' as can be witnessed in some of the developments within humanistic psychology and the 'human potential movement'. But even the more sombre Sartre-inspired forms of existential psychology may be said, from Jung's perspective, to be too much engrossed by the idea of human freedom, thereby forgetting the opposite, the extent of our determination by the maternal earth-ground of the unconscious, the 'Great Mother'.

What sort of connection then does Trinick establish between Jung and Berdyaev and what is its relevance for us? In his book, Trinick develops one central idea. He traces the development of the symbol of the *Coniunctio* through its transformations in alchemy up until the time of Jung's *Mysterium Coniunctionis*. Trinick sees in this historical process a continued development and transmutation of the symbol itself, in which a 'transfiguration of the symbol into its truth (i.e. into the thing signified)' (Trinick 1967: 13) is finally reached.

What the most significant alchemists achieved in their inner consciousness, the lapis, 'was none other than the *Mysterium Coniunctionis*', which signifies 'the mystery of that "round", or "globed" being which Plato adumbrated . . . in the *Symposium*' (ibid.: 88), i.e. the *androgyne*. This symbol lived on in the imagination of poets like Blake and Novalis and philosophers like Baader and Soloviev, and found 'something like an apotheosis . . . in the thought of Nicolas Berdyaev' (ibid.:125).

In Berdyaev's thought, this symbol reaches its 'transfiguration into its truth': it becomes full existential reality in the fully humanised form of a 'dynamic conjunction . . . of two completely differentiated beings of opposite sex' (ibid.: 130). Jung's *Mysterium Coniunctionis*, for Trinick, is ultimately a kind of 'summa' of this mystery, one that masterly gathers together all material and brings 'into the full light of consciousness . . . the obscure roots of this most vital and central of all human verities' (ibid.: 132).

A central thread in Trinick's line of thought is that alchemy in the course of its development shows 'a marked feature of the humanizing process' (ibid.: 16) of the coniunctio symbol. 'If alchemistical philosophy was from the first an empirical philosophy, there was a time, towards its end, when it became most of all an existential philosophy' (ibid.: 86). This is how its central images live on in the imagination of such unorthodox Christian thinkers as Baader, Blake, Novalis, Soloviev and finally Berdyaev. They are now images of the deep mysteries of human existence, not any more of natural substances. These thinkers prepare the ground for a much broader vision of Christianity, which includes the sacredness of the erotic dimension, a 'secular' sphere of life that now becomes the place for a spiritual rebirth of the person in its integrated wholeness.

But the erotic sphere, which Trinick focuses on specifically, is just one aspect of such a broadening into the 'secular'. Berdyaev's philosophy contains other dimensions that are at least equally important, most notably his ethics of creativity. The general motif of the *coniunctio oppositorum* runs through all of Berdyaev's thought on the person. I hope to show in this book that a closer study of Berdyaev's philosophy will not only further substantiate the connection Trinick established between Jung and Berdyaev but also show Jung's criticism to be unjustified. Like Jung's psychology, Berdyaev's existential philosophy of the person itself also amounts to a 'circumambulatio and an approximation of the centrum', not to a 'one-sided spiritualism' to which materialism forms the other side

Nevertheless, Berdyaev's philosophy does also offer a way of critically interpreting Jung's psychology of individuation that puts some of its central theses into a different light. Berdyaev considers freedom as the 'fourth dimension', which breaks out of the closed circle of psychologism. His thought allows for a reading of depth psychology that explores the subtleties of the interaction of the spiritual and the psychological. In this way Trinick's focus on the erotic relationship will be replaced here by an exploration of the relationship between soul and spirit within the person. The two themes are not unrelated, and the same symbolism can be employed for both.

I shall begin by offering an overview of Berdyaev's life because his philosophy has grown out of his life experience and is inseparable from it (Chapter 2). It will also be necessary to offer an introduction into Berdyaev's philosophy, which I will want to present as the living expression of his own individuation process, intended to stimulate an inner revolution in others. At the same time I will also be filling in the picture I began to paint in this introduction concerning the shift towards secularization by looking at the development of an 'anthropological' focus in modernity which owes much to Kant (Chapter 3). An initial comparison of Jung's and Berdyaev's understandings of the person will help to bring out both their striking similarities as well as their equally evident tensions (Chapter 4). One way of describing these tensions is that they amount to a different understanding of the way in which fundamental polarities operate within the total person. To use Erich Neumann's expressions, Jung's alchemical view is founded in the 'mysteries of the feminine' while Berdyaev's existential dialectics are founded in the 'mysteries of the masculine'. As Neumann remarks, 'the two are complementary, and it is only taken together that they yield an approach to the whole truth of the mystery' (Neumann 1971: 149).

But before we can explore their potential harmonization we will first have to go to the root of the tension between Jung and Berdyaev. I will want to propose that this root is in part epistemological. It originates in the use that Jung makes of Kant's epistemology to give a 'philosophical–epistemological' foundation to his psychology. This will be explored in Chapter 5. Kant is maybe even more important for Berdyaev, but the use he makes of his philosophy is strikingly and revealingly different from Jung's. I will want to suggest that Berdyaev's interpretation of Kant opens a way out of what otherwise would remain Jung's 'psychologistic immanentism'. While it is certainly true that Jung moves resolutely beyond a narrow psychologism, I will want to suggest that it is the fateful consequence of his particular form of Kantianism that his psychology ends up potentially (not necessarily) distorting the dimension of human spirituality.

Chapter 6 will offer an in-depth exploration of Jung's and Berdyaev's understanding of Christian revelation, which forms the 'transpersonal' basis for their understanding of the person. Here we will see how the different epistemological foundations find their development in the form of two very different and yet related ways of re-imagining the Christian symbols, i.e. the Trinitarian and the Christological Dogma. If Jung's psychological interpretation of Christian symbols is not to end up as a new 'psychological religion' it is maybe to an approach like Berdyaev's that we need to look as a corrective to this tendency. Berdyaev seeks an interiorization and spiritualization of Christian symbols, which can profit as much from a psychologically refined understanding as this psychological perspective can profit from Berdyaev's 'pneumatology'.

Chapter 7 is perhaps the most important, with the preceding chapters having served to prepare the ground. It will try to offer a comparative analysis of Berdyaev's 'ethics of creativity' with Jung's 'ethics of individuation'. Berdyaev's ethics of creativity is perhaps the most significant potential contribution to Jung's psychology. But for its proper understanding the preceding chapters are a necessary preparation. We will see in Chapter 6 that both Jung and Berdyaev follow a Joachite scheme[5] in which the 'age of the Father', the Old Testament religion of the law, is surpassed by the 'age of the Son', i.e. historical Christianity to be similarly 'sublated' by the new 'religion of the Spirit' in the 'age of the Holy Spirit'. To this new 'aeon of the Spirit' belongs a new form of ethics, the ethics of creativeness in Berdyaev's perspective and the ethics underpinning the process of individuation in Jung's case. Both of these ethical positions come into being within the specific 'religious' context which both thinkers unfold. And this context in turn is shaped by their epistemological assumptions, which in their turn flow from their experience of the individuation process as it crystallizes in their understanding of the person.

The central issue in Chapter 7, which will be explored further in the concluding chapter, will be the problem of good and evil and the issue of the 'privatio boni', over which Jung fell out with Victor White. I hope to show that Berdyaev's religious philosophy offers perhaps the best possibility to create the sort of bridge which Jung and White failed to build. This bridge will, as we shall see, have a lot to do with refining the notion of a new style of consciousness as it develops through the transcendent function by using Jean Gebser's[6] notion of integral consciousness. I believe that this allows us to push open a door which Jung the Kantian seems to have been intent on shutting firmly, but Jung the intuitive knower of souls has left if not opened, then ajar.

Chapter 2

Berdyaev's life

Figure 2.1 Portrait of Nikolai Berdyaev in Paris towards the end of his life.

As most readers will not be familiar with Berdyaev, I want to begin, in addition to offering some biographical details, by conveying a flavour of his personality. The French writer Madeleine Davy, who knew him personally, gives us a particularly vivid description of her impression of Berdyaev:

> Tall, of athletic stature, although fragile, a subtle dignity emanated from his personality. Nothing was vulgar with him or the least bit banal. When one listened to him, his sonorous voice awakened the best in oneself. His sheer presence drew one beyond one's limitations, communicated a new dynamism to the spirit and modified the rhythm of time. Everything received a new clarity. . . . When one was with him one forgot oneself and savoured a strange joy . . . Something became alive . . . to use an expression of Novalis, it seems possible to say that it was the 'divine child' in oneself that moved.
>
> (Davy 1991: 74, trans.)

Berdyaev wrote an autobiography, which is one of his most readable books. Similar to Jung's *Memories, Dreams, Reflections* (1995) it is not so much a factual account but rather a portrait of his journey of individuation in its intimate connection with world events. Neither in his autobiography nor in any of Berdyaev's other writings does one feel any gulf between life and thought, so much so that Berdyaev writes: 'When I think about my life I am led to the conclusion that it has not been the life of a philosopher in the current sense of the word . . . I was always aware of its irrational and unpredictable nature' (Berdyaev 1950: xiii). It is this awareness of the irrational that makes Berdyaev's thinking so rich in psychological insight.

Berdyaev was born near Kiev in 1874 when vague forebodings of the collapse of Tsarist Russia were already in the air. He was imprisoned twice, lived through two revolutions and the First and Second World Wars, and spent the second half of his life in forced exile in Paris. As a consequence, all his thought is marked by an acute awareness of volcanic energies always looming close to the surface of the seemingly solid ground of bourgeois existence, ready to erupt at any moment. The opening sentences of his philosophical autobiography convey to us this mood of soul. Berdyaev never felt at home in the world:

> The first response to the world of a creature who is born into it is of immense significance. I cannot remember my first cry on encountering the world, but I know for certain that from the very beginning I was aware that I had fallen into an alien realm . . . The consciousness of being rooted in the earth was alien to me, and I was strongly attracted by the Orphic myth concerning the origin of the human soul, which speaks of a falling away of man's spirit from a higher world into a lower.
>
> (Berdyaev 1950: 1)

We get a flavour of the 'gnostic' mood that pervades Berdyaev's philosophy here: the world is an alien realm, the exile of celestial souls.[1] With Berdyaev, we find ourselves in a very different world from Jung's. While Jung experiences a strong bond with the earth, nature and its mysteries, Berdyaev's fundamental intuition is that of a spiritual origin of the human soul, which is 'thrown' into an alien realm. Along with the Heideggerian sense of existential *Angst* in relation to 'this world', for Berdyaev there is an equally vivid sense of the reality of the spiritual. Philosophy is for Berdyaev a way to 'renounce and be relieved of this unspeakable anguish . . . anguish takes its rise in life . . . and drives man towards the transcendent' (ibid.: 44). In Berdyaev's inner world there is a constant fiery clash between darkness and light. Out of the darkness, light is born; such is the creative process that overcomes 'the world'. Creativity is for him 'that very movement towards transcendence and the evocation of the image of the wholly other in relation to this life' (ibid.: 44). It is a response of man's total existence to the facticity of his 'thrownness'.

Berdyaev's rich inner life took shape in a protected but also deeply troubled family environment. His family belonged to the disintegrating Russian nobility. In his ancestry 'inbred aristocracy, inherited mysticism, the best traditions of military valour and ancient chivalry, independence of thought to the point of agnosticism' (Lawrie 1960: 13) mingled. This imbued him with a strong, rebellious dislike of control by external authority and an ethos of 'spiritual chivalry'.

His father came from Russian nobility with a long military tradition. He was a freethinker who liked Voltaire and used to make jokes about the Bible at the dinner table to the dismay of his French Catholic mother. But her religious inclinations did not go very deep either. Berdyaev made his way towards Christianity only much later, without the sort of baggage which Jung had to carry from his pastoral home. On his mother's side of French origin 'there was scarcely an ancestor without a title, count or prince or even king' (ibid.: 13). Once again, typical for Berdyaev, he writes: 'I was never conscious of belonging to my parents . . . the ties of blood . . . evoked a strange aversion in me' (Berdyaev 1950: 1). As a student he would rebel against his noble descent and join the social revolutionaries, who sought to overthrow the old order. He was 'unable to recognize true aristocracy, the aristocracy of the spirit' (ibid.: 19) in the aristocratic society to which he belonged. His sympathies were with the misfits of society. He became and remained for all of his life a socialist who at the same time believed in an 'aristocracy of the spirit'.

Berdyaev had one brother, 15 years older than him, who had serious psychological problems and eventually had to be hospitalized. He spent his childhood in Kiev, essentially growing up as a single child, left very much to his own devices, fiercely defending his independence even as a little boy. His room was his kingdom, which nobody was allowed to enter. Illness, neurotic tendencies and outbursts of violent rage were common in the Berdyaev household. Berdyaev himself had a lifelong tendency to fall into rages, and he suffered from hypochondria and a nervous tic all his life. All of this contributed not only to a vivid sense of the frailty of the human condition but also to an intensely introverted attitude, coloured by a sense of alienation from the surrounding world. He lived in his own inner world. He began to read novels and philosophical books at a very early age. He writes that 'already as a boy I became conscious of my philosophical vocation' (ibid.: 11). He read Kant, Schopenhauer and the novels of Tolstoy and above all Dostoyevsky. Dostoyevsky in particular 'shook his soul' (ibid.: 25). One character of Dostoyevsky's novels he felt a special kinship with was Stavrogin, the revolutionary anarchist from *The Possessed*:

> There was, however, an evil spirit in me, since everyone has, as it were, his positive and his negative 'Other one' within himself. My evil spirit was typified by Stavrogin. When I was a young man people used to call me Stavrogin and I used to relish the identification. I liked being 'the aristocrat of the Revolution' . . . There was, as a matter of fact, something of Stavrogin in me, although I believe I have successfully gotten the better of it . . . It is a sign of ignorance and narrow-mindedness to be surprised at contradictions in man. Man is fundamentally a contradictory being; and this denotes something deeper and more important than any seeming absence of contradiction in him.
>
> (ibid.: 25)

The fiery temperament of the revolutionary remained always alive within him but he was able, for the most part, to contain and transmute its destructiveness.

In 1894, now as many other intellectuals of the time a Marxist, he became a student at Kiev University. He was arrested on several occasions and was finally excluded from the university for taking part in illegal demonstrations. At this time demonstrations and student unrest were the order of the day. He began to make a name for himself as one of the leading intellectuals of the Marxist Movement. In his earliest writings he argued for a non-materialistic interpretation of Marxism, which posits as the foundation of the human social world the dimension of the psychic: 'All social institutions are nothing other than the objectified psyche of man' (Roessler 1956: 13, trans.). Both the material, economic basis and the ideological superstructures ought to be dissolved into the psychic basis as the most fundamental reality. We find here already the beginnings of Berdyaev's later metaphysics of the spirit, which is here still termed the psychic. This is an interesting parallel with Jung, which we will be able to enrich and elaborate as we go along.

Gradually Berdyaev's interpretation of Marxism, which was never materialistic, found itself more and more at odds with the economic materialism of the Marxist orthodoxy. He increasingly rebelled against the collectivism of the movement and 'the problem of the revolution becomes for him the problem of the human personality' (ibid.: 20). After being imprisoned in

1901 by the Tsarist regime he studied philosophy in Heidelberg for a short period, and then immersed himself in the literary and philosophical circles in St. Petersburg, before finally moving back to Moscow. In St. Petersburg and Moscow he had contacts with many Russian intellectuals, including Sergei Bulgakov, Lev Shestov and Dimitri Mereshovsky. In St. Petersburg he immersed himself in the eccentric literary world of the Russian cultural renaissance: 'We saw the glow of a new dawn, and the end of an old age seemed to coincide with a new era, which would bring about a complete transfiguration of life' (Berdyaev 1950: 141). But, as with all such movements he got involved in, Berdyaev soon kept his distance, noting 'unmistakable signs of decadence in the whole movement' (ibid.: 141). He felt that 'Eros held decisive sway over Logos: and this involved above all a disregard, especially painful to me, of the problem of personality and freedom . . . these people were vividly and highly pronounced individualities, but they lacked personality' (ibid.: 155).

In Moscow Berdyaev spent much time with the 'pilgrims, tramps and vagabonds of "Holy Russia" (ibid.: 196). It is characteristic that he felt much greater kinship with these simple, uneducated peasants than with most of the educated intellectuals. He admired their vivid language and imagery, which was 'vigorous and daringly original . . . The whole atmosphere was expressive of a passionate concern and search for truth and a great spiritual and intellectual intensity' (ibid.: 197). Among them he found individuals with the elementary visionary temperament of a Jacob Boehme. These for him were 'the true revolutionaries of Russia, more genuine and ultimately effective than the social and political revolutionaries' (ibid.: 200).

In 1904 Berdyaev entered into a marriage with Lydia Trusheva, but they remained childless. In his autobiography he mostly keeps silent about their relationship but it appears that they did have a very close bond of love. Throughout this time Berdyaev was already publishing his work, as well as editing various philosophical journals, and he founded a 'free academy for spiritual culture' in 1919. He became a promoter of the 'New religious consciousness' which sought a fresh, undogmatic approach to Christianity. In 1916 he published his first magnum opus, entitled *The Meaning of the Creative Act* (1962).

Berdyaev had in the meantime moved from his early sociological interpretation of Marxism to an interpretation of it in the light of Kant's and Fichte's transcendental idealism. Their opposition of being and moral obligation became for him a 'revolutionary idea', a 'symbol of the protest against reality' (Roessler 1956: 24). The fundamental ethical idea founded on this opposition was for Berdyaev that of the personality. To be the eternal protestant against all sheer reality was for Berdyaev, like for Max Scheler,[2] a basic human quality, which marks man as a person. Kant's notion of the personality as an end in itself became for him the guiding principle of revolutionary action. *Spirit* now became for him the truly revolutionary force and this meant that a way had to be sought out of the abstractions of transcendental idealism and into a transcendental realism of the person as a living, concrete spiritual reality. Berdyaev found the means for such a breakthrough in the integral epistemology of Khomyakov, Kireevsky and Soloviev. We will see in the course of this book how this spiritual realism becomes refined into Berdyaev's specific form of Christian existentialism.

In the *Meaning of the Creative Act* (1962/1916) he finally offered *his* vision of a new Christianity, which integrated a radical notion of freedom and creativity and was strongly inspired by Jacob Boehme's theosophy. The writing of the book was precipitated by an overwhelming experience of a sudden illumination.

After having been a professor without a proper degree at Moscow University Berdyaev got imprisoned once more, this time by the new Soviet government, and finally was exiled from Russia along with a number of other Russian intellectuals. After a short time in Berlin, where he met Max Scheler, he finally settled in Paris. Just as in Russia, Berdyaev was in steady contact with a large number of intellectuals there, including Jacques Maritain, Gabriel Marcel, Etienne Gilson and E. Mounier. Apart from various gatherings of like-minded spirits, including regular weekly meetings at his home and the occasional delivery of a talk, Berdyaev's life in Paris was concentrated on writing (including a vast amount of daily correspondence) and contemplation.

Berdyaev was extremely well read but his thinking 'had another source and proceeded from some primal experience which cannot be acquired by means of study and reading' (Roessler 1956: 82). What interested him was the raw eruption of the untamed creative impulse, which was 'absolutely unique, unbidden and lawless' (ibid.: 218). He wrote 'in response to an inner voice which commands me to transmit my spiritual experience'. His writing was for him 'no luxury but a means of survival, an almost physiological necessity' (ibid.: 218), a 'form of spiritual hygiene, meditation and concentration, a way of life' (Berdyaev 1953a: 246, trans.). He describes how 'the discursive and deductive processes of reasoning give place in my mind to sudden disturbing visions. The thoughts to which I attach most importance came to me like flashes of lightning, like instantaneous illuminations' (ibid.: 219).

We could say that for Berdyaev the creative process of his writing had the psychological significance of actualizing the transcendent function. We would therefore expect his thought to penetrate beneath the surface and offer us a perspective that draws upon the sort of 'primitive' visionary consciousness of the Russian God seekers, which he so loved, giving it the refinement of philosophical reflection.

In Paris Berdyaev wrote a number of books in which his theory of personalism gained its final definition, in dialogue with contemporary existentialist thought. Berdyaev's wife, Lydia, died in 1945 and he died three years later, on 23 March 1948, while writing, the finished manuscript of his last work, *The Existential Dialectic of the Divine and the Human* (1949a) on his desk.

Chapter 3

An introduction to Berdyaev's philosophy

Writing was for Berdyaev a means of survival, an almost physical necessity. His philosophy may be seen as born out of a 'necessity of adopting some kind of answer to the problem of psychic suffering' (Jung 1956b: para. 1578) in the form of a *Weltanschauung*. Like Jung's psychology, Berdyaev's thought is the fruit of an individuation process, which transforms the psychic suffering of living through the historical crisis he found himself in into a creative response. This creative response is shaped by the spiritual atmosphere of the Russian origins of Berdyaev's thought.

Jung and Berdyaev also share a similar context, which I will characterize as the shift of modern man away from an orientation towards transcendence to an anthropological focus, as he is moving into a post-religious age. While Jung offers his psychology as a way to recover the lost religious contents Berdyaev develops what we could call a 'pneumatology'. I will outline the foundational concepts of this pneumatology: spirit, freedom, objectification and creativity as a necessary foundation for a deeper exploration of Berdyaev's understanding of the person.

Weltanschauung *and individuation*

While Berdyaev's thought is religious, it is characteristic that he identifies a *philosophical* rather than a religious experience of insight as 'the most powerful and perhaps only' conversion experience of his life:

> Once, on the threshold of adolescence, I was shaken to the depths by the thought that, even though there may not be such a thing as a meaning of life, the very search for meaning would render life significant and meaningful. It is to this that I desired passionately to dedicate my life. This insight marked a true inner revolution.
>
> (Berdyaev 1950: 78–79)

From this time onwards Berdyaev was convinced of his vocation as a philosopher and never doubted it. 'My conception of this vocation,' he writes,

> was in some way very similar to Marx, who proclaimed . . . that hitherto philosophy had been concerned with knowing life, but that the time had come to change life. It was therefore conceived by me primarily as a creative vocation, committing me to the fulfilment of a creative task.
>
> (ibid.: 86)

Thus, for Berdyaev philosophy is a function of life: it ought to transform life itself from its very foundations, not just externally. Berdyaev, as we have seen, changes from being primarily the political activist to becoming the existential philosopher who finds the most radical changes occurring in the 'deep heart' of the person and radiating out from there as a ferment of true change.

Philosophical truth that can catalyze such a radical transformation cannot be subordinated to practical considerations, as it is in Marxism or pragmatism. Only a 'subjective–existential concept' of truth reaches the foundations of life (Berdyaev 1952: 15). This does not imply subjectivism, but an understanding of truth, which links it insolubly with a personally appropriated trans-subjective dimension of meaning. This depth-dimension is, in Berdyaev's view, opened in an act of philosophical faith: it is not an objective 'given', but a given only by virtue of the existential *act* of overcoming apparent meaninglessness. While not being objective, what is thus given is nevertheless more than 'just subjective', i.e. it is trans-subjective, otherwise it could not constitute meaning. Personal meaning is neither 'nothing but' subjective, nor can it be captured within an objectivistic framework. It is meaning, which, while it can only be disclosed in interiority, nevertheless elicits my faith and existential commitment to it as to something transcending my subjectivity. Such a philosophical faith implies a total engagement of the whole person. Philosophy becomes 'the integral reaction of the human spirit to the totality of being' (Berdyaev 1962: 32f) which aims at a more radical revolution than political activism could ever attain.

Berdyaev follows K. Jasper's distinction between two fundamental types of philosophy, scientific and prophetic, and understands his own philosophy as prophetic. According to Jaspers,

> *Weltanschauung* is not only a knowledge, but it reveals itself in valuations, ways of life, destiny, in the experiential scale of values . . . When we talk of *Weltanschauung*, we mean ideas, the ultimate and the totality of man, both subjectively as experience and strength and fundamental attitude (*Gesinnung*), and objectively as objectively shaped world.
>
> (Jaspers 1985: 1, trans.)

Philosophy seeks an understanding of the whole, but this alone does not make it a *Weltanschauung*. Dilthey claimed that 'the ultimate root of any world view is life itself' (Dilthey 1957: 21). Jaspers alludes to this rootedness in life when he writes: 'Universal contemplation is not yet a *Weltanschauung*, for this there have to be the impulses which affect man in his totality and which issue from his totality . . . such philosophy we call prophetic philosophy' (op. cit.: 2). Prophetic philosophy is, then, a living expression of the totality of a man's existence, which moves beyond detached contemplation towards an involvement of the total existence of the person. The term *Weltanschauung* emphasizes this intimate link between the creative activity of 'philosophizing' and the process of individuation, which engages the whole person.

In his essay *Analytical Psychology and 'Weltanschauung'* (1928/1931) Jung suggests precisely such a close connection between the formulation of a worldview and the development of personality. A need for a *Weltanschauung* will arise for someone who believes with Goethe that 'the highest joy of man should be the growth of personality' (Jung 1928/1931: para. 731). A purely objectivistic perspective will have a 'withering of the human personality' (ibid.: para. 736) as a consequence. Our need for a *Weltanschauung* is rooted in our need to realize personality as an integral whole. 'Only when mirrored in our picture of the world can we see ourselves in the round. Only in our creative acts do we step forth into the light and see ourselves whole and complete' (ibid.: para. 737). The shaping of a worldview is an implicit component of the overall process of the shaping of the personality. It is integral to the process of individuation. Insofar as it stems from a subjective, psychological/spiritual need, it cannot make any claims to objective truth. Nevertheless, it will have to balance the mutually contradictory claims of both consciousness/adaptation to objective reality and of the unconscious/ the equally 'objective' factors of the inner world.

Jung speaks in this context of the '*symbol* of a *Weltanschauung*' (ibid.: para. 738) in which the 'historical, universal man in us joins hand with the new-born, individual man' (ibid.). *Weltanschauung* in this sense has to be understood as being more than just the result of a purely conscious reflection. It is the result of the transcendent function operating through philosophical creativity, which generates the symbol. Berdyaev's term 'trans-subjective' suggests such a third possibility that emerges between the 'purely subjective' and the 'purely objective'.[1]

I understand Berdyaev's philosophy as such a prophetic *Weltanschauung* as *symbol* in the service of individuation. The two characteristics of the 'prophetic' in this context are an active opposition to the given world and an inner force stemming from a spiritual experience, which seeks a clear formulation in philosophical thought (Segundo 1963: 12, trans.). In order to gain a full understanding of Berdyaev's prophetic philosophy, its specifically 'Russian' character has to be taken into account[2]: 'I regard my contribution as an eminently Russian one: I came to the West with a particularly "Russian Idea" ' (Berdyaev 1950: 250). J. L. Segundo offers a succinct summary of Berdyaev's position: 'Russia is for Berdyaev the privileged soil for personalism' (Segundo 1963: 24, trans.).

Russian orthodoxy

In his late essay *Personality and Community in Russian Thought*, Berdyaev writes: 'only a Christian Renaissance uniting the principle of personality with that of community is capable of assuring victory over the depersonalisation and dehumanisation now menacing the world' (Berdyaev 1949b: 70). Whereas western humanism led only to individualism, he believes that in Russia a form of personalism had been evolving which belongs to an eschatological interpretation of Christianity.[3] Berdyaev's socialism is a 'personalist socialism' which, he says, 'starts from the belief in the supremacy of personality over society' and which is 'simply the social projection of personalism' (Berdyaev 1943: 17).[4] The foundations for this vision are provided by Russian Orthodoxy, and had been developed within Russian religious thought. What marks out Berdyaev's thought within this movement is that it is 'an integration of the revolt of modernity into a renewed Christianity' (Clement 1991: 19, trans.).

Berdyaev regards himself not as a theologian but 'as a Christian theosophist, in the sense in which Clement of Alexandria, Origen, St Gregory of Nyssa, Cardinal Nicolas of Cusa, Jacob Boehme, St Martin and Vladimir Soloviev were Christian theosophists' (Berdyaev 1935a: xix).[5] It has to be emphasized that Christian theosophy as Berdyaev understands it has nothing to do with the 'theosophy' of H. P. Blavatsky, of which Berdyaev, like Soloviev, was highly critical.[6]

For Berdyaev, the term 'Christian theosophy' simply denotes a more individual, freer approach to the contents of revelation than ecclesiastic theology generally allows for, inasmuch as the latter is inevitably more socialised and collective. Theosophy in this sense does not oppose the authentic tradition of the Church, but rather seeks to penetrate more deeply into its living essence, which 'is deeper than any objectification and socialisation and . . . is a living creative link with the creative spiritual experience of the past' (Berdyaev 1953a: 67).[7]

Not surprisingly then, what attracts Berdyaev to Orthodoxy is that it is 'less susceptible of definition and rationalisation than either Catholicism or Protestantism. For me this was significant of greater freedom' (Berdyaev 1950: 177). Orthodox theology itself already has an experiential and existential basis: 'Theology . . . must necessarily conceal a Gnostic dimension, in the sense of the theology of contemplation and silence' (Lossky 1978: 13). The Orthodox are not fond of western legalistic metaphors of salvation and see theology more as a therapeutic science based on spiritual experience (see Hierotheus 1994, Larchet 2008).

Orthodoxy emphasizes apophatic theology. The distinction between apophatic and cataphatic or negative and positive theology comes from Dionysius the Areopagite. Positive theology proceeds by affirmations, negative theology by negations. This is not to be confused with agnosticism, but constitutes a supreme form of knowledge: 'It is by unknowing that one may know Him who is above every possible object of knowledge' (Lossky 1976: 25). The corollary of 'knowing by unknowing' is symbolism: what is known mystically can only be adequately expressed in the medium of symbolism, which avoids the straitjacket of univocal rational concepts and gives space to soul. The same apophaticism applies to the human person: 'The human person cannot be expressed in concepts. It eludes all rational definitions, indeed all description, for all the properties whereby it could be characterised can be met with in other individuals. Personality can only be grasped . . . by direct intuition' (ibid.: 53).

The understanding of the human being as person has a central place within Orthodox thought. According to Genesis 1: 26–27 man is created in the image and likeness of God. For Orthodox theology this means that 'man is in the image of the Word and . . . he is in the image of God through the mediation of the Word. He is therefore an "image of the image" ' (Spidlik 1986: 57). The image is, we could say, as yet only the unconscious potentiality of actualized personhood (likeness). We become persons by responding to the deeper promptings of the heart and unfolding in this way the potentials of the image in the likeness. We are, as the existentialists would say, called to become what we are out of our own free, creative effort.

Second, this understanding is, in the Christian interpretation of the Old Testament, closely connected to the biblical notion of the heart as the existential centre of the human being. In the heart the biological, psychological and spiritual dimensions form one single unity, that of the human person. The person is the inner man and 'the inner man is the heart' (ibid.: 1986: 91). The heart as 'the principle of unity within a person' (ibid.: 105) is also the place in which man becomes united with God and the Cosmos: 'If the heart is at the centre of man's being then it is through the heart that man enters into relationship with everything that exists' (ibid.: 106).

The reality/symbol of the heart in Orthodox thought can easily be related to the depth psychological notion of the unconscious, as the following quote makes evident:

> The heart includes what we today tend to describe as 'the unconscious'. The heart, that is to say, includes those aspects of myself which I do not as yet understand, the potentialities within myself of which I am at present largely or totally unaware . . . we may say that the heart is open both below and above, to the abyss of the subconscious below; above, to the abyss of mystical supraconsciousness.
>
> (Ware 2002: 15)

For Orthodox thinkers 'the person is a mystery, intelligible only by the contemplation of the Trinity' (Clement 2000: 27) and the Trinity, 'the Identity of Unique Persons, signifies that love is not merely the fulfilment of personal existence but its origin' (ibid.: 29). The fundamental Christian doctrines of the Trinity and the Divine–human nature of Christ form the foundation of the process of *theosis*, the transfiguration of the human being by the Holy Spirit into a person: that is, a participant in Christ's divinity. St Athanasius has expressed this doctrine in the famous words that 'God became man so that man may become divinized'.[8] According to the definition of Chalcedon in 451 AD, the one Christ

> makes himself known in two natures without mixture, without change, indivisibly, inseparably, in such a way that the union does not destroy the difference of the two natures, but on the contrary the properties of each remain more firm when they are united in a single person or hypostasis.
>
> (Cited in Lossky 1978: 98)

This is the basis of *theosis*, which means neither the dissolution of the human in the Divine, nor the separation of the human from the Divine, but the fulfilment of personal existence.

This concrete and personalistic focus, which is connected to a love of freedom, finds expression in Dostoyevsky's 'Legend of the Grand Inquisitor', which is of absolutely central importance for Berdyaev:

> It might be said that taking my stand as a Christian I accepted the picture of the Christ in the legend of the Grand Inquisitor; I turned to Him and in my Christianity I was opposed to everything which could be ascribed to the spirit of the Grand Inquisitor.
>
> (Berdyaev 1943: 16)

This Christ is a 'Kenotic Christ' (from *Kenosis*, self-emptying) who renounces the power principle to give man his full freedom. It is a human Christ who emptied himself of his divinity to be in the world 'incognito', forcing nobody to anything. He is the source and fulfilment of human freedom. The Grand Inquisitor on the other hand 'protects' men from their freedom and appropriates the power principle for his own manipulative aims. He is a 'friend of humanity' who wants to take the burden of freedom, which Christ has laid on their shoulders, away from them.

The vision of the Trinity as a communion of unique persons in love gains a universal social significance in Russian Orthodoxy. It is extended into a vision of the all-unity of men with each other and with the cosmos, so that 'everybody is responsible for everybody else' (Dostoyevsky, cited in Spidlik 2002: 176). At least equally if not more important for this universalistic vision is the power of the 'fundamental category of motherhood' in the Russian soul: 'The mother of God takes precedence of the Trinity and it is almost identified with the Trinity' (Berdyaev 1992: 24).

Berdyaev sees in the Russian people a people incapable of establishing itself firmly in this world. The Russian soul is as yet unformed and exposed to the volcanic energies of the unconscious in all their rawness. Russian Orthodoxy has within itself an as yet untapped future potential, which will become significant for humanity as a whole. A figure that embodies some of this potentiality, for Berdyaev, is Dostoyevsky's Staretz Sossima in *The Brothers Karamazov* (1993). Berdyaev felt that Dostoyevsky's portrait of Sossima was inadequate, but that it still expressed a vision of a 'new holiness', which will be born 'out of the depth of the Karamazov-realm', but only after modern man has 'trodden his tragic path' (Berdyaev 1925: 188). This new holiness would, he thought, be open to the world in a whole new way, and capable of integrating the shadow.

Russia is chaotic and full of contradictions, but for Berdyaev it is precisely within this demonic darkness – the 'Karamazov-element' of inner contradiction and dividedness – that, once man/woman has passed through the trials it imposes upon him/her, the new light can be born. In Dostoyevsky's *The Brothers Karamazov* it is Alyosha who is touched by this new spirituality. In the chapter *Cana of Galilee* he encounters the dead Staretz in a dream and he tells him: 'let us drink the new wine, the wine of new and great joy'. After he wakes up, he stumbles out into the night,

> above him the wide and boundless keeled cupola of the heavens, full of quiet, brilliant stars . . . The earth's silence seemed to fuse with that of the heavens, the earth's mystery came into contact with the stars . . . Alyosha stood, looked and suddenly cast himself down upon the earth like one who has had his legs cut from under him. Why he embraced it he did not know, he did not try to explain to himself why he so desperately wanted to kiss it, all of it, but weeping he kissed it, sobbing and drenching it with his tears, and frenziedly he swore to love it, love it until the end of the ages.
>
> (Dostoyevsky 1993: 417)

The coniunctio experience which is described here informs Berdyaev's philosophy and takes it beyond 'gnostic' pessimism towards a full affirmation of life: a new spirituality of individuation. All these latent elements found their further unfoldment within the philosophical movement of Russian religious thought.

Russian religious thought

The representatives of Russian religious thought sought a 'third way' between conservative Orthodoxy and the simple adoption of western rationalistic ideas. The central figure of this movement was Soloviev. He was preceded by the Slavophil thinkers, of whom Kireevsky and Khomyakov are noteworthy. Soloviev was then followed by a whole group of thinkers, Berdyaev among them.

These thinkers developed an integral epistemology which takes up Schelling's notion of a 'positive philosophy' and resolutely intensifies its existential orientation by drawing on elements of the Orthodox contemplative tradition[9], which locates the *nous* in the heart. The opening of the 'eye of the heart' involves a total effort of the whole person in which reason is elevated 'above its usual level' and raised 'to the level of sympathetic agreement with faith' (Kireevsky in Jakim and Bird 1998: 259) through a striving to 'gather into a single undivided whole all one's individual powers' of reasoning, feeling, aesthetic and moral sense. As a result of this inner 'concentration of all spiritual forces' one realizes 'integral thinking' in which 'all the soul's strings should be audible in full accord, blending into a single harmonious sound' (ibid.: 260). The elevation of thought is here clearly related by a movement of interiorization and centring, psychologically speaking, towards the Self:

> The very manner of human thought is constantly elevated by the inner consciousness that, in the depth of the soul, there is a shared living center of all the separate forces of reason, which is hidden from the usual state of the human spirit, but accessible to the person who seeks it, and which alone is worthy to attaining the highest truth.
>
> (ibid.: 260)

The highest truth is here not a truth separate from and 'above' the concrete but a mode of 'capturing, in an integral way, the meaning of being and life' (Berdyaev in Jakim and Bird 1998: 344). The force, which makes such an integrality of knowledge possible, is love. 'Love is the door to knowledge' (Evagrius Ponticus cited in Spidlik 2002: 124). This principle is as fundamental to Russian religious thought as it is to the contemplative tradition of Orthodoxy. Pavel Florensky offers a succinct summary:

> Knowing is a real *going* of the knower out of himself, or (what is the same thing) a real *going* of what is known *into* the knower, a real unification of the knower and what is known. That is the fundamental proposition of Russian . . . philosophy.
>
> (Florensky 2004: 55)

From this centrality of love as an ontological principle comes the notion of *sobornost* which means as much as conciliarity or free communion in love. According to Khomyakov,

> Communion in love is not only useful but wholly necessary for the attainment of truth, and the attainment of truth is based on communion and is not possible without it. Inaccessible to individual thought, truth is only accessible to the combination of thoughts linked in love.
>
> (in Jakim and Bird 1998: 339)

This concept of *sobornost*, of the essence of the Church as free unity or communion in love by which the truth is disclosed, is essential to Berdyaev's personalism. Berdyaev emphasises the universalistic aspect of this conception and moves it beyond confessional and institutional boundaries. The mystical essence of the Church is 'a Divine–human process . . . that will attain fullness at the end of history ... The new religious consciousness begins when one becomes conscious of Christ's Church as the cosmic kingdom' (ibid.: 334, 336).

This emphasis on the eschatological conception of the *ecclesia spiritualis* provides Berdyaev with the means to open up his religious thought to include the 'secular' sphere as belonging into the Divine–human process which embraces not only all of humanity but the whole cosmos. It is the same conception Jung is referring to when he writes that 'an *Ecclesia spiritualis* above all creeds and owing allegiance solely to Christ, the *Anthropos*, is the real aim of the alchemists' endeavours' (Jung 1955/56: para. 12). From this perspective, the division between the realm of the 'Grand Inquisitor' and that of Christ runs now right through all manifestations of human spirituality, be they secular or religious. The means of 'discerning the spirits' is for Berdyaev the '*Theandric* principle' of 'Divine–humanism'. What accords with it is accepted and developed and what contradicts it is rejected because, whereas in the first case personality is affirmed, in the second it is destroyed.[10]

Berdyaev's more universalistic understanding of *sobornost* is underpinned by his belief in a universal mysticism: 'There are greater affinities between the mystics of various religions than between the religions themselves. The depth of spirituality may manifest a greater community than objectified religions' (Berdyaev 1946: 134). Jung sees the Church as a projection of the Self or total psyche. A more conscious relation to the psyche would then at the same time be a move towards the sort of *ecclesia spiritualis* Berdyaev envisions.[11]

What Berdyaev seeks to give expression to is a genuinely Christian humanism, a very broad, in fact all-encompassing, *ecclesia spiritualis* of true humanness. The foundations for this humanism had already been laid in Soloviev's Sophiology. 'The doctrine of *Sophia* asserts the principle of the divine wisdom in the created world, in the cosmos and in mankind. It does not allow an absolute breach between the creator and creation' (Berdyaev 1992: 189). It is a 'holistic' doctrine that affirms divine immanence without thereby becoming pantheistic, a 'pan-entheism'. Even though he is not a *Sophiologist* in the strict sense, the synthetic element of *Sophiology*, which aspires to an intuitive vision of the whole, permeates all of Berdyaev's thought. In emphasizing divine immanence, *Sophiology* bestows a new dignity on the human person. Soloviev opens on these grounds new perspectives on the sublime humanism inherent in 'the religion of God-manhood', which has not yet been allowed its full expression in history:

> In the person of Jesus Christ there took place the union of the divine and the human nature and the God-man appeared. The same ought to take place in humanity, in human society and in history. The realisation of God-manhood, the Divine–human life presupposes the activity of men. In the Christianity of the past there was not enough of the activity of men . . . man was often crushed. The liberation of human activity in the new history was necessary for the realisation of God-manhood.
>
> (ibid.: 109)

In this spirit, Soloviev envisioned a 'free scientific theosophy' (see Soloviev 1978: 515), which would constitute a synthesis of the eastern focus on mystical communion with the divine with western humanism, philosophy and science. Such knowledge is inseparable from a total transformation of the human being, and must lead to an active, creative transformation of reality or true art by way of 'free *Theurgy*'.[12]

It is precisely this active–creative reinterpretation of philosophical knowledge as *theurgy* that Berdyaev develops. Truth is not understood to be a positivistic account of factual givenness or as systematic thought relying on logical coherence, but 'expressionistically', as a living force which transforms reality.[13] Berdyaev places Soloviev's thoughts on an existential basis already provided by him by emphasizing the creative, *theurgic* aspect of knowledge. Philosophy becomes transformed into an active realization of the person as the truth of human existence. Berdyaev interprets the totality of scientific, philosophical and theological knowledge from the existential viewpoint of the person, the existent subject.

The foundations of Berdyaev's personalism

The manifestation of the latent potentials of the 'Russian Idea' presupposes a passage through the 'Karamazov-element' of atheism and nihilism, with the attendant psychological–existential upheavals characteristic of the modern psyche. The modern soul is a divided soul, with a 'subterranean psychology' unknown to the older Christian and 'humanistic' consciousness (Berdyaev 1925: 200).

For Berdyaev, Nietzsche's philosophy in particular marks a transition into something new: 'European humanistic philosophy has found its spiritual end in Nietzsche, who is flesh from its flesh, blood from its blood' (ibid.: 49). The 'Death of God' proclaimed by Nietzsche means also the death of the old image of man: the modern soul enters new territory. Modern man's soul is not better, but 'his soul is infinitely more complex, his consciousness infinitely sharper' (ibid.: 47). Berdyaev shares with Jung a similar depth analysis of the psychological–existential condition of modern man, and both address the need for a response, which ought to face the problem at its roots in the human psyche.

Philosophical anthropology

Symptomatic of this need for a reorientation is the rise of philosophical anthropology. In 1930, Max Scheler stated that 'the problems of a philosophical Anthropology have become the centre of all philosophical problems . . . and that far beyond the circles of philosophical specialists. Biologists, doctors, psychologists and sociologists work on a new image of the essential structure of man' (Scheler 1930: 11, trans.). We possess a

> scientific, a philosophical and a theological anthropology but a unified idea of man we do not have. The growing multiplicity of specialist sciences studying man obscure . . . the essence of man much more than illumining it . . . one can say that at no time in history has man become so problematic to himself than at the present.
>
> (ibid.: 14)

Berdyaev is similarly convinced that 'the time has come to formulate a philosophical anthropology which has not existed in the past' (Berdyaev 1945a: 45) and that in fact such an anthropology should constitute the very foundation and centre of philosophy. In fact, philosophy had always been anthropocentric, but now 'philosophy must become consciously not instinctively anthropological' (ibid.: 45).

A quick glance at the history of the concept of philosophical anthropology will be useful at this point. Between the sixteenth and eighteenth centuries, anthropology was understood as *psychologia empirica*, in contradistinction to *psychologia rationalis*. Thus it became established as a study of man based on knowledge of nature and life-experience, rather than on metaphysical speculation or mathematical, experimental science. This understanding of anthropology was taken up by Kant:

> Kant's turn towards anthropology is thematically linked to the formulation of the critical insight that the metaphysics of the past is only concerned with mental objects (*Gedankendingen*), mathematical natural science only with appearances. But the human life-world, which cannot be reduced to the totality of the world of understanding (*Verstandeswelt*) lacking in reality and not to the reality of the 'world of sense' lacking in totality . . . demands a philosophical theory.
>
> (Marquart in Ritter 1971/I: 365, trans.)

In fact, philosophical anthropology was, for Kant, not only a special field, to which he devoted special lectures, but summed up the fundamental questions of his philosophy (see Heidegger 1991: para. 36ff.). The problem of man comes to the fore because metaphysics is shown to deal only with concepts, and natural science only with appearances. As a consequence, the focus inevitably shifts towards man himself. Philosophical anthropology had already gained huge popularity by the first half of the nineteenth century, and was by now based on the Romantic *Naturphilosophie*. This is largely the philosophical matrix from which Jung's theory of the unconscious originates (see Ellenberger 1994).

An important turning point, which has reverberations up until the present day, comes with Ludwig Feuerbach. For Feuerbach man, with the inclusion of nature as the basis of man, becomes the 'universal . . . object of philosophy – anthropology therefore, including physiology, is the universal science' (Feuerbach 1904: para. 1, trans.). Berdyaev subscribes fully to Feuerbach's 'anthropological reduction'[14] but, following the Russian theologian Nesmelov,[15] gives it an interpretation which is diametrically opposed to the atheistic naturalism of Feuerbach. For Nesmelov, the 'mystery of Christianity is above all an anthropological mystery and Feuerbach's atheism can be understood as a dialectical moment of the Christian apprehension of God' (Berdyaev 1992: 204).

By the beginning of the twentieth century, with ever increasing bodies of specialist knowledge, man had become profoundly problematic to himself and philosophical anthropology had correspondingly increased in importance. Succinctly, one could say that philosophical anthropology aspires 'to interpret philosophically the facts that the sciences have discovered concerning the nature of man and the human condition. It presupposes a developed body of scientific thought, and accordingly, in its programmes aspires to a new, scientifically grounded metaphysics' (Pappe 2006: 317). It is therefore primarily a 'reactive philosophical discipline' (Habermas in Pappe ibid.). This definition reveals the problematic nature of the project, which led Heidegger to dismiss it. If philosophical anthropology remains a 'reactive discipline', how can it integrate the ever increasing proliferation of specialist knowledge in a philosophically convincing way? Because the foundations to ask the question 'what is man?' philosophically were not yet in existence, Heidegger embarked on his analytics of *Dasein* in *Being and Time* (see Heidegger 1991: para. 36ff.).

One can see in Jung's psychology another project designed to offer an integrative centre for the various sciences that study man from different angles (see Shamdasani 2003: Ch. 1). Seen in this way, Jung's psychology would offer itself as another alternative to a 'philosophical anthropology'. Jung was deeply interested in scientific, empirical anthropology, and used its theories (e.g. Levi-Bruhl, Bastian; see Shamdasani 2003) but felt that it lacked a proper psychological foundation. For Jung, analytical psychology could provide such a foundation. If we were to use the term 'anthropological reduction' for Berdyaev's philosophical anthropology, we could use the parallel term 'psychological reduction' for Jung's project.

What then is Berdyaev's conception of philosophical anthropology? When Berdyaev writes that 'Philosophy must get rid of psychologism, but it cannot get rid of man. Philosophy must be consciously, not instinctively anthropological' (Berdyaev 1945a: 45), we have the beginnings of an answer to this question. For Berdyaev, man as he becomes conscious of himself through philosophy is more fundamental than the man of history, sociology, empirical anthropology, biology, or experimental or depth psychology. What Berdyaev claims is that philosophy itself is unconsciously anthropological right from the start. For philosophy to become *consciously* anthropological, what is needed is nothing less than a total revolution in its self-understanding. Instead of philosophical anthropology being oriented towards the special sciences of the humanities and somehow trying to integrate them, philosophy itself has to become conscious of its most persistent and ineradicable presupposition: Man himself. It is always man himself who philosophises, and any attempt to get rid of man for the sake of objective philosophical truth has not understood that this anthropological nature of philosophy is not to be equated with psychologism. On the contrary! On it rests the very nature of philosophical truth, as opposed to the relative truth of specialist knowledge within regional ontologies. It is easy here to discern the parallel to Jung's universal claim for psychology as a foundational science. But for Berdyaev it is now the spirit, not the psyche, which is foundational. Philosophy is a creative manifestation of the human spirit.

What Berdyaev means by the anthropological presupposition of philosophy becomes therefore clear for us if we reflect on the audacious nature of the project of philosophy itself. Berdyaev argues that man's metaphysical hunger, as displayed in the philosophical quest, is testament to man's consciousness of himself as an 'equal' to the world. He asserts that 'Man is a small universe – that is the basic truth for knowing man and the basic truth *which precedes the very possibility of knowing* . . . man and the cosmos measure forces against each other, as equals' (Berdyaev 1962: 58, emphasis mine).

But man is even more than a 'small universe'; he is also a 'break in the world of nature' (ibid.: 60), a *microtheos*. Berdyaev's notion of philosophical anthropology has to be understood in terms of a development of the Feuerbachian 'anthropological reduction' along the lines suggested by Nesmelov. Nesmelov formulated the fundamental anthropological insight also found in Pascal, namely that 'man is a twofold being' (ibid.). This insight, that man contains both a natural and a spiritual dimension, is fundamental for Berdyaev and thus 'anthropological theories depend on the way in which the relation between the two is defined' (Berdyaev 1945a: 49).

Furthermore, if 'humanness' or closeness to the 'facts of human existence' are seen as more truly anthropological, i.e. if anthropology is not a theory about man, but itself an *authentic expression of* humanity, then it will be, above all, the writers and intuitive, existentialist thinkers who will be relevant, not the scientists and academic philosophers. Berdyaev mentions Shakespeare, Tolstoy, Dostoyevsky, Stendhal and Proust:

> With these great artists may be ranked a few thinkers such as St Augustine, Jacob Boehme and Pascal in the past, Bachofen, Feuerbach and Kierkegaard in the nineteenth century and Max Scheler in our day. And among the men of science the first place belongs to Freud, Adler, Jung.
>
> (ibid.: 49)

To return to Heidegger's criticism of philosophical anthropology, and his postulated need for an analytic of *Dasein* as a new 'fundamental ontology', Berdyaev both endorses Heidegger's project and criticizes it. On the one hand, Heidegger is right to subvert the subject–object division of traditional ontological metaphysics. On the other hand, however, his phenomenological hermeneutics of *Dasein* is self-contradictory, because it misunderstands the element of transcendence inherent in it (see Segundo 1963: 229).

> Berdyaev wants to complete the view 'from below' or 'from outside' in which human *Dasein* is revealed as care and anxiety . . . he wants to revolutionize it through the view 'from above' or 'from within' in which 'existing is revealed as spirit'.
>
> (Dietrich 1975c: 222, trans.)

For Berdyaev, the transcendence of *Dasein* does not lead to some Kantian or Husserlian transcendental ego, but to 'transcendental man'. In this concept lies the key to understanding why Berdyaev is so intent on distinguishing his anthropological approach to philosophy from psychologism. 'Reason and logic in man are human if regarded as belonging to the transcendental man . . . The task which faces existential philosophy consists in the attempt to make reason itself turn towards humanity' (Berdyaev 1953a: 20).

What is important about this concept is that it combines within itself the opposites of 'man', in all his concreteness, and the 'transcendental', which in Kantian terminology refers to the generally valid and necessary preconditions of objective rational cognition. What Berdyaev wants to say is that the transcendental condition of the possibility of all knowledge is man, as a concrete, embodied, spiritual being who is not above and outside empirical reality and yet is nevertheless distinct from purely natural, empirical man. We do well to think back to the biblical notion of the 'hidden man of the heart' who knows truth not abstractly but through his total existence:

> If the existence of transcendental man be not admitted, it is impossible to make any pretensions to the knowledge of truth, it is a priori to any apprehension of truth and even to the existence of truth. It is not a logical a priori or an a priori of the abstract reason, it is an a priori of the whole man, of spirit.
>
> (ibid.: 19)

Personality is spirit embodied in nature. Naturalistic anthropologies focus so exclusively on the nature-aspect that the spiritual dimension gets lost. But the concrete complexities of personality stem precisely from the paradoxical and dialectical opposition of these two dimensions. The full scope and nature of this dialectical tension within the personality is not seen by naturalistic anthropologies. Modern sciences, including depth psychology, like Heidegger's analytics of *Dasein*, are 'concerned not so much with personality as with its disintegration, with the impersonal' (Berdyaev 1945a: 72).

Berdyaev esteemed the contribution of modern depth psychology, the work of 'Janet, Freud, Adler, Jung' as being of 'tremendous importance for philosophical anthropology' (ibid.: 68) because they corrected the erroneous image of man as primarily rational and unmasked his deeply irrational nature. That 'man is an irrational being and may long for suffering and not for happiness', as the optimistic rationalists of the humanistic past assumed, is shown 'in a masterly way' by Dostoyevsky. 'This is confirmed by modern psychology' (ibid.: 74). Nevertheless: 'True anthropology is bound to be personalistic' (ibid.: 54), which means that it does not give the last word to a naturalistic self-interpretation of man, but remains mindful of his dual nature. In order to understand how this personalistic philosophical anthropology unfolds, we now need to turn to the meaning of a number of other fundamental terms in Berdyaev's philosophy: spirit, freedom, creativity and objectification.

Spirit, freedom, creativity and objectification

If our reflections on the central role of philosophical anthropology have brought us to the 'entrance door' of Berdyaev's philosophy, his understanding of spirit is this very door itself (Gagnebin 1994). We have already mentioned that early on Berdyaev employed the term 'the psychic' for what he later was to call spirit. Jung's psychological reduction posits psychic reality, *esse in anima*, as fundamental. Psychic reality is for Jung a dynamic process, which finds its primary expression in archetypal images and then crystallizes into conscious representations and ideas. Jung believes that psychology ought to be rooted in psychological experience and present a faithful phenomenology of it. Thus psychology replaces abstract metaphysics as *prima philosophia*.

For Berdyaev 'an abstract metaphysics cannot exist, but a philosophy as a *phenomenology of the spiritual life* is possible' (Berdyaev 1935a: 6, emphasis mine). By combining the two notions of *integral epistemology* and the *transcendental man* that we have already touched upon, we are able to see how spirit for Berdyaev is the very essence of reality as it is know by the transcendental man, a knowledge that is rooted deeply in life. Spirit then holds for Berdyaev the same place that psyche does for Jung – it designates the totality of lived experience and not just an abstracted, etherealized segment of it: 'We may conclude therefore that philosophy is determined by life because spirit is life, and because the knowledge which spirit has of itself is the knowledge that life has of itself' (ibid.: 4).

Spirit is dynamic, living process, it is 'creative becoming' (ibid.) and in this capacity it represents a concept designating primary reality: life itself in all its heights and depths. Metaphysics fails to grasp life because it results from a fixation or freezing of creative becoming, a hypostatization of dead, frozen concepts. This is the domain of secondary reality determined by the subject–object division.

But Berdyaev's anthropology from above by no means avoids facing the dark abysses of life. As Spirit is essentially the innermost concreteness of life itself, it is life in all its heights and depths envisioned from within: 'Spirit is both fathomless depth and heavenly height' (Berdyaev 1946: 33).

Nowhere is this more evident than in his book on Dostoyevsky, which may be read as an exposition of his own philosophical ideas. Dostoyevsky is a ' "pneumatologist"; his "psychology" always penetrates into the spiritual life . . . the subterranean psychology of Dostoyevsky is only a moment of the spiritual path of man. He does not leave us in the closed circle of psychology, he leads us out of it' (Berdyaev 1925: 200, trans.). Dostoyevsky is 'the poet of the "subterranean" movements of the spirit' (ibid.: 10). He has 'something of the spirit of Heraclitus. Everything in him is fiery and dynamic, everything is in movement, in contradictions and battle. Ideas in Dostoyevsky are not static categories but a stream of fire'. In Dostoyevsky, 'Religion is finally transferred into the depths of the human spirit. To man is given back his spiritual depth' (ibid.: 191).

This subterranean aspect of the spirit has some kinship to the symbol of the 'spirit *Mercurius*', in its aspect of the 'ambivalence of the spirit archetype', which Jung develops (Jung 1943/1948: para. 288). For Berdyaev, spirit has a twofold origin: 'Spirit emanates from both God (Godmanhood) and from primordial Freedom (*Ungrund*)' (Richardson 1968: 87). *Mercurius* would, in this context, refer to its origins in primordial freedom, the chthonic aspect of spirit, which, all the same, is also the *anthropos* in potentia.

In fact, Jung's remarks on the Augustinian distinction between *cognitio matutina* and *cognitio vespertina*, at the end of his essay on *Mercurius* (1943/1948), throw some light on the whole dynamic into which I have placed Berdyaev's 'anthropologism'. The *cognitio vespertina* is the *cognitio hominis* (see Jung 1943/1948: para. 301) in which man's consciousness is darkened, not the *scientia creatoris* or true self-knowledge, *cognitio matutina*, which is the *aurora* after the *cognitio vespertina*, rising out of the darkness.

In his essay The New Middle Ages, Berdyaev writes:

> Men of intuition perceive, all the signs and proofs show that we have passed from an era of light into an era of darkness . . . Night is not less wonderful than the day . . . it is lit by the splendour of the stars and it

> reveals things to us that the day does not know. Night is closer than day to the mystery of all beginning. The abyss (Jacob Boehme's *Ungrund*) is open only by night: day spreads a veil over it.
>
> (Berdyaev 1933: 71)

If we add to this the following statement about Dostoyevsky, we have a characterization of the new dawn of the *cognitio matutina* emerging out of the darkness that is very similar to Jung's:

> [Dostoyevsky] penetrates into the dark abysses and reveals light there. Light does not only belong to the well-behaved surface. Light can also flame forth in the dark abyss, and this is the truer light. This fiery movement in man is generated from the polarity of human nature, the clash of hidden contradictions. This polarity, this antinomy, extends right into the deepest depths of human nature.
>
> (Berdyaev 1925: 43)

Thus, for Berdyaev, spirit is not the same as rationality. It is in a certain sense even diametrically opposed to it, because Berdyaev understands rationality in a Kantian sense as that which constitutes objectivity and is 'designed' for a pragmatic–scientific type of knowing. Jung writes in a similar vein: 'The spirit may legitimately claim the *patria potestas* over the soul; not so the earth-born intellect, which is man's sword and hammer, and not a creator of spiritual worlds, a father of the soul' (Jung 1934/1954: para. 32). Nevertheless, Berdyaev's understanding of spirit includes aspects different from Jung's. This is indicated by his distinction between *pneumatology* and 'psychology'. For Berdyaev, spirit is not only, nor even primarily, 'subterranean', nor is it purely 'transpersonal' (i.e. 'spirit' as the 'archetype as such'; cf. Jung 1947/1954: para. 420). It is essential to *distinguish* between the spiritual and the psychic, even though 'spiritual life is a spiritual–psychic life' (Berdyaev 1946: 40). Neither should the spiritual be subsumed under the psychological; nor should it be separated from it. In the first case we remain locked 'in the closed circle of psychology', and in the second the result is a dehumanizing spirituality hostile to concrete personhood.

Berdyaev sees the integration of the spiritual and the psychic realized in eastern Christianity, in which 'there is a special comprehension of the heart as the kernel of the human creature and his spiritual life. In the light of this conception the heart appears not as man's emotional–psychic nature but as a spiritual–psychic whole comprising also a transfigured mind' (Berdyaev 1946: 41). Berdyaev's notion of spirit is to be seen in this context as opening out into the depth of human existence, which while transcending the psychological–subjective is nevertheless not abstracted by a process of depersonalization from our concrete humanity. The heart can become an integrating spiritual centre of the person. It is the symbol of the person as a spiritual reality characterized essentially by *apophatic* concreteness and uniqueness, a non-subjective (i.e. non-'psychological') interiority.

Within the reified naturalistic perspective spirit is either absorbed into soul as 'man's emotional–psychic nature' or it is placed high above the natural human being as a 'supernatural' reality of divine spirit or grace. Berdyaev rejects both of these perspectives by placing spirit right into the heart 'as a spiritual–psychic whole' designating a reality of an entirely different order from both the material and the psychological. By removing grace and spirit into the realm of a transcendent above 'not only nature but grace is naturalized because it is objectified and because it is put "outside" and not "in the depth" ' (Berdyaev 1935a: 7). The mind–body dualism on the other hand stems from a false hypostatization of concepts, which now appear as two things (Descartes' *res cogitans* and *res extensa*). If we were to use the tripartite model of the human being as composed of body, soul and spirit on this false basis the human spirit appears as nothing more than discursive consciousness, an impotent epiphenomenon. But for Berdyaev all of this is nature. Spirit is on an entirely different level, it is

> life, experience, destiny. A purely rational metaphysics of the spirit is impossible . . . The life of spirit is not set over against knowledge as an objective thing, such as nature. Everything that transpires in the life of the spirit and in its own knowledge of itself lies within the unfathomable depths of spirit.
>
> (ibid.: 9)

In order to understand Berdyaev it is essential to grasp this key point. It can be clarified by using the two terms 'epistemological subject' and 'existential subject'. These correspond to the terms of primary and secondary reality.

> The 'secondary' consciousness originates in the process of objectification, whereby reality is broken up into the realms of subject and object. The 'primary' consciousness, on the contrary pertains to the subject, and proceeds from it *as from a fountain of living water*: it marks the fundamental identity of subject and object.
>
> (Berdyaev 1950: 97 emphasis mine)

The *gnosis* of the existential subject is creative, living, fluid. While the epistemological subject is invariably actualized in developed ego consciousness, the existential subject may remain latent. It is only actualized through individuation in Jungian terminology. The existential subject has to do with what goes on 'behind the back' of the knowing subject. While the knowing subject is oriented towards the object, the existing subject comes only into view when the object-constituting activity of the knowing subject is 'seen through' as the expression of something going on in the existential sphere.

The epistemological subject lacks the 'presence' for this awareness. It comes, so to speak, always too late. Objectification is a spiritual phenomenon, a process in the existential depths of life, which eludes the *ego cogitans*.

'The mystery of reality is not solved by concentrating on the object, but by reflecting on the action of the subject' (Berdyaev 1946: 9), where the action of the subject is that of spirit. Spirit is integral, whereas the knowing subject is partial. Spirit cannot be abstracted from the existential subject; it needs to be interpreted 'above all in a personalistic way' (ibid.: 16). The existential subject is symbolically located in the heart, just as the knowing subject is symbolically located in the head. It knows directly and intuitively because 'knowledge of life is life itself' (Berdyaev 1935a: 9).

The ego of consciousness (i.e. the knowing subject) is rooted in the spirit (i.e. the existential subject): 'Spirit is not the same thing as consciousness, but consciousness is formed through spirit and through it again reaches superconsciousness' (Berdyaev 1946: 35). The reality of spirit is therefore an 'altogether different reality' (ibid.: 10) from objective reality: it is, in Kantian terminology, 'that of freedom rather than that of nature. Spirit is never an object; nor is spiritual reality an objective one' (ibid.).

The real dualism for Berdyaev then is not the one of 'mind and body' or 'spirit and matter' understood as differerent 'things' but, following Kant, that of *freedom* or *spirit* and *nature*. The key point here is that what Berdyaev has in mind when he talks about the Kantian dualism of spirit and nature is 'not an ontological dualism' but a '*dualism of modes of existence* [which we have explicated as the modalities of the epistemological and the existential subject], *of qualitative states in man and in the world*' (Berdyaev 1976: 87, emphasis mine). Therefore, as he writes elsewhere, 'spirit is freedom and objectification is nature (not in a Romantic sense)' (Berdyaev 1946: 52). In fact, 'nature in a Romantic sense' (i.e. not conceived as object and mathematically calculable mechanical necessity but as cosmos or macrocosm in inner relation to the microcosm) belongs in some sense on the side of spirit: 'In spirit man encounters the cosmos, and man is not separated from it but rather united to it . . . Concrete spirituality contains within itself the fullness of cosmic life in all its varying degrees' (Berdyaev 1935a: 41).

The dualism of spirit and nature also has to be distinguished from that of spirit and body. The body, as well as the soul, can be spiritualized, and it belongs to the wholeness of the person; it is therefore not the opposite of the spirit. Both body and soul can be transformed by the spirit from within or can remain in a 'natural', objectified condition.

The defining element of 'nature' in opposition to spirit therefore is the 'qualitative state' of objectification, which implies a loss of interiority and a subjection to exterior, mechanical necessity. One of the defining marks of objectification is 'the rule of necessity, of determination from without, the crushing of freedom and the concealment of it' (Berdyaev 1976: 62). Objectification means 'the estrangement of the object from the subject', which means that the object now turns into the dead weight of extrinsicism, which crushes anything personal, anything free and anything which displays genuine interiority, and which consequently cannot be subjected to the common and impersonally universal without thereby becoming tragically alienated from itself.

The distinction between the two qualitative states that Berdyaev puts forward here closely resembles Buber's distinction between the 'I-Thou' and the 'I-It' (see Buber 2002). 'Objectification is the uprising of an exteriorized "not-I" in place of the "Thou", which exists interiorly' (Berdyaev 1976: 60). The knowing subject lives in a world of exteriorized objects, whereas the existential subject lives in a world of interiority of the Thou and We known through inner communion. The dissociation of the knowing subject and the existential subject (one might say, the dissociation of head and heart) leads to the 'estrangement of the object from the subject', resulting in the subjection of both to pure extrinsicism, which, in the case of the subject, means egocentricity.

For Berdyaev, the generic term for all philosophical perspectives that are, to varying degrees, caught up in this fundamentally alienated viewpoint is 'naturalism'. Naturalism in this sense covers everything from blunt materialism, to a traditional ontological metaphysics. What is common to all these viewpoints is that in them the *personal*, the interiority and freedom of the spirit, gets crushed and subjected to the impersonal, the common and the extrinsic that obey some mechanical order of necessity. From all of this it also follows that, for Berdyaev, the naturalistic mentality in all its forms is in itself also 'nature'. According to this view, all talk of freedom within the 'qualitative condition' of naturalism becomes pointless, and those who argue against 'freedom of the will' are in fact more right than those who argue for it.

Freedom is a reality of the sort of experience of the existential subject, which found its symbolic expression for example in Boehme's image of the *Ungrund* (abyss). The word *Un-grund* suggests a 'groundlessness', an absence of any conceivable foundation, which is inaccessible to rational knowledge. The symbol of the *Ungrund* points to the direct, intuitive apprehension of the existential reality of freedom itself, because any truly free act arises from a fathomless depth utterly beyond rationalization.

This sort of experience of freedom is 'not natural to man; it is rather a new birth in which the spiritual man makes his appearance and which is only revealed in the experience of the spiritual life' (Berdyaev 1935a: 121). Spirit is freedom – this is repeated by Berdyaev over and over again – and it is freedom because it implies the absence of any exterior determination; it is pure interiority: 'Freedom is Nothing, in the sense that it is not one of the realities of the natural world' (Berdyaev 1949a: v).

Naturalism, with its blindness for the existential reality of freedom, is an expression of a particular qualitative condition of human existence, which has its roots in depths beyond the cognitive activity of the knowing subject.

This gives naturalism a certain incontestable reality and justification. The 'new birth' is not under the control of the conscious subject. Nevertheless, viewed existentially its naturalistic blindness is an expression of its spiritual destiny, not something mechanically imposed from outside. Existential philosophy, as Berdyaev understands it, tries to go back to the existential 'conditions of possibility' of this condition of objectification and the naturalism resulting from it. It seeks these in the dimension of freedom, the normally unconscious domain of the existential subject:

> The philosophy of freedom begins with a free act before which there is not, nor can there be, existence, being. If we were to begin with being as a basis, and recognise this primacy of being over freedom, then everything, including freedom, is determined by being. But a determined freedom is not a freedom at all. Another type of philosophy however is possible, which asserts the primacy of freedom, of the creative act over being. And only this second type is favourable to freedom.
>
> (Berdyaev 1952: 102)

Berdyaev's understanding of creativeness is as intimately linked to freedom as freedom is to spirit. Just as he often repeats that 'spirit is freedom', so he also writes: 'creativeness is the mystery of freedom' (Berdyaev 1962: 134). Thus we can say: spirit is only known in freedom and creativeness, and it needs to be interpreted above all in a personalistic way. A philosophy which asserts the primacy of freedom, of the creative act over being, is a personalistic philosophy in which the person created in the image and likeness of God is characterized by its spirituality, freedom and creativeness.

It is above all this element of creativeness which Berdyaev sees as the essentially new ingredient of a philosophical anthropology of the future. He sees Nietzsche as 'the forerunner of a new religious anthropology' (ibid.: 86). Berdyaev passionately pursues the new perspective which Nietzsche's thought opens. For Nietzsche creativity is not limited to cultural creativity, rather 'life is a creative process in which all values are created' (Berdyaev 1949a: 37), even the Divine, which Nietzsche sought to create in the superman. Berdyaev believes that Nietzsche was right in his view that 'truth is created and not revealed. Truth is not a datum and is not received passively by man' (ibid.: 37).

Yet, for Berdyaev, it is not 'the will to power' but 'the will to meaning and freedom' (Dietrich 1975c: 26, trans.) that drives this creation of truth. Because in Nietzsche's view only the human dimension existed, he sought the superhuman in 'an old form which did not become clarified into the human' (ibid.: 32), i.e. in the realm of the subhuman. For Nietzsche, 'the *eschaton* implies the "going under" (*Untergang*) of the human in the pre-human as the supposed primal ground of lasting forces' (ibid.: 32). In Nietzsche's philosophy the lower wants to create the higher, which is impossible. The thirst for creativeness therefore demands a new anthropology, a 'Christology of man' that leads not to the Superman but to the God-man. But in order to reach this new anthropology one has to 'share Nietzsche's torment; it is religious through and through' (Berdyaev 1962: 86). Overcoming Nietzsche from within, by sharing his torment, implies the passage into a new, eschatological understanding of Christianity in which the religious meaning of creativeness is revealed; it 'does not come from above but rather from below – it is an anthropological, not a theological revelation' (ibid.: 92).

Berdyaev's conception of creativeness leads him to re-evaluate the relationship between potency and act, to put it in Aristotelian terms. In Greek and medieval Scholastic philosophy it is the actualized, accomplished form of being that is seen as superior to potency, which by its nature implies imperfection. But creativeness, or the emergence of newness, requires the existence of potency, where potency is re-evaluated and seen as not inferior to the act. 'The possibility of accomplishing a creative act, of disclosing change and newness, is due to imperfection' (Berdyaev 1976: 159).

We can see the closeness of Berdyaev's conception of creativeness to Jung's notion of the unconscious. The unconscious, we could say, is the *potentia* in man, in the human soul. But at the same time we may wonder how much of his criticism of Nietzsche's attempt to create a new image of the human out of the realm of the subhuman would be applied by Berdyaev to Jung's conception as well. To gain some perspective on this question, we have to reflect more deeply on the distinction we made earlier between Berdyaev's 'anthropological reduction' and Jung's 'psychological reduction'.

Anthropological and psychological reduction

Our exploration of the rise of philosophical anthropology has placed us at the point of origin of both Berdyaev's philosophy and Jung's psychology. Both sought, by 'anthropological' and 'psychological' reduction respectively, a new foundation for a worldview in which we as persons 'see ourselves as whole' (Jung 1928/1931: para. 737). Berdyaev's 'philosophical anthropology' stands against the background of *Sophiological* Russian religious thought, which resulted from an assimilation and critique of German Idealism in the light of the concept of God-manhood. Jung's psychology of the unconscious, on the other hand, as far as its philosophical origins are concerned, is set against the background of the type of anthropology which developed in Romantic thought, and was inspired by Schelling's *Naturphilosophie*.

In 1874, Soloviev wrote, in an essay entitled *The Crisis of Western Philosophy*, about 'the essential significance of the *Philosophy of the Unconscious* [i.e. Hartmann 1923] in that centuries-old intellectual development of the West whose final crisis is expressed in this philosophy' (Soloviev 1996: 104). This early work was Soloviev's starting point for a philosophy which he believed united both logical and empirical elements within the domain of 'inner experience', in which an 'a priori synthesis' is given 'which is prior to consciousness and presupposed by the latter' (ibid.: 138). In this domain of the unconscious, which ought more properly to be called 'superconscious', 'an essential identity between metaphysical essence and the knower, i.e. our spirit, is presupposed' (ibid.).

Yet, whereas for Soloviev and his followers the focus on the spirit prevailed, through the integration of this theory into a 'philosophical' development of the Orthodox tradition, in the West, what ultimately gained precedence was 'the idea of nature as an intrinsic source [which] goes along with an expressive view of human life' (Taylor 1992: 374). According to Charles Taylor, these two ideas – which are born from the matrix of Romantic *Naturphilosophie* – lead to the notion of 'expressive individuation, [which] has become one of the cornerstones of modern culture' (ibid.: 376). He formulates this notion, which can easily be discerned as influential in Jung's psychology, as follows: 'If nature is an intrinsic source, then each of us has to follow what is within; and this may be without precedent. We should not hope to find our models without' (ibid.: 376).

Within this Romantic view, by which Jung's psychology is clearly shaped, nature is imagined to be imbued with an unconscious spirit, and an 'essential unity of man and nature' (Ellenberger 1994: 203) is posited. C. G. Carus' quintessentially romantic view of the unconscious 'shows the shape reached by the theory of the unconscious at the end of the romantic period' (ibid.: 208) and is a clear prefiguration of Jung's psychology.[16]

The dynamics of this historical background provide the context for a tension which will have become evident to the reader: Berdyaev's focus on the spirit and his criticism of depth psychology as an 'anthropology from below' stands in marked contrast to Jung's focus on the unconscious psyche as 'nature'. Jung's own notion of spirit is that of a 'spontaneous principle of movement and activity', which has the capacity of the 'free production of images beyond sense-perception' as well as for the 'autonomous and sovereign manipulation of . . . images' (Jung 1945/48: para. 393). For Jung, the emphasis is on the autonomy of this image-producing factor and on its ambivalence. Spirit, where it is not consciousness, is, in a very Romantic sense, operating just like a 'force of nature'. It is mercurial, hiding a sting of darkness even where it is light and inspiring, awaiting the transformative action of the alchemist-psychologist.

Even though we have seen in Berdyaev a notion of the ambivalent character of spirit, we cannot overlook the fact that this notion is intrinsically connected to his 'mysticism of freedom', whereas Jung's emphasis on the ambivalent character of the spirit-archetype is connected to his focus on the autonomy of unconscious contents. For Jung, the central position of the 'personal spirit' appears to be 'downgraded' in favour of a plurality of autonomous 'spirits', i.e., archetypal agents, which, in their interaction with the 'heroic' ego, potentially lead to individuation (see Jung 1945/1948). While the Self 'comes close to expressing the universal archetype of spirit' (Samuels *et al.* 1986: 140), it does not necessarily amount to a personal spirit in Berdyaev's sense of the term.

While Berdyaev's asymmetrical dialectic of spirit and nature within the person has clear roots in the orthodox-theological notion of the person, Jung's conception favours the path of 'alchemical' individuation, which 'is not an upward going straight line f.i. from Earth to Heaven or from matter to spirit, but rather a *circumambulatio* of and an approximation to the *Centrum*' (Jung 1976: para. 396). In Berdyaev's philosophy we find a non-naturalistic 'expressivist' notion of individuation and creativeness. How do these differences shape Jung's and Berdyaev's understanding of the person?

Chapter 4

Person in Jung and Berdyaev

I have tried to show how the new understanding of the person developed by both Berdyaev and Jung takes shape within the context of the crisis of historical Christianity, which was epitomized by Nietzsche. If God is dead, so is the *imago dei* in man. The source of integrality in the psyche, and with it the personality, disintegrates: 'The destruction of the God-image is followed by the annulment of the human personality' (Jung 1951: para. 170). But 'is God really dead, because Nietzsche declared that he had not been heard of for a long time? May he not have come back in the guise of the superman?' (Jung 1944: para. 560).

This observation by Jung makes evident that the reconstitution of identity goes hand in hand with the transformation of the God-image and vice versa, a transformation fraught with the danger of inflation. In the post-humanist (today we would say postmodern) era, which Berdyaev sees prophetically declared by Dostoyevsky and Nietzsche, 'men with duplicitous thoughts appear' (Berdyaev 1925: 183, trans.). The image of Christ, of which the *imago dei* in man is a reflection, 'is no longer clearly felt, it gets contaminated with the image of the Antichrist' (ibid.: 183). The 'Antichrist', we could say, is an image of quintessential inflation.

This crisis led to an intensification of anthropological consciousness, which led Jung to assign a fundamental role to psychology and Berdyaev to what Bulgakov called his 'mystical Feuerbachianism' (Meerson 1998: 168). Also for Jung's psychological position Feuerbach's *Essence of Christianity* (1956) can be viewed as 'its closest philosophical relative' (Lammers 1994: 32). For both it is *from within man* that a profound 'revaluation of values' based on a new God-image flowing from a new understanding of personhood now has to emerge. The process of individuation and the centrality of human creativity are in this way inseparably linked to these overarching collective transformations. For Jung it is wholeness, which ought to replace the earlier ideal of perfection, while for Berdyaev a 'new Christological anthropology must reveal the secret of man's creative calling and thus give to man's creative impulses a high religious meaning' (Berdyaev 1962: 88). While distancing themselves from Nietzsche, both at the same time also seek to offer a response to his challenge. Healing does not lie in shunning those dangerous ambiguities but in transforming the poison into a medicine. The task is to shape a new authentic unity out of the duplicity and disintegration of contemporary man/woman, who is often incapable of any deeply rooted, unambiguous commitments.

In this chapter I will want to consider some of the main features of this new understanding of the person as it emerges in both Berdyaev's and Jung's writings. We will discover many common features but it will be the differences that are most interesting for us. Their implications will be unfolded in the later chapters in epistemological, 'theological' and ethical respects.

First, a terminological clarification is required. Berdyaev distinguishes, in line with the theological tradition, between the biological individual and the person. 'The individual is a category of naturalism, biology and sociology. The individual is indivisible in relation to some whole; he is an atom' (Berdyaev 1943: 35). But precisely because individualistic man is an 'atom' in opposition to the whole he 'is invariably thought of as part of a whole' (ibid.). Self-absorbed individualism and subjection to biological and sociological process thus go hand in hand, while man 'as a person, the same man, gains mastery of the egocentric self-confinement, discloses a universe in himself, but insists upon his independence and dignity in relation to the surrounding world' (ibid.: 36). This pathos of independence and dignity shapes Berdyaev's view of the person deeply.

Jung also repeatedly emphasizes that individuation is not individualism. But the term *individuum* itself has for him virtually the reverse meaning to the one it has for Berdyaev, while the term *personalistic* often refers in his language to the unindividuated state. Whenever Berdyaev talks of personality he has in mind a dimension of human existence which corresponds to what Jung calls the process of individuation without being exactly identical to it.

Berdyaev's understanding of the person

Personality as existential centre

For Berdyaev, 'the fundamental problem of Existential philosophy is that of the personality. I am an ego before I become a personality . . . The ego's purpose is to realize its personality . . .' (Berdyaev 1938: 159). The dramaturgy, dynamics and implications of this process of realization are the themes of existential philosophy as Berdyaev understands it. It offers us an existential perspective on the very phenomena that Jung considers from a psychological point of view.

In fact, 'the personality is the principal category of existential knowledge' (ibid.: 173). Another way of expressing this fundamental thesis is: 'Personality is the absolute existential centre' (Berdyaev 1943: 26). Berdyaev believes that 'true anthropology is bound to be personalistic' (Berdyaev 1945a: 54). Only the person integrates all dimensions of reality within itself. It constitutes a synthesis of body, soul and spirit. Any theory that does not consider man from this integral vantage point will not be sufficient for a *philosophical* anthropology, but will end up by reducing the human image to the structural necessities of a particular regional ontology.

Because the human personality is a microcosm,[1] it alone opens to us a truly 'holistic' perspective and thus 'the key to reality is to be found in man' (ibid.: 45). Thus, far from excluding the world, existential philosophy offers us the key to its meaning. Something analogous happens in Jung's psychology because he sees the psyche as the originating source of all other forms of knowledge.

According to the traditional doctrine of hermetic philosophy, knowledge is gained through recognizing the correspondences between microcosm and macrocosm.[2] In Berdyaev's philosophy, this idea receives an existential interpretation: knowledge of reality is bound up with the concretely lived experience of the person. Inasmuch as the person is in its innermost core also a *microtheos*, it is ultimately impossible for this experience to remain confined to the purely 'cosmic' dimension. In its fullness, it takes shape as the experience of living through the fundamental existential tensions between 'nature' and 'spirit'. Man is a finite being that is nevertheless oriented towards transcendence and the infinite. But, more than this, this aspect of the phenomenology of existential experience also tells us something about the deeper foundations of the world: the life of the world itself has to be thought of as permeated and shaped by spirit and freedom. For Berdyaev this is not a matter of projecting psychological contents onto an objective world but of the primacy of an integral epistemology over the derivative mode of objectifying cognition.

A purely rationally constructed philosophical system is therefore not possible. Instead, 'true integrality of thought is bound up with the integrality of personality, is an existential unity, not a logical [one]' (Berdyaev 1943: 8). The personality thus becomes the principal category of existential knowledge, the existential equivalent to a fundamental principle, which unifies a rational system of thought. But unlike various philosophical notions of the 'absolute', this 'principle' is not abstract but concrete, not static but dynamic, not totalitarian but pluralistic and at the same time oriented towards communion.

Integrality of thought in this case becomes bound up with destiny, just as for Jung psychology becomes inseparably bound up with the process of individuation (see Jung 1947/1954: para. 429). It represents an inner coherence that is not logical, but results from living through the dynamism of the life-process of the person; 'man is after all an inconsistent and polarized being' (Berdyaev 1943: 8). Existential thought, which remains true to real lived existence, is therefore inevitably dynamic and dialectical. Within this dynamic, personality as the existential centre is at the same time the 'changelessness in change' (ibid.).

In psychological terms we find in Berdyaev's thought an existential description of the circumambulation of the Self in the journey of individuation, which increasingly leads beyond the narrow confines of the ego. In a similar manner, Jung's psychology of individuation draws ever wider circles to include both broad historical perspectives and tentative speculations on the *unus mundus*.

Sphaera infinita cuius circumferentia numquam, centrum ubique

Berdyaev's existential perspective endows the human dimension with supreme value in a way comparable to Jung when he writes in *Mysterium Coniunctionis* that:

> A psychological approach to these matters draws man more into the centre of the picture as the measure of all things cannot be denied. But this gives him a significance, which is not without justification. The two great world-religions, Buddhism and Christianity, have, each in its own way, accorded man a central place, and Christianity has stressed this tendency still further by the dogma that God became very man.
>
> (Jung 1955/56: para. 789)

Like Jung's psychology, Berdyaev's existentialism shifts the spiritual centre of gravity into the dimension of human interiority, which escapes the calculating rationality of objective science. Both at one and the same time radicalize and overcome the subjectivism of the anthropological focus, which threatens to cut the individual off from the objectified world.

The objectively oriented anthropological sciences, such as biology, psychology and sociology, regard man only as an object, 'but there is in that case no mystery of man, as personality, as an existential centre of the world. Personality is recognised only as a subject, in infinite subjectivity, in which is hidden the secret of existence' (Berdyaev 1943: 22). The existential centre, unlike the superficial ego, is open to infinity. In order to understand what Berdyaev means here by 'infinite subjectivity', let us recall the passage, quoted earlier, in which Berdyaev states that, unlike ontological philosophy '[t]he philosophy of freedom begins with a free act before which there is not, nor can there be, existence, being' (Berdyaev 1952: 102). We are challenged to undergo a radical shift of perspective from the 'ontological' viewpoint, which remains caught up in the subject object division, to the existential viewpoint, which asserts the primacy of the existential dimension of 'infinite subjectivity', i.e. freedom and spirit. This could be understood as an act of the 'philosophical imagination'.

We can refer here to Jung's psychological description of the Indian concept of *tapas* as a total introversion which leads to the state of 'meditation without

Figure 4.1 A mandala from Kunrath's Amphitheatrum Sapientiae, depicting a scheme of Christian Kabbalism with Christ as a hieroglyph of the philosopher's stone at the centre.

content', resulting in a 'complete identity of inside and outside, which is technically described as *tat tvam asi* (that art thou)' (Jung 1921: para. 189).

It is Berdyaev's fundamental intuition that the 'secret of existence' disclosed in this state of mystical concentration is precisely that of the 'eternal freedom' which Boehme ascribes to his *Ungrund*, and that existence and being come about when the *Ungrund* concentrates a centre, thereby becoming *Grund*. This is, of course, symbolic language (for which see Grunsky 1956: 77ff.). It is based on the 'definition' of God as an infinite sphere whose circumference is nowhere and whose centre is everywhere (Mahnke 1937), a much quoted phrase by Jung in relation to the archetype of the Self.

The centre, like the Leibnitzean Monad, is to be imagined as a microcosm.

It is not cut off from the object/circumference, but concentrates within itself the quality of 'infinite subjectivity'.[3] Nikolaus Cusanus elaborates this very same image and envisions each person as a unique individuality, a living image (*viva imago*) of the infinite Godhead, a particular 'individual infinity' (Mahnke 1937: 103). Applied to the human person this image at one and the same time overcomes any notion of cut-off subjectivity and endows subjectivity with infinite value. The *mana* of the Divine takes residence in the soul. But, unlike the windowless monad of Leibnitz, for Berdyaev 'personality . . . *admits infinity into itself*; in its self-revelation it is *directed towards* an infinite content' (Berdyaev 1943: 22, emphasis mine).

According to Boehme, there exists a structural analogy between the human soul (*Gemuet*) and God: 'As you are, thus also is the eternal birth in God. Because God is spirit and your regiment in your love is also spirit' (Boehme 1955/1960: III, 4, 75, trans.). Thus the 'infinite centre' is also present by analogy in the unconscious depths of the human centre or *Gemuet*. It is the point which 'is identical with the . . . scintilla, the "little soul-spark" of Meister Eckhart' (Jung 1955/1956: para. 42). According to Boehme this inner centre in man is 'not a piece of the whole . . . but everything entirely . . . in every point there is a whole' and 'heaven, earth, stars and elements, everything is in man, also the triune Godhead' (cited from Mahnke 1937: 36, trans.).

But we ought to take careful note of Boehme's exact formulation: *your regiment in your love* is also spirit. Our 'roots are . . . in God, and also in the nethermost depths' we are children 'of God and of non-being, of meonic freedom' (Berdyaev 1945a: 46). Infinite subjectivity *without love* would introduce us to Boehme's 'wheel of anxiety'. Here in these depths then are the deepest roots of Berdyaev's existential dialectics, which drive human destiny and history. What Berdyaev says of the twofold origin of the spiritual core of the person, something equally expressed in Boehme's Mandala *Die Philosophische Kugel oder das Wunder Auge der Ewigkeit* in his *Viertzig Fragen von der Seelen* (1942),[4] points towards the mystery which Jung approaches in *Aion* concerning the paradoxical nature of the Self. Only by entering into love can we realize that 'God himself is the being of all beings, and we are gods in him, through which he reveals himself' (Boehme, cited from Mahnke 1937: 36).

Where we would speak of the Self here in Jung's psychological language, Berdyaev refers to 'the depth of my ego [which] is steeped in infinity and eternity' (Berdyaev 1976: 42). The ego in this depth 'participates in the *Ungrund* . . . The pure willing, which in the basic ego is not consciousness, nor a self-apprehension: but is the fecundating source, which freely seeks illumination' (Richardson 1968: 102).

The symbolism of centre and circumference is central to one of Jung's key themes, the mandala (von Franz 1998: Ch. 7).[5] Berdyaev's understanding of the person as 'existential centre' does probably have its roots in Boehme's use of the term *Centrum*. Berdyaev himself offers an explanation of this term in his commentary to his French translation of Boehme's *Mysterium Magnum*.

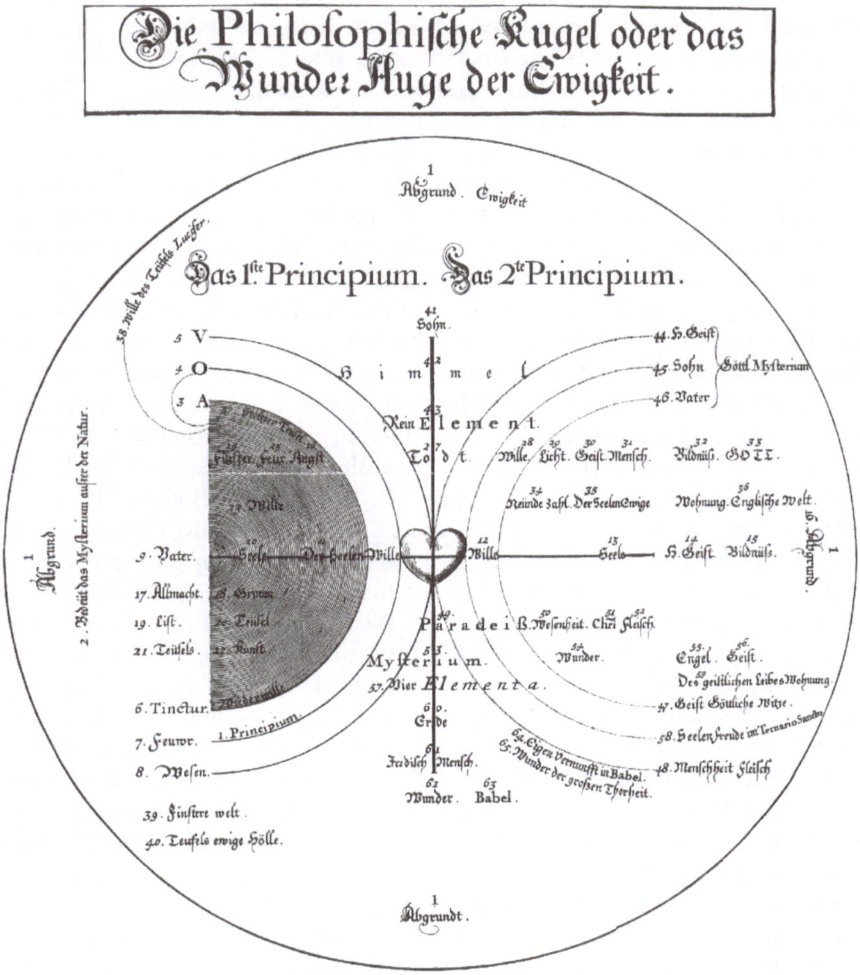

Figure 4.2 Boehme's philosophical globe, symbolizing the dialectic of light and darkness in the innermost depths of the soul. From Boehme's *Viertzig Fragen von der Seelen*.

Centrum, he says, is 'the most intimate part of a being, the irreducible factor of personification, the ray (*faisceau*) of forces which constitute the distinct' (quoted in Segundo 1963: 376, trans.). Segundo sees in the term 'existential centre' the 'imaginative scheme of a centre of force' (ibid.: 376), which is necessary for re-educating our imagination, leading it from a condition of being locked into a static, ontological scheme of reality towards a dynamic, existential philosophy of freedom in which static 'being' appears as the 'frozen' product of the creative power of freedom. In other words: being is reduced to occupying a secondary, derivative place. 'Primary existence is freedom and act, it is creative power' (Berdyaev 1953a: 70). It is for this reason that the person as 'an existential centre of the world' is the 'principal category of existential knowledge' (Berdyaev 1943: 22).

Anthropos and Uebermensch

As von Franz writes, the 'symbols of the cosmic *anthropos* and the mandala are synonymous; they both point to an ultimate inner psychic unity, to the Self' (von Franz 1998: 141). The symbol of the *anthropos* emphasizes that the process of centroversion (Neumann 1954) is a process of humanization. Teilhard de Chardin's 'omega point' can be mentioned here (see Teilhard de Chardin 1965: 283ff.). It emphasizes the cosmic dimension of this principle of which the psychological drive for individuation is a specific manifestation. Berdyaev follows Boehme's intuition in positing the drive towards personalization or individuation as animating the innermost heart of reality, the life of God (and thus also of the cosmos) itself. Koyre interprets Boehme's theosophy as 'personalistic': 'Boehme describes the conditions of the absolute person' (Koyre 1929: 318, trans.). For Boehme,

> it is by realising himself in that which is the most personal and the most profound that man attains his authentic perfection, which is to incarnate and express God. Thus it follows that finitude and determination are not imperfections. To the thesis: *omnis determinatio est negatio*, Boehme implicitly opposes the belief *omnis determinatio est positio*.
>
> (ibid.: 319)

We may express this also by saying: God seeks to become man just as man seeks to become God. In Berdyaev's first major work, *The Meaning of the Creative Act* (1962), Boehme occupies a central place. It is in Boehme 'that anthropological visions are revealed which rise above and beyond time itself' (ibid.: 64). In Boehme, Berdyaev finds a Christian version of the doctrine of the *anthropos* comparable to that of Hermetic philosophy and the Jewish Cabbala. The *anthropos*, the divine man, is what finally stands behind Berdyaev's exalted understanding of the value of human personality. He thereby develops a core theme of the Christian renaissance humanism of Paracelsus, Cusanus, Pico della Mirandola and Marsilio Ficino.

The Cabbala, Hermeticism and Boehme's theosophy all reveal a fundamental anthropological truth which, in Berdyaev's eyes, has remained largely obscured, both in official Christian theology and in academic philosophy. But it is only in Boehme's voluntarism that this truth gains the existential quality Berdyaev is looking for. While 'the Kabbala reveals the truth about man as the image and likeness of God . . . this truth about man has not yet become dynamic and creative' (Berdyaev 1962: 64).

The existential dimension of this truth is only becoming fully revealed in the intense dramaturgy and dynamism of existential dialectics. For Berdyaev – like for Nietzsche, the 'disciple of Dionysus'[6] – the tragic is a fundamental category. Such a dynamic and creative view, which reveals the truth about the volcanic energies in the depths of existence, is, for Berdyaev, to be found in Boehme, who arguably was the originator of the dialectics of later German idealism. Jung, who has undeniable attachments to this tradition, which came to him via Romantic thought, says: 'the Self is not just a static quantity or constant form, but is also a dynamic process' (Jung 1951: para. 411).

Jung himself summarises in *Aion* Boehme's interpretation of the figures of *Adam Kadmon* (the first Adam, in his as yet unfallen state) and Christ, the second Adam: 'Boehme's first Adam is the same as the Heavenly Adam of the Cabbala. And Christ, the Absolute Man, is the Heavenly Adam' (1951: para. 411).[7] It is within this context that, for Berdyaev, 'the fact of Christ's appearance in the world is the basic fact of anthropology' (Berdyaev 1962: 75), because this appearance of Christ marks the birth of personality in man, the appearance of the inner man.

Christ is, in the Pauline sense, not a single individual 'out there', but, as the second Adam, encompasses all of humanity within Himself. In this way the appearance of Christ restores to humanity its original royal dignity. More than that, it potentially bestows on man a consciousness 'which surpasses the self-consciousness of the first Adam: it marks a new phase in the creation of the world' (ibid.). The self-consciousness of the first Adam was not, properly speaking, a self-consciousness at all, because 'Paradise is the unconscious wholeness of nature, the realm of instinct' (Berdyaev 1945a: 38).

Only through the new Adam does man become a person. But man is 'reborn into the new Adam only if he has had *an immanent experience* of the crucifixion' (ibid.: 93, emphasis mine). Therefore Berdyaev says about the Christian epoch of redemption that 'on the way of the spiritual life this is the crucifixion on the cross of the rose of life' (Berdyaev 1962: 90). Initially, the Christian epoch violently eradicates any 'pagan' remnants of paradisiacal innocence. But the 'force of personalisation' which has entered humanity through Christ strives not only for redemption but also for creative fulfilment, for the *fresh blossoming* of the rose of life: 'Redemption from sin, salvation from evil, are in themselves only negative, and the final aims lie beyond, in a positive, creative purpose' (ibid.).

These are the deeper forces that finally led to the emergence of secularized humanism in the Renaissance. Not being able to find their adequate development within institutional Christianity itself, these forces sought other outlets and found powerful expression in Feuerbach's anthropology and even more so in Nietzsche's idea of the *Uebermensch*. For Berdyaev these developments are an indication that we are entering a new 'postmodern' historical period in which the religious significance of human creativeness has to be revealed as a divine potential 'by man's own free initiative . . . In creativeness man himself reveals the image and likeness of God in him . . . the breathing of the spirit is not only divine, it is Divine–human as well' (Berdyaev 1962: 93). Jung has perhaps a similar emphasis on the *human*, immanent dimension of the 'breathing of the spirit' in mind when he writes to Victor White in a letter from 5 October 1945: 'My personal view in this matter is, that Man's vital energy or libido is the divine pneuma alright' (Lammers and Cunningham 2007: 7).

The meaning of personality, which, for Berdyaev, is connected with the archetypal image of the *Anthropos*[8], i.e. the original, prelapsarian Adam *Kadmon* who is restored to humanity in Christ, becomes fully manifest as an inner experience to the individual only in free creativity. This ought to be the new religious signature of our time: the immanent and therefore *individuated* experience of the Divine–human mystery, which is fully revealed only in the Spirit. As a consequence of this emphasis on individuation '[p]ersonalism is most profoundly opposed to monism. Monism is the domination of the "common", of the abstract universal, and the denial of personality and of freedom. Personality and freedom are linked with pluralism' (Berdyaev 1943: 68). Each person is a microcosm and *microtheos*, an 'image of the image of God' (i.e. of Christ the *Anthropos*) which stands in a relation of existential participation, not of monistic identity to the one Christ-*Anthropos*. This existential participation amounts to a 'Christification' of man, which is not to be confused with a monistic dissolution of the human in the divine. But neither does it have anything to do with the rampant individualism of the *Uebermensch*. In a very similar way Jung talks of a 'Christification of many' (Jung 1952/1967: para. 758). The parallel to Jung's psychology of individuation is further emphasized when Berdyaev writes:

> The Coming Christ will never appear to him who by his own free effort has not revealed within himself the other, creative image of man . . . The third creative revelation of the Spirit will have no holy scripture . . . it will be accomplished in man . . . it is an anthropological revelation, an unveiling of the Christology of man . . . The virtue of accepting a dangerous position, the virtue of daring to do, is the basic virtue of the creative epoch.
>
> (Berdyaev 1962: 101)

While creative daring has to risk the encounter with the potentially destructive and chaotic Dionysian wellsprings of creativity in the unconscious 'creativity is never the revolt of ancient chaos. . . . Creative Dionysism is a Dionysism transfigured, Dionysism which has passed through the law and the redemption, and is joined with Apollonism' (ibid.: 251).

We can see how Berdyaev's personalism develops similar themes to Jung's psychology of individuation: the Self becomes manifest as a new quality of consciousness in the *coniunctio oppositorum* of the Dionysian unconscious and the Apollonian consciousness. We will therefore want to take a closer look at Berdyaev's understanding of the unconscious.

Subconscious, conscious, superconscious

The 'archetypal' images/symbols which underlie Berdyaev's understanding of the person would be misunderstood if they were taken literally, in an ontological/naturalistic sense. They are symbolic of processes in the unconscious. But the unconscious contains within itself clearly distinct dimensions. It designates the height and depth dimensions of existential experience.

Only because there is also a spiritual or 'superconscious' dimension of the unconscious does the experience of an 'immanent transcendence' become possible: 'Consciousness recognizes as transcendent to itself that which is immanent for supraconsciousness. For that reason I can say that the transcendent is not outside me but on the contrary within me' (Berdyaev 1976: 81). The formation of personality requires the development of consciousness. But consciousness creates divisions between subject and object, immanence and transcendence and is therefore intrinsically 'unhappy consciousness', as Hegel terms it. Our experience is subject to qualitative fluctuations, to different degrees of consciousness. According to Berdyaev:

> Consciousness must needs be thought of dynamically, and not statically, it can shrink or it can expand, it can hide away whole worlds or it can reveal them. There is no absolute nor impassable boundary, separating the conscious from the subconscious and the supraconscious. That which presents itself to this median-norm consciousness . . . is but a certain degree of petrification of the consciousness, relative to certain norms of social life . . . But an egress from this median-norm consciousness is possible and with it are connected all the utmost attainments of man, with it are connected sanctity and genius, contemplation and creativeness.
>
> (Berdyaev 1936b: 18).

The person has within itself a 'subconscious elemental basis, connected with cosmic life and with the earth, a cosmic telluric element' (ibid.: 17) and it is vital for it to stay connected to this root-ground because:

> The very passions connected with the natural-elemental basis would seem to be the material, from which also are created the greatest virtues of the person. The intellectual-moral and rational denying of the natural-elemental within man leads to the dissociation and stoppage of the wellsprings of life.
>
> (ibid.)

Nevertheless, if either the subconscious, on one side, or the rational consciousness, on the other, dominate, see-sawing back and forth in seemingly interminable conflict, then we become cut off from reality. Only the supraconscious is the sphere in which genuine self-transcendence (*agape*) with respect to the other as Thou, to nature, to the human other and to God, takes place.

The dialectic between these three dimensions within the person is complex, and is one aspect of the existential dialectic which characterizes the person. 'Person is a unity of destiny. This is its basic definition' (ibid.: 13). The destiny of the person is characterized by conflict, tragic contradictions and tensions, and the person is that which holds the unity, which bestows meaning by moving towards a continuous self-transcendence without ever 'arriving' with all conflict resolved in Hegelian harmony. Berdyaev favours the categories of the tragic, the aporetic and the paradoxical as being fundamental to human existence. Like Kierkegaard he breaks open the closed circle of Hegel's 'absolute system', which promises universal rational control.

The resolution of conflict is only found in the superconscious, but never permanently, only momentarily in the timeless instant of 'existential time'. Nevertheless, the gradual 're-centring' of the person in superconsciousness is the source of true integration. This journey towards wholeness paradoxically happens by *suffering through* the paradoxes of existence: the *immanent experience* of the cross. We can think here of Jung's words: 'Whenever the archetype of the self predominates, the inevitable psychological consequence is a state of conflict vividly exemplified in the Christian symbol of the crucifixion – that acute state of unredeemedness which comes to an end only with the words "consummatum est" ' (Jung 1951: para. 125)

Ethics is, for Berdyaev, principally a study of these existential tensions within the personality. If 'something be affirmed in man at the one pole, then this is compensated for by the affirmation of the opposite at the other pole' (Berdyaev 1936b: 5). Berdyaev formulates the dynamic nature of this opposition with respect to consciousness and the unconscious in a way reminiscent of Jung's basic developmental scheme:

> There are three stages in the development of the spirit: the original paradisiacal wholeness, which has not yet had the experience of thought and freedom; division, reflection, valuation, freedom of choice; and, finally, superconscious wholeness and completion that comes after freedom, reflection and valuation. Those stages cannot of course be understood merely chronologically – they express an ideal successiveness.
>
> (Berdyaev 1945a: 39).

The 'fall' from paradisiacal wholeness (which is not to be confused with the state of 'primitive man') marks not only the emergence of divided consciousness, but also a change in the unconscious itself: 'a dark void formed in it, and consciousness was needed to safeguard man from the yawning abyss below. But consciousness also shuts man off from the superconscious' (ibid.).

Both the unconscious (which has now become the 'subconscious') and consciousness are now highly ambivalent and locked in battle, a battle which can only be resolved in the superconscious, which plays a similar role to the transcendent function in Jung's psychology. 'True spiritual victories are won in the domain of superconsciousness, i.e. in spirit, and not in consciousness' (ibid.: 78). Berdyaev does not envision a return to the (illusory) innocent integrity of the 'primitive' but neither is the superconscious simply an intensification of consciousness. It implies a qualitative shift of consciousness from rationality to the integral intelligence of the total, existential self. This 'holistic' intelligence of the spirit, as opposed to the rational, objectifying mind, is able to integrate the natural, instinctive wellsprings of life.

Berdyaev's understanding of the dialectic of these dimensions within the person – a dialectic of freedom – is different from the notion of a naturalistic evolution of consciousness. It is much more dramatic and turbulent, as it is in Dostoyevsky's novels.

Despite the emphasis on the need to distinguish the superconscious and subconscious, Berdyaev also uses the term unconscious *pars pro toto*. The realization of personality is a creative process and therefore involves the potential dimension of the unconscious – the source of creative impulses – as much as consciousness. The tension of opposites means that 'personality cannot be a complete whole; it is not an objective datum; it fashions and creates itself, it is dynamic' (Berdyaev 1938: 174). Personality is always much more *in potentia*, i.e. unconscious, than *in actu*, and as a living dynamic process it is constantly called upon to 'actualize' its potential. The unconscious has a dual aspect: it 'includes automatism, the lower unconscious or the subconscious in the strict sense. But it also contains the sources of human creativeness . . . Creative inspirations always have their original basis in the unconscious or the superconscious' (Berdyaev 1945a: 75). This formulation shows his recognition that, from one perspective, the unconscious and the superconscious appear as the same depth-dimension of the person.

Person as a unity of acts and a unique Gestalt

In order to emphasize the creative nature of personality and its fundamental difference from an objective datum, which can be studied scientifically, Berdyaev follows Scheler, who defined the personality as a 'unity of *acts*' (Scheler 1973: 383).[9] 'Personality is not a substance but an act, a creative act' (Berdyaev 1943: 24). If personality is thought of as a substance, it appears as something objective, readily given and fixed. But personality is the very opposite of automatism or static 'thingness'; it is free being. It is an integral unity of creative acts, the existential centre of all these acts: 'Personality is my whole thinking, my whole willing, my whole feeling, my whole creative activity' (ibid.: 25).

Personality is free being. It is experienced only through the activity of creative expression. Nevertheless, for Berdyaev, unlike Sartre, the actualization of personality as free being cannot be an actualization out of nothing, in the sense of a pure nihilistic absence of any 'ideal blueprint' (see McLachlan 1992). The unity of acts that personality represents – the existential centre – must already exist, though not as a substance, just as for Jung the Self is both pre-existent and yet also resultant from the process of individuation:

> Personality is not made up of parts, it is not an aggregate, not a composition, it is a primary whole. The growth of personality, the realization of personality certainly does not mean the formation of a whole out of its parts. It means rather the creative act of personality, as a whole thing, which is not brought out of anything and not put together from anything. The form of personality is integral, it is present as a whole in all the acts of personality, personality has a unique, an unrepeatable form, *Gestalt*.
>
> (Berdyaev 1943: 23)

This integral unity, or *Gestalt*, therefore becomes actualized in all the acts of personality. This *Gestalt* can be thought of as a 'time-*Gestalt*'. As it gives cohesion, shape and inner coherence to temporal experience, this 'time-*Gestalt*' cannot itself be temporal.[10]

This means nothing else than that personality is spirit, because spirit is free, creative activity and as such is the opposite of objectivity, which is always only the *result* of the activity of spirit. For Berdyaev, being is, as we have seen, secondary to freedom. What belongs to the sphere of being is investigated by the different sciences, and in the final analysis it lacks all uniqueness. The quality of uniqueness so essential to personality has its origin in the non-objectifiable spirit.

In living out its destiny, personality is forging its unique *Gestalt*, and it does so only if it is not merely passively carried along and 'well-adapted' but actively realizing its unique and unrepeatable vocation. 'Personality is bound up with the consciousness of vocation . . . Personality which is conscious of itself listens to the inward voice and obeys it only' (Berdyaev 1943: 48). It manifests something unique in the world, which is incompatible with the purely passive adaptation and imitation of collective standards: 'only determination from within and arising out of freedom is personality' (ibid.: 27).

The 'cosmotheandric' character of personality

From this it is clear that the *Gestalt* through which personality realizes itself cannot be any objective standard or fixed ideal, because personality is constantly changing, or, more precisely, it is 'the unchanging in change, unity in the manifold' (ibid.: 22). Personality realizes this constancy within fluid change by faithfulness to its vocation, which springs from an inward, existential communion with God, not from a static set of objective norms.

> God does not exist as an objective reality found to be necessary by me, as the objectivization of a universal idea. He exists in existential contact and meeting, as the process of transcension, and in that meeting God is personality.
>
> (ibid.: 39)

The consciousness of vocation is the result of existential communion with the non-objectifiable, eternal Thou, to use Buber's expression. This Thou exists only *as* the process of transcension. Where I do not live this process, no 'eternal Thou' exists for me. But this does not mean that it is *produced by* my activity. In the act of transcension I known the eternal Thou as the *other* that addresses me and yet is, in the words of St Augustine, 'more I than I am myself'. God is personality for me because he is the *other* which calls my innermost identity to life and mysteriously evokes and sustains the act of transcension in which this unique identity unfolds in a way that is experienced as the most intimate meeting and communion possible. In this communion I am freed from the tyranny of static, abstract norms. They become the instruments for my creative shaping of reality. I am also protected against the inflationary, dehumanizing consequences of the Nietzschean vision of the *Uebermensch*.

Personality is thus characterized by the *synergy* between the Divine and the human: it is Divine–human. Personality, Berdyaev often says, is God's idea of man, and that idea is the *Gestalt* man is called to realize, not a general idea, but an absolutely unique and yet universal content. God calls each one of us by a 'secret name'. Far from being a passive reception of this content, the realization of personality is a creative manifestation of uniqueness born from an existential communion of the Divine and the human, which, while communing in spirit, nevertheless at the same time remain distinct. And it is this distinctness which marks out the existential 'space' in which newness emerges. Far from extinguishing uniqueness and free creative initiative, *synergy* is precisely the condition for the creative shaping of one's own identity and of objective circumstances. Grace, for Berdyaev, only operates within freedom. Creative freedom *is* a state of grace.

The combination of uniqueness and universality that characterizes personality means that it is not a closed spiritual monad that somehow inhabits body and soul, but it is open; it potentially includes and integrates the whole cosmos; it is the only centre of integration. It is not a part of anything, neither the cosmos nor society; rather, both cosmos and society are a part of it. This conception does not imply egocentric grandiosity but points towards the non-objectifiable and communal nature of personality. Personality flourishes in overcoming egocentricity in favour of communion with God and with others in love.

The notion of the person as microcosm implies a robust refutation of 'psychologism', which 'sees in man a closed individual being, a fractional part of the world' (Berdyaev 1962: 62). If man is considered to be 'not as a fractional part of the universe . . . but [as] a whole small universe including in himself all the qualities of the great universe, imprinting himself upon it and receiving its imprint upon himself' (ibid.), then the psychology which follows from such a view will be 'cosmic':

> For instance anger . . . is not only an element in man but an element in the cosmos. The subject is visible in the object and the object in the subject. A spiritual materialism characterises the mystics. In the mystical teachings of Jacob Boehme there is much water, fire and sulphur, spiritual material and material spirituality.
>
> (ibid.)

Personalization, like individuation for Jung, moves towards an increasing sensibility for what Jung called in his later work the *unus mundus*.

Thus, the affirmation of personality as a microcosm which is itself a whole and not part of any objective whole is the very opposite of narcissism and solipsism; it is a 'throwing open in love' (Berdyaev 1943: 44). Only through love and communion is the universal content of personality actualized. What is overcome in the realization of personality is the alienation of the biological individual within impersonal social structures; realization allows it to attain living, existential communion with the Thou, the We and the cosmos. Personality lives in communion.

It is this inner, existential communion with God which gives personality its independence from the world of objects, and thus at the same time frees it to attain communion. Personality 'is not formulated by the world of objects but by subjectivity, in which is hidden the image of God' (ibid.: 45). In this lies its Divine–human quality. The inner vertical movement of transcension in which the ego liberates itself from its objectified condition is a liberation from the egocentric greed and concupiscence that go along with this state of objectification.

In Jungian terms we would say that this state results from the ego being caught up in projections. The more I experience myself as an object in a world of objects, the more the hunger for infinity inherent in subjectivity will manifest itself as insatiable greed. The objectified world is essentially a social construct, a sort of 'collective idol', which obscures the true reality of others and the cosmos. It is the world that the ego, which is cut off from the Self, constructs for itself through projections.

Personality as embodied

The spiritual nature of personality does not imply that it is abstracted from body and soul. Spirit, for Berdyaev, is not abstract and ethereal. On the contrary, it is the most concrete and dynamic dimension of existence. It is precisely in the depth of the person that the living essence of existence is disclosed. Spirit defines the unique, integral *Gestalt* of the personality, which is only real if it is creatively expressed in soul *and* body:

> The spirit gives form to the soul and to the body and brings them into a unity; it does not crush or destroy them . . . the spirit gives form to the personality, into which the body enters, into which there enters the face of man.
>
> (ibid.: 32)

Inasmuch as the body expresses or *is* form, *Gestalt*, it is essentially a spiritual phenomenon, an existential reality, not a 'material object'. The meeting with the other as Thou is a meeting with an embodied other. In particular, the face is an embodied expression of personality: personality in its concreteness is an integral whole comprising body and soul, which receives its *Gestalt* from the spirit.

By communicating form to the soul, the spiritual centre of the personality is the force of integration. Loss of personality means disintegration of the psyche, while its actualization means wholeness and integrality. Personality 'is linked with character . . . Character is the victory of the spiritual principle in man, but victory in a concretely individual form, which is bound up with the soul–body constitution of man' (ibid.: 47). Once again, this integrality is not a false 'properness' enforced by the ego, which tries desperately to fulfil superego standards. It is rather a capacity to resist the pressures for adaptation both to psychic automatism and to the social pressures coming from the collective.

Such integrality is never totally realized in temporal existence. Personality is and remains an 'axiological category', an ideal – not an abstract one but one constantly realizing itself in the shaping and integration of the chaotic psychic *prima materia*. We are thus suspended between these two poles of disintegration and integration, oscillating between them. This oscillation is inherent to the dynamic existence of personality and this dynamic existence of personality is a concrete, embodied existence.

The creative function of memory and moral creativity

In this dynamic existence of personality, memory plays an important role. For Berdyaev memory 'is a spiritual phenomenon, it is a spiritual endeavour to preserve man's being from the disintegrating influence of time' (Berdyaev 1938: 167). That memory is a spiritual phenomenon means that it has a creative function. It is not just the passive, mechanical activity of recollecting facts, but the active shaping of a story, a personal myth in which the meaning of my personal biography is disclosed.

The individual biography as a meaningful whole has as its 'background' a mythical perspective on universal history which presupposes both creative memory and the creative anticipation of future potentials. We see this same focus on the historical and on the need for a new myth that gives meaning to our history also in Jung. As the collective myths that we absorbed passively lose their force, we are faced with the task of creatively shaping our own myths as part of the process of individuation. But such myths have real, living force and reality only if they have deep historical roots in the collective memory of humanity.

Berdyaev's emphasis on the importance of memory may also help to understand an important dimension of in-depth therapy, which could be interpreted as an in-depth exercise in creative recollection: the gradual shaping of a story, of a personal myth which weaves together the personal and the universal. Therapy thus emerges as a creative process that is contained within and nourished by the field of the therapeutic relationship, which can facilitate an opening of the heart, the integral, spiritual core of the person, which is the source of creativeness. This process implies the overcoming of unconsciousness, i.e. impersonal, mechanical automatism: 'Everything that is personal in man is set in opposition to any kind of automatism' (Berdyaev 1943: 36).

The most marked opposite of automatism is geniality, and for Berdyaev there is *always* an element of geniality in personality. 'Geniality is the whole nature of man; it is its intuitively creative relation to life . . . Geniality is potentially inherent in personality . . . The image of God in man belongs to geniality, but this geniality can be concealed, crushed, obscured' (ibid.: 57). The ethics of personality are, for Berdyaev, the ethics of creativeness, which presuppose a quality of moral genius. Conscience here becomes the creative centre of the person, not the compulsion to adapt to external norms. The heart as the 'kernel of the human personality . . . is the seat of wisdom and the organ of moral conscience, which is the supreme organ of all evaluation' (ibid.: 196). As the integrating centre of the person it is a heart of flesh, alive with feeling, broken, sorrowing, loving, longing, living: personal, not abstract. It points us to the Self in Jung's psychology, to which we will now turn.

Jung's understanding of the person

While Berdyaev's response to the crisis of modernity, which threatens to lead to a dissolution of the person, takes the form of a new Christian 'Divine–humanism', Jung seeks to revision the Christian myth in terms of his empirical study of the individuation process, for which he identifies alchemy as a historical precursor. The 'alchemical' theme continues into Nietzsche's *Zarathustra* and Goethe's *Faust*. In both works the death of the traditional

God-image initiates a process of individuation. The dying God has gone underground and is now to be found in Faust's 'kingdom of the mothers where everything is in a continuous state of self-renewal, a continuous rearrangement' (Jung 1988: 54). And Nietzsche, by declaring that God is dead 'immediately gets into the process of [the] . . . archetype of rebirth, because those vital powers in us which we call "God" are powers of self-renewal, powers of eternal change' (ibid.). Like Nietzsche, who gets 'into the mill, the alchemical melting pot where he is cooked and transformed' (ibid.), contemporary man is facing a similar predicament and Jung's psychology seeks to assist the process of rebirth of a larger, individuated personality. Considered within such a broad context, personality can legitimately be seen as a central theme of Jung's psychology.

Nevertheless, certain questions present themselves. To begin with, how does this square with one of his most important contributions to depth psychology, i.e. the theory of the collective unconscious, which is clearly impersonal? Furthermore, Jung called his psychology 'complex psychology', which appears to emphasize his interest in the dissociability of the psyche and a 'pluralistic' understanding of personality. How compatible is this with the 'monotheistic' view of the person? To answer these questions, we will want to form a clearer idea of how these notions fit into what we might call Jung's alchemical notion of personality.

This alchemical understanding of the person does not so much point in the direction of a 'Divine–humanism' but more in the direction of what we might perhaps call a 'humanistic pantheism', to use a term which Rose Pfeffer employs to characterize Goethe's and Nietzsche's position: 'In Goethe's and Nietzsche's pantheism, man is central; but it is man as a part of nature' (Pfeffer 1972: 233). Although Jung does not want to use any metaphysical framework but rather to do empirical psychology, his romantic roots and his kinship to Goethe and Nietzsche leave their unmistakeable traces.

'Personalistic' ego-personality versus total personality as a task of individuation

A first testimony to the importance of the notion of the person for Jung is his account of the decisive effect that reading Krafft-Ebbing's *Textbook of Psychiatry* had on him; it made him decide to turn towards psychiatry while still a medical student:

> I thus read in the preface: 'It is probably due to the peculiarity of the subject and the incompleteness of its elaboration that psychiatric text-books are stamped with a more or less subjective character'. A few lines further on, the author called the psychoses 'diseases of the person'. My heart suddenly began to pound. I had to stand up and draw a deep breath. It had become clear to me in a flash of illumination that there

> could be no other goal for me than psychiatry . . . Here was the empirical field common to biological and spiritual facts, which I had everywhere sought and nowhere found. Here at last was the place where the collision of nature and spirit became a reality.
>
> (Jung 1995: 130)

We get the impression that Jung is hit by a flash of intuitive insight, showing him the shape that his later work would take. Three closely interrelated themes can be identified:

- the subjective character of psychological knowledge
- the understanding of psychological pathologies to be diseases of the person
- the understanding of the person to be the meeting place of biological and spiritual facts.

All of these are fundamental themes of Jung's psychology. Jung continuously emphasizes the subjective and provisional character of psychological knowing, due to the 'personal equation'.[11] Second, he aspires towards a 'holistic' understanding of psychological processes that is synthetic rather than analytic. This means that 'Jung envisaged the totality of the human personality so as to gauge the particular phenomena from the standpoint of the whole' (Frey-Rohn 1974: 67). Third, Jung considers this psychic totality to be a polar union of tension between the opposites of spirit and nature. This notion of the person is a psychological one. Not person as spirit – as in Berdyaev – but *esse in anima* is what captivates Jung's intuition.

Krafft-Ebbing's use of the term 'person' suggests an organic, holistic and phenomenological–hermeneutic mode of psychological understanding. The 'holistic' understanding of psychic processes has important consequences for Jung's understanding of psychotherapy. First of all, it leads Jung to trust in the self-healing and self-regulating capacity of the psyche. Furthermore, as a 'healing art', therapy for Jung is not just a 'method' based on a fixed theoretical system, but essentially 'a dialogue or discussion between two persons . . . A person is a psychic system which, when it affects another person, enters into reciprocal reaction with another psychic system' (Jung 1935a: para. 1). A psychic system is characterized by two features: on the one hand it is always individual and unique, but on the other hand it shares collective, universally human characteristics. If the latter were not the case, no psychology would be possible. If the former were not the case, there would be no unique person.

While individual differentiations can be made the object of a psychological theory, as Jung did in *Psychological Types* (1921), this element of uniqueness cannot. Therefore all psychological statements are provisional. Jung takes account of the non-objectifiable personal dimension by proposing a 'dialectical formulation, which tells us precisely that psychic influence is the reciprocal reaction of two psychic systems' (Jung 1935a: para. 1).

Therefore, the therapeutic dimension of the personal comes into play by the introduction of an 'apophatic' dimension. To be present to the other, to give him/her one's full attention with a mind emptied of preconceived notions, is a fundamental gesture in the therapeutic process. 'In the end,' Jung writes in one of his letters, 'personality is the most powerful therapeutic agent' (Jung 1973: 112). What is most powerful and essential is also most elusive and incapable of psychological systematization. And yet, this element of uniqueness is nevertheless a central psychological reality.

But it is not only impossible for psychology to grasp the reality of the personal beyond giving it a place in the spontaneous unfoldment of the therapeutic process. From the psychological perspective it is the collective, not the existential dimension, which appears to be primarily in charge: 'human personality is certainly not individual only, it is also collective, and to such a degree that the individual is rather like an underprivileged minority' (Jung 1959b: para. 888).

Therefore, despite what has been said so far, on examining his writings, one might initially not get the slightest impression that the theme of the person is centrally important to Jung.[12] On the contrary, one might be inclined to think that he attempted, with his concepts of the collective unconscious and the objective psyche, to provide precisely a counterweight to the excessively 'personalistic' Freudian approach, which is, for example, incapable of understanding the psychology of schizophrenia.[13] Indeed, the term 'personalistic' is often used by Jung to criticize an excessively ego-centred psychology: a 'narrowly personalistic psychology' (Jung 1944: para. 40) is not only incapable of mastering the archetypal material which becomes manifest in psychotic states, but also that which can emerge from the depths of the psyche in healthy individuals and is closely related to religious phenomena. A 'personalistic' psychology is 'egocentric' because 'the ego is the subject of all personal acts of consciousness' and as such forms 'the centre of the field of consciousness' which 'comprises the empirical personality' (Jung 1951: para. 1).

Unlike Freud, Jung represents the unconscious as something that includes but transcends the 'personal unconscious' and coincides in its deepest reaches with the total impersonality of natural processes. Archetypal psychologists hail Jung as the liberator from the prison of western individualism and personalism. Is not the alchemical symbol of the 'philosopher's stone', which is taken by Jung to be a symbol of the Self, precisely the thing most removed from the personalistic human realm? What could be more impersonal than a stone? Is not this movement beyond the 'personalistic' and towards the 'archetypal' much more characteristic of Jung's work?

To address this question, we must first of all differentiate between the 'personalistic' meaning of personality and the meaning of personality that focuses on its character of unrepeatable uniqueness, which Jung terms 'the individual' or 'individuality' (Jung 1921: para. 755ff.), giving the term, as we have pointed out earlier, a completely different meaning to Berdyaev.

The development of the whole personality requires the union of 'biological duty' (or nature tasks) and 'culture tasks' (see Jung 1930–1931). Personality is a wholeness in which the biological and the spiritual dimensions meet. Its realization will therefore have to do with resolving the conflict and collision between these dimensions and creating a harmonious whole. In this process individuality is shaped. Life poses the problems and each individual contains a new, unique possibility for their solution. We all have to find our own 'philosopher's stone'.

This harmonious whole, which increasingly finds expression in the process of individuation, is something which inevitably escapes any final definition. A 'total description of the personality is, even in theory, absolutely impossible' (Jung 1951: para. 7), because it comprises not only conscious but also unconscious elements, which, by definition, escape description. We are alive, and that means always unfinished. Wholeness is not static but dynamic, just as the alchemists sometimes describe the stone as liquid, not solid.

From his 'non-personalistic', archetypal perspective, Jung develops an 'apophatic' approach to the person. Personality as a value to be realized primarily in the second half of life is a value which orients the ego towards a continuous self-transcendence into the unknown. We are always more than we know ourselves to be. 'Clearly then, the *personality as a total phenomenon* does not coincide with the ego, that is, with the conscious personality, but forms an entity that has to be distinguished from the ego' (Jung 1951: para. 8). This total personality 'which, though present, cannot be fully known' Jung suggests we call the Self (Jung 1951: para. 9). Jung's alchemical notion of personality focuses on this process of the creation of the *lapis*, the Self. In the Self the unique and the universal coincide. Individuation is a uniquely individual process, which at the same time leads to an ever deepening participation in the vast tides of life moving through the *anima mundi*.

The 'secret of personality': Jung, Goethe and alchemy

Is it possible to give more precision to this idea of an 'alchemical notion of personality' in Jung? Uniqueness emerges as a result of the lived response to a calling to the *opus* of transformation which may reach us through chaos and neurotic suffering: 'Because neurosis is a developmental disturbance of the personality, we physicians of the soul are compelled by professional necessity to concern ourselves with the problem of personality and the inner voice, however remote it may seem to be' (Jung 1934: para. 316). The birth of true individuality is often precipitated by a crisis, which commits us to find our own path, our own solution. Jung connects personality closely to the inner voice and the phenomenon of receiving a calling or vocation. 'True personality is always a vocation' (ibid.: para. 300).

The actual phenomenology of psychological experience shows that this inner voice, far from being harmless, is something irrational, supernatural or godlike, a daemonic factor, which somehow intervenes in the life of the individual and calls her out of her immersion in the collective into a situation of isolation. So, for example, Goethe's Faust is desperately lonely on that Easter Sunday when he hears the Church bells ringing, and recognizes that the message has lost its meaning for him. He is in a state of what we would now call 'clinical depression', and contemplates suicide. All his life energy has dried up; nothing has any meaning any more; he has reached a total dead end. At this point Mephisto enters the stage, and the profound drama of transformation begins. The 'inner voice' here takes on anything but a harmless character; rather, it is ambivalent, dark and threatening: it appears to be even plainly 'evil'. But for Jung, Mephisto is not so much the Christian devil, but rather a personification of *Mercurius*.

Here we strike a crucial spot in Jung's psychology and in his understanding of neurotic symptoms. Jung always asks: What is the soul saying through the symptom? How can it be recognized as the inner voice of this individual, which has not been heeded and now demands attention in an apparently menacing form? 'The neurosis is thus a defence against the objective, inner activity of the psyche, or an attempt, somewhat dearly paid for, to escape from the inner voice, hence from the vocation' (ibid.: para. 313).

Thus, when Jung characterizes neurosis as a 'developmental disturbance of the personality', he does not so much have in mind of developmental psychology in the Freudian sense, but rather a disturbance of the relation of the ego to the objective, inner activity of the psyche, because this activity is a process that fosters transformation and urges us towards it. If it remains unconscious, this urge may have uncanny, seemingly hostile, and clearly dangerous and destructive consequences. The psyche's urge is towards wholeness and will appear to oppose the limited goals of the ego and if someone 'voluntarily takes the burden of completeness upon himself, he need not find it "happening" to him against his will in a negative form' (Jung 1951: para. 125).

When he had familiarized himself with the principles of alchemy, Jung realized that

> the unconscious is a *process*, and that the psyche is transformed and developed by the relationship of the ego to the contents of the unconscious. . . . Through the study of . . . collective transformation processes and through understanding alchemical symbolism I arrived at the central concept of my psychology: *the process of individuation*.
>
> (Jung 1995: 235)

Somehow, during this process, the self-regulating capacities of the psyche, which compensate for one-sided developments of consciousness and drive it towards the realization of a larger wholeness, become manifest. What calls is 'the God within', like the Son of the King in the alchemical parable who is calling to be saved from the depths of the waters (see Jung 1944: para. 434).

In the same chapter of Jung's autobiography we find a passage which will lead us right into the heart of Jung's thinking about the unique or individual personality that results from this process of individuation:

> I regard my work on alchemy as a sign of my inner relationship to Goethe. Goethe's secret was that he was in the grip of that process of archetypal transformation, which has gone on through the centuries. He regarded his Faust as an *opus magnum* or *divinum*. He called it his 'main business' and his whole life was enacted within the framework of this drama. Thus, what was alive and active within him was a living substance, a supra personal process, the great dream of the *mundus archetypus* . . .
>
> I myself have been haunted by the same dream, and from my eleventh year I have been launched upon a single enterprise, which is my 'main business'. *My life has been permeated and held together by one ideal and one goal: namely, to penetrate into the secret of the personality. Everything can be explicated from this central point, and all my works relate to this one theme.*
>
> (Jung 1995: 232, emphasis mine)

The idea of personality which Jung has in mind is thus one that is most intimately linked with vast historical perspectives. In its uniqueness personality does not take shape without deep roots in the *mundus archetypus*. Each one of us is a new and unique way in which a supra personal process which unites all of humanity takes shape. And in this hidden *rhizome* the personal and the historical are woven together with the rhythms of nature itself.

A quick glance at the mind of Goethe will give us, I believe, a way into the deeper aspects of Jung's thinking about 'the secret of personality' which, as we have seen up to now, has something to do with the opposition and union of nature and spirit. As is well known, the study of the processes of transformation or metamorphosis was fundamental to Goethe's work on natural science.

> The path of research which he took in botany, the way in which he found his fundamental principle of his doctrine of metamorphosis of plants, and this principle itself become for Goethe the prototype of all his other studies and researches in various fields. From plants he turns to animals and discovers there an analogous developmental law . . . Finally he also says of his study of colours that 'it rests with the metamorphosis of plants on one and the same principle'. But also the development of man is drawn into this circle.
>
> (Leisegang 1932: 49ff., trans.)

Therefore, Goethe's *Faust* is a study of the metamorphosis of the human soul.[14]

Furthermore, polarity was, for Goethe, another fundamental principle along with metamorphosis. Goethe developed a form of thought which understood all things

> as if they were living totalities, to find everywhere polarities which unite within a circle, so that not only life and death, but also self-determination and destiny, freedom and necessity, moment and eternity, man and world, good and evil all mutually condition each other and are all thought together into the same unity, like the whole and its parts, the one and the many contained in it.
>
> (Leisegang 1932: 39, trans.)

Goethe was familiar with alchemy, which can be seen as the study of metamorphosis, of transformation processes in nature and in the human soul. Jung sees Goethe's *Faust* as 'an alchemical drama from beginning to end' (Jung 1944: para. 85).[15]

Alchemy is the study of the archetypal patterns underlying all transformation processes. Within the human psyche, the fundamental transformation process is that of the 'second birth', i.e. the birth of a new, *vaster* personality that is supraordinate to the ego. It is this process which is described in *Faust*, where Faust is the representative of modern man. In this way Goethe unveils a 'process of transformation' in the human soul, a process of collective dimensions 'which has gone on through the centuries'. The collective and the personal in this *vaster* non-'personalistic' sense are most deeply connected.

To penetrate into the 'secret of personality' therefore means to unveil a substratum in which the individual is connected in mysterious ways to the collective, to the historical process, and even to nature and the cosmos. But, at the very same time, this does not entail the dissolution of the personal within the cosmic–impersonal dimension. The treasure obtained from these depths, the 'larger personality', is instead a *coincidentia oppositorum* of the personal and the impersonal.

It appears, therefore, that on the individual and the collective human level, 'nature', i.e. the psyche, constitutes a 'process', which, if the ego begins to consciously relate to it, incessantly drives towards individuation, the production of the *aurum non vulgi* of true personality. But the very same process may take on destructive characteristics if the ego is out of touch with it. In either case, an element of crisis and danger is involved.

In Boehme's theosophy, 'eternal nature' is initially dark and terrifying, a consuming wrath-fire (which could be interpreted psychologically as symbolizing a condition of madness and chaotic disintegration) that strives to be reborn as light: there can be no light without this dark fire. We have already mentioned Goethe's principle of polarity, which rules all of nature. The same idea can be found in Hegelian dialectics and, with significant modifications, in Berdyaev's 'existential dialectics'.

The *nigredo* is the beginning of the work, and the unsuspecting 'victim' of the process falls into this 'dark world' like Alice in Wonderland. A 'descent into chaos' initiates the birth process of the larger, renewed personality. 'We must not underestimate the devastating effects of getting lost in the chaos, even if we know that it is the *sine qua non* of any regeneration of the spirit and the personality' (Jung 1944: para. 96).

At this point it might be fruitful to ask, returning to the previously mentioned quote from Jung's autobiography: what happened to Jung when he was 11 years old? Why was his life permeated from then on by one ideal, one goal: to penetrate into the secret of personality?

When Jung was 11 years old he had an 'active imagination' experience which was, for him, a profoundly religious and numinous revelation. He had initially an innocent fantasy of God being enthroned in the sky, high above Basel Cathedral. When he dared to give into his frightening urge to bring this fantasy to its conclusion, God defecates on the Cathedral (see Jung 1995: 52 ff.). Here, in this crude image, the theme of opposites contained within the God-image appeared to Jung for the first time, with overwhelming force. He had dared to imagine the unimaginable, what is always left out, and in precisely that moment he experiences the reality of 'God'. This is what comprises the innermost secret of personality: this root, origin and source of all psychic dynamism which people have always called 'God'. Thus we can see how Jung's intuition of a psychological notion of personality is linked to his psychological notion of 'God'.

From the psychological perspective 'God' appears as a force of nature, which drives everything towards individuation and which is far more ambiguous than theology allows for. Historical processes, just like processes in nature, are shaped by it. The closer one moves to the Self, the more deeply linked does the psychological process appear to that which infinitely surpasses the individual in its vastness. In a text from Islamic tradition it is said that 'God is the hidden treasure who desired to be known and created the world for this end' (cited from Faivre and Needleman 1995: 212). This mythical image resonates well with Jung's psychological understanding of 'God'. The place where the hidden treasure can finally become known is the human personality. Thus all nature drives towards the creation of an organism, which can be the vessel of consciousness.[16] The 'hidden treasure' which desires to be known is a paradoxical union of opposites, and therefore the individuation process is, on the one hand, a 'process of nature' and, on the other hand, an *opus contra naturam*, a process which unites in itself both a biological and a spiritual aspect.

Personality and (sub-)personalities

We can now see that for Jung the 'personal' in a narrow sense refers to the untransformed ego-personality, whereas personality in the deeper sense, i.e. as a value to be realized in the second half of life, results from a 'second birth', an alchemical 'transmutation' of the original ego-personality. A religious, numinous factor intervenes, a process which is almost invariably precipitated by a crisis that challenges the spurious integrity of the ego-personality. What underlies this seeming unity and integrity of the ego?

The ego-personality has two characteristics: it is closely related to consciousness (see Jung 1928: para. 392), and it is largely cut off from the deeper, 'impersonal' or collective aspects of the unconscious. But precisely because it is cut off from them, it is that much more 'collective', i.e. driven by them. Not only does the ego-complex originally emerge as a coalescence of initially separated 'islands of consciousness' or luminosities (Jung 1947/1954: para. 387), the psyche also maintains a constant dissociability (ibid.: para. 365ff.), and the identity of the everyday ego-personality is therefore anything but stable. It is more often an amalgam of different personae, which surface in different social circumstances.

The term 'personality' thus has various levels of meaning. On the one hand, the ego-personality can be understood as a 'distinct, defined functional complex' (Jung 1921: para. 799). On the other hand, various complexes can themselves be said to have some sort of quasi-personality. Archetypes such as anima and animus operate like personalities within us. As long as the ego is unconscious of these inner dynamics, there is actually no true personality, but only a more or less 'arbitrary segment of the collective psyche – often fashioned with considerable pains' (Jung 1928: para. 245).

The ego-personality is thus a unity only in a very limited sense, established by a defensive attitude towards complex unconscious dynamics which, in the case of an *abaissment du niveau mental*, may lead to a total disintegration of the personality, i.e. schizophrenia or, in the case of neurosis, a dissociation 'which is bridged over by a unity of personality which still functions' (Jung 1939: para. 509). In such cases, and even in 'normal' psychology, 'the affect that binds the complex together could easily be interpreted as milder, preliminary forms of schizophrenic symptoms' (ibid.: para. 578). If Schelling says that all personality rests on a dark ground (cf. Schelling 1990: 413) we could say, along with Jung, that all personality rests on a dark ground of dissociation from which it is never entirely free. Conversely Jung finds a 'normal personality' present in the psychic background of so-called mad people: 'More than once I have seen that even with such patients there remains in the background a personality which must be called normal. It stands looking on, so to speak' (Jung 1995: 148).

From all this we can see that the 'personalistic', conscious ego-personality is something very precarious, which can maintain a semblance of 'character', stability and permanence only through a ruthless repression of everything that doesn't fit into the adaptive pattern of the persona. Outwardly it is at the mercy of collective standards and modes of thinking; inwardly it is unconsciously swept along by everything that moves in the collective psyche. One could say that 'normality' is an acceptable degree of insanity; and insanity, for Jung, is more meaningful and intelligible than it appears on the surface. But for the ego-personality, because it is uncomfortably closer to the condition of madness than it would like itself to believe, this condition appears alien and frightening.

This fundamentally defensive character of the largely collectively determined ego-personality has another consequence. The 'personalistic' consciousness represses not only those personality-fragments which do not fit into the persona that it has built with great pains, but also those unconscious contents which have 'never entered into consciousness at all because no possibilities exist for apperceiving . . . [them]' (Jung 1947/1954 para. 366). We cannot assimilate contents into consciousness that are entirely foreign to its current *Gestalt*. This *Gestalt* may act like a barrier against the new, which may confuse us and upset the more or less precarious equilibrium that we find in the stable little world that we have constructed for ourselves. This close proximity to the genuinely new can be called the 'repression of the sublime' (see Assagioli 1975: 48, 66). The fear of madness lodged in the recesses of the ego-personality here becomes the fear of the unknown, even where the latter may be sublime, graceful and redeeming.

The new, vaster personality on the other hand has a capacity of integration, which is not anxiously contracted onto the ego's little world but open to the new and unknown, able to change and to progressively include more and more of the vast ecology of life and meaning (*anima mundi*) beyond the boundaries of the ego. The crossing of the threshold which separates the ego from this encompassing sense of identity has a numionus-initiatic, a 'religious' character. Jung locates religion right in this experiential core of transforming and expanding personal identity.

The 'vaster personality'

The '*vaster* personality' that seeks to be born within us has a sublime quality, which is as foreign to the ego-personality as the disintegrating forces that threaten it from 'below'. In his autobiography, Jung talks about how, as a child, he began to discover that he was actually two personalities: 'personality No. 1' and 'personality No. 2'. Jung gives an account of how it transpired that a sense of 'authority' awakened in him, which formed the seed of what would become 'personality No. 2'.

> I was taking the long road home from school . . . when suddenly for a single moment I had the overwhelming impression of just having emerged

> from a dense cloud. I knew all at once: *I am myself*! It was as if a wall of mist were in my back, and behind that wall there was not yet an 'I'. But at this moment I *came upon myself* . . . This experience seemed to me tremendously important and new: there was 'authority' in me.
>
> (Jung 1995: 49)

The 'other', i.e. Jung's 'personality No. 2', which now started to emerge, was not the insecure schoolboy but 'a high authority' (Jung 1995: 50) who lived in 'another realm' than the schoolboy, 'like a temple in which anyone who entered was transformed and suddenly overpowered by a vision of the whole cosmos . . . Here lived the "Other" who knew God as a hidden, personal, and at the same time supra-personal secret. Here nothing separated man from God . . . At such times I *knew* I was worthy of myself, that I was my true self' (Jung 1995: 62).

We may remember here Berdyaev's insight, drawn from his own experience, that 'It is necessary to distinguish in man the superficial and the profound ego . . . The superficial ego in man which is socialised, rationalised and civilised, is not the personality in man' (Berdyaev 1943: 25). What Jung seems to be describing is his own discovery of the 'profound ego', which leads to a gradually developing fantasy of the 'personality No. 2' which is not socialized, rationalized, civilized, but which lives in its own world. This discovery takes the form of something entirely 'new' and unsuspected breaking into the consciousness of the young schoolboy. Paradoxically, 'personality No. 2' was somehow an 'unconscious personality', which nevertheless had something to do with the awakening of a highly distinct sense of self-consciousness.

This relationship is elucidated further in a dream that Jung had towards the end of his life, in which he entered a chapel where a Yogi sat meditating. On waking up, Jung thought: 'Aha, so he is the one that is meditating me. He has a dream, and I am it' (Jung 1995: 355). Jung considered the dream to be a parable: 'My self retires into meditation and meditates my earthly form' (ibid.: 356). The aim of the dream, he believed, was

> a reversal of the relationship between ['personalistic'] ego-consciousness and the unconscious as the generator of the empirical personality. This reversal suggests that in the opinion of the 'other side', our unconscious existence is the real one and our conscious world is a kind of illusion, an apparent reality constructed for a specific purpose, like a dream which seems a reality as long as we are in it . . . Unconscious wholeness therefore seems to me to be the true *spiritus rector* of all biological and psychic events. Here is a principle, which strives for total realisation – which in man's case signifies the attainment of total consciousness.
>
> (Jung 1995: 356ff.)

In a passage from *Mysterium Coniunctionis*, Jung formulates this peculiar nature of the ego – of being at once 'superficial' and 'profound' – theoretically. After discussing the fact that the alchemists 'came very close to realising that the ego was the mysteriously elusive arcane substance and the longed-for *lapis*' and thus established 'an intimate connection between God and the ego', an intuition of 'man's hidden Godlikeness' which 'Angelus Silesius finally expressed . . . without disguise' (Jung 1955/1956: para. 131), he goes on to say that it could seem self-contradictory that he here attributes to the ego qualities that are, in all his other writings, attributed to the Self. He responds to this by saying that the ego 'is an essential part of the self, and can be used *pars pro toto* when the significance of consciousness is borne in mind. But when we want to lay emphasis on the psychic totality, it is better to use the term "self" ' (ibid.: para.133).

If the ego appears, in this light, to be much more mysterious than we might initially suspect, this applies equally to the 'personality'. The personal and the personality are, in one sense, clearly linked to ego consciousness; that is, the consciousness of Jung the schoolboy, or, more generally of the superficial, socially adapted ego that resides on the persona level. But at the same time, the ego is not identical to the persona, although this is most often what we refer to when we talk of 'the ego'. The ego is in one sense dispersed amongst different 'subpersonalities' with which it identifies at different times, i.e. different 'personae', and it is also somehow driven by an 'inner personality', by the animus/anima and by various complexes which all have a degree of personality in themselves. But clearly none of these is identical with the ego, and by dissolving its unconscious identity with them the ego may come into a position of authority in relation to them.

It is quite a different situation with the Self, the 'psychic totality' or 'total personality' as Jung often calls it, because here the ego finds itself in a relationship similar to that which Jung's dream portrays. It is as if it finds itself to be a projection of the Self, a much vaster, wiser, infinitely older and superior personality, which always remains a supraordinate personality because it can never be made fully conscious. Nevertheless, in one of its important symbolic aspects the Self is symbolised by *Sol*, the sun. It appears as the source of ego consciousness in such a way that we can imagine the ego in its 'solar' nature as emerging from the sun/Self like one of its rays.

The 'superficial ego' then appears as 'the veil of Maya' (Jung 1955/56: para. 132), behind which is hidden the 'profound ego' or 'total personality'. Jung's 'personality No. 2' is not an impersonal 'universal *atman*' (ibid.), though, but a personality of a quite distinct character. The term 'total personality' suggests a distinct, individualized identity that is already differentiated from an impersonal 'universal *atman*', but is nevertheless much vaster and infinitely wiser than the superficial ego-personality. In Jung's case, his fantasies about a man of high authority in the eighteenth century etc. are obviously highly particularized. They seem to form a kind of 'imaginal veil', which, like any other archetypal image, mediates something of the archetype to consciousness, but also limits and obscures it. In the dream he has in old age, the same 'personality No. 2' appears as a meditating Yogi.

In the case of the Self, the term 'archetype' becomes strictly speaking problematic if we consider the fact that, in its aspect of being the 'profound ego', it is precisely that which is least collective and most individual. It is only in its other aspect as 'psychic totality' that its collective aspect is emphasized. This brings us back to the already mentioned mystical saying: *Deus est sphaera, cujus centrum ubique, circumferentia nusquam*. The 'solar' aspect of the Self is the *centrum*, the *scintilla animae*. So, in one important aspect, to which Jung points in the passage quoted from *Mysterium Coniunctionis*, the Self is the seed of individuality, very closely related to the ego itself in its mysterious depths and origins.

The seed of individuality slumbers in the depths of the psyche and presses towards its unfolding; for Jung it operates in mysterious ways through all the different symptoms, dreams, moods and affects which the psyche produces, and which tend to throw the superficial ego-personality out of kilter. It may appear as a hostile *diabolos*, like Faust's Mephisto, or in countless other guises. Somehow it may even, and to an unknown extent, synchronistically orchestrate outer events to drive the ego towards certain realizations. In all these forms it manifests itself, often unheeded and unrecognized, as the 'inner voice' addressed to the ego from the depths.

This 'inner voice', as we have seen earlier, is ambivalent. To follow it is therefore a dangerous undertaking. Nevertheless, faithfulness to one's own unique law, although often severely punished by the collective, is at the same time praised as the highest value. 'True personality is always a vocation and puts its trust in it as in God, despite it's being, as the ordinary man would say, only a personal feeling' (Jung 1934: para. 300). One has to risk following this calling from the depths. Jung interprets the Christ-life as a symbol and a template for this sort of faith. It 'became a sacred symbol because it is the prototype of the only meaningful life, that is, of a life that strives for individual realization – absolute and unconditional – of its own particular law' (ibid.: para. 310).

In place of the effort to adapt oneself to a dogmatic representation of Christ as an external ideal of perfection, Jung sees as the only valid meaning of the *imitatio Christi* for contemporary man the struggle to realize inner wholeness by being courageous enough to live out fully and passionately the unrepeatable meaning of one's unique existence. Jung's faith is not a faith in a transcendent God, but a faith in the soul's mystery as it becomes manifest in psychological experience. This mystery is 'God' experienced as a numinous force welling up from the depths. If Christ is 'the way' (John 14: 6) this way now has to be found in the depths of the soul: 'Personality is Tao' (ibid.: para. 323), the way which is the soul's own *immanent* law, demanding truthfulness to oneself, not to dogmatic formulations.

Personality is Tao: The transcendent function

The formation of a personality as 'a well rounded whole that is capable of resistance and abounding in energy' (ibid.: para. 286) is dependent on the container which religion provides. Having lost the collective safeguards of traditional religion, modern man is confronted with this task often in harsh and challenging ways. In his paper 'The Development of Personality', Jung refers to Schiller as the genius who first divined 'the problems of adult education' (ibid.: para. 284) as they present themselves to modern man.

The birth of the vaster personality depends on the presence of the living, uniting symbol traditionally provided by religion. The conflict and crisis resulting from the loss of living religious symbols, both in the individual and in the culture, can and ought to lead to new creative responses from the depths. Schiller's ideas are for Jung precursors to his own notion of the transcendent function, which is capable of creating new symbolic containers (see Jung 1921: Ch. 2).

Schiller sees two opposing fundamental drives at work in man. We are beings who are, at one and the same time, entirely absorbed by the outer world and tied to it by bonds of desire, yet also finding within ourselves an equally strong drive towards the spiritual, the ideal, the realm of eternal form and values. If we only follow the impulse to immerse ourselves in the sphere of sensations we become savages, in whom 'feelings reign over principles' (Schiller 1991: 14, trans.), but if, on the other hand, we follow our nobler, rational–spiritual natures, we become barbarians who 'scorn and dishonour nature' (ibid.). It is in the aesthetic sphere that both these aspects of the personality are united in effortless play, and therefore 'man is only truly man where he plays' (Schiller 1991: 63). This creative play happens in the sphere of artistic creation or in the element of beauty. Beauty unites rationality/ spirituality and sensuality/emotionality without doing violence to either.

Jung sees Schiller's solution as too naïve, because it already presupposes what in reality still needs to be realized. By seeing beauty as the mediator between the spheres of the rational, rule-abiding consciousness and the 'wild' irrational unconscious world of desires, affects and chaotic emotions, Schiller precisely prevents the possibility of a synthesis of these two warring spheres, because beauty excludes ugliness, chaos, and everything dark and terrifying, and is therefore likely to become another repressive agent on the side of consciousness.

Nevertheless, Jung believes that Schiller touches upon something essential: when we play, and when fantasy and the imagination are left to play freely, we enter a realm in which we are not identified with either of the two opposites: either the conscious, collectively well-adapted primary function, or the largely unconscious, 'primitive', unadapted inferior function.[17] The effortless play of the imagination can produce a uniting symbol which harmonizes the opposites and constitutes a manifestation of the psychic totality, the seed of individuality or the *spiritus rector*, hitherto existing in the background. The Self, or total personality, is not identified with the dominant function of consciousness, like the ego, but located at the centre of the circle of the four functions.

In the play of the mythopoeic, symbol-producing imagination, which flows from a state of effortless meditative concentration, a solution to the inner conflict can be found which is neither rational nor irrational, but means a return to Tao. 'Tao is the right way, the reign of law, the middle road between the opposites, freed from them and yet uniting them in itself' (Jung 1921: para. 192). This is the process of the development of the transcendent function, which, by uniting the opposites in the imaginal–symbolic sphere, allows for the development of the ego–Self axis (see Neumann 2002: 26–57,148). It is the way in which the ego heeds the 'inner voice'.

So to become a personality, for Jung, is a process which entails harmonizing with the 'right path', which for each one of us is our own innermost, unique law: unique, yet in effortless harmony with the flow of life, an effortlessness most difficult to attain. Everything is renewed this way, a way that brings fresh imagination to everything:

> Classical Chinese philosophy names this interior way Tao, and likens it to a flow of water that irresistibly moves towards its goal. To rest in Tao means fulfilment, wholeness, one's destination reached, one's mission done; the beginning, end, and perfect realisation of the meaning of existence innate in all things. *Personality is Tao.*
>
> (Jung 1934: para. 323, emphasis mine)

Tao, the midpoint between the opposites, is that seed-place from which the organic and natural growth of the *entelechy*, the seed of individuality, can proceed. This is the 'central point', the 'secret of personality' into which Jung penetrated more and more deeply throughout his life. 'This something is the desired "midpoint" of the personality, that ineffable something betwixt the opposites, or else that which unites them, or the result of conflict, or the product of energic tension: the coming to birth of personality' (Jung 1928: para. 382). Personality is living form, which grows according to its own inherent living dynamism; the 'living form needs deep shadow if it is to appear plastic. Without shadow it remains a two-dimensional phantom, a more or less well brought up child' (ibid.: para. 400).

Tao is 'the Way' which reunites that which has been separated – life and consciousness – into its original unity, the unity of living form. The living form is gradually realized by a *circulatio* around the centre, which has 'the moral significance of activating the dark and the light forces of human nature' (Jung 1929: para. 39). Through this circulation one gains depth and reality, one moves from being just a well brought up child to becoming a real person. The 'sun wheel', the wheel of one's destiny, begins to turn and Tao, the path of self-knowledge, is activated. The 'intuition of the self, of one's own individual being' which results from such self-knowledge enforces 'an attitude of devotion to life' (ibid.: para. 36). In fact, life itself, 'lived with utter devotion, brings an intuition of the self, of one's own individual being' (ibid.).

The union of the opposites, symbolized as Tao in Chinese alchemy, becomes not only the theme of *Mysterium Coniunctionis*, Jung's monumental study of alchemy, but also of his other writings on Christianity. Jung attempts to reconnect the Christian dogma (which in its consciously elaborated and differentiated 'scholastic' form alienates consciousness from its natural roots) to the unconscious psyche (see Jung 1944: para. 40). In *Aion*, Jung is centrally concerned with the assimilation of the Christ-figure to the human psyche. 'The result appears in the emergence of the human personality and the development of consciousness' (Jung 1951: para. 346). And we can see in *Aion* how Jung depicts this assimilation as a move towards a conscious engagement with the principle of polarity underlying the psychic process.

Alchemy, the precursor of depth psychology, was 'ceaselessly engaged in preserving the bridge to nature' (ibid.: para. 346). The Tao, the natural way, the flow of life, is the energy of 'God', the 'hidden treasure which desires to be known', and creates for this purpose the sacred vessel of the human personality in which nature finds its fulfilment through the 'creation of consciousness' (see Edinger 1984). 'What the symbolism of alchemy describes is the whole problem of the evolution of personality' (Jung 1944: para. 40). Thus it becomes clear how Jung can say in his autobiography that all his 'life has been permeated and held together by one ideal and one goal: namely, to penetrate into the secret of the personality. Everything can be explicated from this central point' (Jung 1995: 232).

The anthropos-*image*

Inasmuch as the Self unites the individual and the collective, Jung's alchemical understanding of the person links the theme of individuation closely to a broad historical perspective. The transcendent function is the source of both individuation and of cultural creativity. The Self, the 'archetype that underlies ego consciousness' (Jung 1951: para. 347) is not a static entity but a process. This process 'goes on through the centuries', i.e. it has an *'aionic'* quality. In Ch. 14 of *Aion*, it is presented by Jung in relation to the *aion* of *pisces* as a vast alchemical *opus circulatorium*, which begins with the *anthropos* and ends with the *rotundum*. The *rotundum*, as the innermost secret of matter, is mysteriously identical to the *anthropos*. Thus the archetypal image of the *anthropos*, buried under the ashes of materialism, may (*Deo concedente*!) renew itself, rising out of these ashes like the Phoenix. Thus we see the mandalic space of individuation extend into ever widening dimensions. To be cut off from these dimensions means to become a faceless number.

This vast historical process is not simply a return to the beginning, the spiritually oriented *anthropos*, but leads to the new position, which Jung's psychology aims to give expression to. This new position constitutes a 'third', sublating both materialistic science and spiritualistic religion. 'The movement does not go on in circles; it goes forward in spirals. This means that you always return to the same point but on a higher level' (Hannah and von Franz 2004:164).

Jung finds in Ezekiel's vision of the *Merkhaba* an imaginal expression of the archetypal pattern underlying this historical process. In his vision, Ezekiel sees 'One who had the appearance of a Man' (Ez. 1: 4–30) seated upon a throne carried by the *Merkhaba*. The *anthropos* uses the historical process of transformation as its vehicle to bring about an increasingly humanized manifestation of the God-image.

What is significant for our theme is the link between the psychological concept of the 'collective unconscious' and this *anthropos*-image. It helps to further substantiate the central argument supporting a 'personalistic' reading of Jung. A further amplification of this image will make this even more evident.

The gnostic *anthropos*, the 'Light-man . . . the personified principle of light' is, according to gnostic myth, 'broken up into thousands of sparks of light or is scattered throughout matter as a "crucified world-soul" there to await his redemption. . . . This gnostic *anthropos* myth lived on, underground, in the alchemical tradition and hermetic philosophy' (von Franz 1998: 123). Jung's collective unconscious is set against the background of this archetypal image as a 'collective soul', the soul of the *anthropos*, the 'crucified world soul' which awaits redemption from the individual: 'He is buried like a corpse in matter, awaiting his resurrection, which comes about through the efforts of the single individual in the interest of the development of the "inner man" ' (ibid.: 123).

The link between the archetypal image of the *anthropos* and the 'abstract' psychological notion of the collective unconscious makes it clear how this chaotic *massa confusa* of the unconscious has in it the potentiality, the unconscious drive towards individuation and personification (the *massa globosa* or *rotundum* of the alchemists, i.e., in psychological terms, the 'pre-conscious Self' (cf. Hannah and von Franz 2004:160). Quite clearly, then, we can see that the notions of personality, *anthropos*, God-man and collective unconscious are linked. The *anthropos* that is buried in 'matter', appearing to us in psychology under the guise of the 'collective unconscious', makes his appearance within the psychological sphere as *Mercurius*, the chthonic counterpart of Christ, the God-man. In his initial, untransformed state he is experienced as the serpent, the Mephistophelian tempter, but he is also, potentially, the *lapis* in which above and below, the God-man and the chthonic 'old Adam', mysteriously become reconciled. Herein lies the secret of personality.

Individuation and spiritual experience

Jung and Berdyaev's notions of personality are closely related to the emergence of a new God-image that takes shape for both as a consequence of their confrontation with the nihilistic condition of modern man. The reconstitution of the human image in the nihilistic climate of modernity depends on a renewal of spirituality. In this new spirituality, the point of gravity shifts from a focus on transcendence to the inner experience of the process of individuation/personalization. This shift, anticipated by the mystics, emphasizes the individually unique character of authentic experience. Personality has to do with the experience of a vocation, the following of a calling. Its realization is driven by the dialectical tension of opposites, which is resolved in the superconscious and by the transcendent function respectively. The new God-image takes shape in this process, it is no longer dogmatically imposed from outside but born out of this process of individuation. Through this process, the individual at the same time finds a new mode of creative participation in the historical process. These are in broad strokes some of the parallels in Jung and Berdyaev's thinking about the person.

Nevertheless, on closer scrutiny we have to differentiate more carefully by using our hermeneutic principle, which states that while Jung focuses on *psychological* experience, Berdyaev focuses on *spiritual* experience in a more precise way. However closely Berdyaev's notion of the spiritual experience of freedom in becoming a person may be related to Jung's notion of individuation, the two are not the same. And this has evident repercussions on their understanding of personality and, as we shall see, for their relationship to traditional Christianity.

Even though, for Jung, the person is the place where the spiritual and the biological meet, the term 'spiritual' does not necessarily have the same meaning as it does for Berdyaev. The polarities within the personality are, for Jung, fundamentally psychological polarities. The life-process which operates within the unconscious depths of the psyche, and which drives the ego towards individuation, is a process of nature,[18] because psyche *is* nature and psychology is nowhere concerned with transcendent notions of spirit *as such*, but only with empirically verifiable psychic processes. The spiritual dimension in itself as it is considered in religious traditions is for Jung the domain of metaphysical speculation, not of verifiable facts. Psychology brings consciousness to the psychic processes evident in religious experience, and thereby becomes a psychology of individuation. 'God' appears within this perspective as a force of nature that drives the individuation process.

For Berdyaev, on the other hand, everything in his 'anthropology from above' is considered from the viewpoint of the creative–active spirit, and thus the oppositional structure of the person and the dynamics of development flowing from it are essentially characterized by an existential dialectic, in which the active, spiritual centre of the person strives to fully actualize its freedom. The dialectic here is asymmetrical, and is clearly weighed towards the spirit, which for him is a trans-psychic reality given in experience. Berdyaev is not operating, like Jung, with the principle of polarity understood as a natural process. His notion of existential dialectics does not refer to a natural process. Nothing for him has the character of a natural process with which the ego seeks to cooperate consciously; rather, Berdyaev seeks to understand the spiritual destiny of the person. Freedom, not nature, is the fundamental category.

This results in a different interpretation of the same phenomena of existential experience. We do not find in Berdyaev the same ambivalence of the 'voice' as in Jung. Ambivalence in existential experience stems from the inherent dialectics of freedom, not from the 'voice' itself. To follow one's calling means to be addressed by the 'eternal Thou' (Buber 1979), the *personal* God. This personal God is encountered in existential–spiritual communion, in freedom, and not as a force of nature.

Whereas Berdyaev reflects philosophically on the existential reality of the person given in spiritual experience, Jung deals with philosophical, theological terms such as 'God' or 'the *Anthropos*' purely as psychic images, which express something of the unknowable archetypal background to the psychic processes. This background tends to be implicitly conceptualized as a monistic All-unity (see von Hartmann 1923(2): 155ff.) or *pleroma* (see Segal 1992: Ch. 10; Maillard 1993). With regard to its philosophical origins, this implicit mode of conceptualizing empirical findings has its roots in the Romantic background to Jung's psychology. This has important implications for Jung's writings on Christianity. Charles Taylor writes that, in Romantic thought

> God . . . is to be interpreted in terms of what we see striving in nature and finding voice within ourselves. A slide into pantheism is all too easy . . . this slide can go further and take us outside Christian forms, until we get a view like Goethe's, for instance, or the views which were reflected in the widespread invocation of Spinoza in the Romantic period.
>
> (Taylor 1992: 371)

What is at stake here is the position one takes on the possibility of differentiating the immanent and the transcendent. Jung's psychology tends to interpret the spiritual, that which transcends nature, in terms of the immanent. This implicit conceptual background does not allow for a sufficiently clear differentiation of the spiritual and the psychological. In Berdyaev's philosophy this transcendent dimension is secured by his notion of the superconscious. The 'superconscious' denotes the dimension of the spirit, which, he claims, becomes present in a non-objectifiable experience that goes right to the core of the person, to its existential centre. In this dimension a dialogic experience with the eternal Thou becomes possible, which provides the foundation for the freedom and integrity of the human person. His conception of the Divine–human character of the person rests on this notion of the superconscious. Through it, the 'closed circle of psychologism' is opened.

Now, Jung does appear to affirm, in certain places,[19] that the unconscious also has such a dimension of the superconscious. His notion of the transcendent function seems to point precisely in this direction, as do certain motifs connected to the 'larger personality', which we have explored in this chapter. The unconscious, he affirms, cannot be called 'subconscious' because it 'is not merely "below" consciousness but also above it' (Jung 1945/1948: para. 433). But this affirmation of the superconscious as a dimension of the unconscious confers on it a different meaning to Berdyaev's apparently similar formulation. In reality, for Jung

> This 'upper' unconscious, however, is far from being a 'superconscious' in the sense that anyone who reaches it, like our hero [Jung talks here of the hero in a fairy tale who climbs the world tree] would stand as high above the 'subconscious' as above the earth's surface.
>
> (ibid.)

The psychological realism of this statement is only too well founded. Psychologically speaking 'spiritual' contents that are located beyond human consciousness have

> a share on the one hand in the daemonically superhuman and on the other in the bestially subhuman. It must be remembered, however, that this division is only true within the sphere of consciousness, where it is a necessary condition of thought. Logic says *tertium non datur*, meaning that we cannot envisage the opposites in their oneness.
>
> (Jung 1945/1948: para. 419)

In psychological experience 'superconscious' and 'subconscious' are linked as two inseparable twins. No light without shadow. But it is easy to go on from there to the further conclusion that in actual reality the only God we can ever know is the God-image, as the empirical psychology of the unconscious has to portray it. What this psychological phenomenology of the God-image excludes are qualitative differentiations based on a stronger notion of truth than empirical psychology allows for. Empirical psychological data become surreptitiously transformed into a psychological religion if they are furthermore mixed up with the sort of implicitly Romantic metaphysics discussed earlier.

A 'personal God' in the sense of Berdyaev is not conceivable within such a psychological–theological framework because what is given as 'higher', beyond human consciousness, is a 'daemonically superhuman' element, which is as unconscious as the 'bestially subhuman', and thus – paradoxically – *identical* to it. Jung's 'superconscious' is a latent unconscious potentiality, not a 'higher consciousness'. Psychological religion knows of no other God than the 'unconscious God', 'God' as a force of nature. This is simply a more religious poetic expression for the psychological notion of the Self.

From all this it becomes evident how much closer Berdyaev's God-image remains to the traditional Christian one, while at the same time emphasizing the notions of immanent transcendence and incarnational spirituality: The notion of the person is inseparable from the incarnation as an *inner experience* which increasingly releases forces in history which press towards a new humanism that bestows a *religious* dignity on human creativity.

Jung's more marked departure from the traditional Christian God-image, on the other hand, flows from his inclination to conceive of 'transcendence' exclusively in terms of an 'absolute unconscious' akin to Spinoza's *deus sive natura*. Besides this implicit Romantic background of Jung's psychology, it is his Kantian epistemological stance which leads him to disregard any recognition of a dimension of spiritual experience which would transcend psychological experience as we find it in Berdyaev. It is to these epistemological issues that I will now turn.

Chapter 5

Esse in anima and the epistemology of the heart

Religion has to do with an existential relation to transcendence. In its traditional more developed form metaphysical thought constituted initially an organic unity with (see Hossein Nasr 1989) and later the rational framework for this existential relation. Through Kant's philosophy, the point of gravity shifted from the metaphysical realm into the anthropological dimension. Pascal's 'God of Abraham, Isaac and Jacob' had first become the God of rational metaphysics, to be finally put to rest by Kant, the 'destroyer of all metaphysics'. If the God of metaphysics is dead it has to be from within the human experiential dimension that for both Jung and Berdyaev a new God-image now has to take shape. We will want to understand more clearly what role Kant plays for both as a necessary prelude to a deeper exploration of the inner connection between their conception of the person and the God-image.

Berdyaev posits the existence of a primary and a secondary sphere of knowing. Being *qua* existence is primary, precedes the process of rationalization and is, in this respect, 'unconscious': 'Viewed from the point of view of contemporary psychology, my original theme could be formulated as the distinction of the conscious and the unconscious' (Berdyaev 1953b: 110). As we have seen though, the term 'unconscious' has a different meaning for Berdyaev than for Jung. The nature of this difference is essential for us and will become clarified further in this chapter. A clearer appreciation of Jung's and Berdyaev's conception of the relationship to transcendence and of the person as rooted in this relationship hinges on such a clarification.

Berdyaev offers the possibility of an immanent critique of what I want to characterize in this chapter as Jung's Kantianism, which, if accepted uncritically, leads Jungian thinking about religion to a curtailing of the relationship to transcendence and its substitution by psychological religion based on a metaphysics of the unconscious. Berdyaev's conception of an existential metaphysics opens a door which Jung's Kantianism threatens to shut. This door leads beyond a purely psychological conception of the human being. It does not negate the insights of psychology but adds another dimension, which accommodates the specific nature of religious experience.

The opening of this door hinges on Berdyaev's conception of the spirit, which is, as we have seen, personal. Rationally conceived, the transcendent God is an object. But in Berdyaev's conception of the spirit, God is a Thou that is encountered in inner communion in the spirit. The Thou is not an object. But neither can it be monistically absorbed into the subject, nor the subject into it. While Jung's Self can be interpreted as an 'inner other', this otherness is conceived psychologically (the 'God-image') while real authentic transcendence dissolves in the unconscious as *pleroma*, the *theos annoetos* (God = the absolute unconscious). Jung's Kantianism might be transformable into the logical form of Hegel's philosophy of the absolute, as Giegerich (e.g. 2001) has attempted, but from Berdyaev's point of view this would be a solution that undermines the possibility of accommodating for the genuine character of (at least Christian) religious experience: psychology 'sublates' religion, just like Hegel saw his philosophy as sublated religion. Neither Hegelianism nor 'Jungianism' of this kind is capable of conceiving of authentic transcendence. The image for both is the uroboric serpent biting its tail: no exit. The issue that arises in this case has been expressed aptly by Charles Taylor: '[H]ow does a Hegelian philosopher *pray*? . . . What he can do is to contemplate his identity with cosmic spirit, which is something quite different' (Taylor 2005 [1975]: 494).

Epistemology of the heart

Existential metaphysics and the 'metaphysics of the unconscious'

That Kant should have such an overriding importance for Berdyaev may seem surprising. But in fact he goes as far as to even call him 'the greatest and most original philosopher in the history of human thought' after Plato (Berdyaev 1976: 5). In his autobiography, Berdyaev states: 'My true master in philosophy was Kant, and I have devoted most of my studies to his thought: to Kant himself rather than to Kantianism or neo-Kantianism' (Berdyaev 1950: 93). What made Kant so important for him?

Berdyaev is not a Kantian, nor does he have any interest in developing Kant's philosophy in a systematic way. He offers us instead '*une sorte de psycho-analyse existentielle*' (Segundo 1963: 60) of philosophers. Berdyaev is interested in the *existential* substance of Kant's thought. He is convinced that this substance has not really been understood by his followers. Even Kant himself did not follow through on the existential implications of his insights. Berdyaev's reading of Kant therefore implies an endorsement just as much as an immanent criticism of Kant. This criticism comes not from a rational, but from an existential point of view.

Berdyaev seeks in Kant a philosophical basis for his personalism, while at the same time rejecting his formalism. The real importance that Kant held for him, notwithstanding his formalism, is expressed by Berdyaev as follows:

> I am convinced that Kant has not been accurately understood. He was a metaphysician and he ought to be interpreted from the metaphysical point of view. He was a metaphysician of freedom, even, it may be, the only metaphysician of freedom and in this respect my attempt to set forth my own metaphysics of freedom will be derived from Kant. When Kant appeared the tragic side of the act of knowing came to light. It was an important event in the history of European thought. It is essential to grasp his vital and existential meaning.
>
> (Berdyaev 1976: 8)

Thus the 'vital and existential meaning' of Kant has to do with his status as possibly the 'only metaphysician of freedom'. Berdyaev is not at all interested in the formalism of Kant, but rather in the *voluntarism* latent in his thought, which ultimately goes back to the mysticism of Eckhart and Boehme (see Kroner 1977a: 10ff.). If Kant, for Berdyaev, is a metaphysician then his significance consists precisely in the fact that he was the initiator of a completely new and different type of metaphysics: the metaphysics of freedom, which Berdyaev calls 'existential metaphysics' and which is characterized by an ethical voluntarism. It is not a science of concepts but has a phenomenological basis in the actual lived experience of freedom. It constitutes itself as a 'depth phenomenology' of existential experience for which Kant paves the way by clearing out the metaphysical clutter.

Like Jung, Berdyaev fully accepts Kant's trenchant criticism of traditional metaphysics. He even welcomes it enthusiastically as a profound act of liberation of the human spirit. Traditional metaphysics tended to make man into a means in relation to transcendent norms, which were the real ends. The new existential metaphysics of freedom, which puts the human person into the centre, is therefore something entirely different – something perhaps even diametrically opposed to the old type of metaphysics. Nevertheless, it is a genuine metaphysics in its own right, founded in an 'ontology of the *ens morale*', and its object is 'man as a being of freedom, in which his personhood is founded' (Kobusch 1997: 20, trans.). By formulating this new metaphysical paradigm with unprecedented clarity, 'Kant's discovery . . . makes a sharp cut in the whole history of human thought and divides it into two parts' (Berdyaev 1976: 9). Kant offers the opportunity to find a philosophical language for existential experience.

Similarly Jung, in one of his letters concerning his controversy with Martin Buber, says:

> Here that threshold which separates two epochs plays the principal role. I mean by that threshold the theory of knowledge whose starting point is

> Kant. On that threshold minds go separate ways: those who have understood Kant, and others that cannot follow him.
>
> (Jung 1976: 375)

Clearly for Jung this implies the end of all metaphysics. But, as Edinger has suggested, we also see in Jung just like in Berdyaev the birth of a new metaphysics of a very different kind, namely an 'empirical metaphysics of the unconscious' raised on Kantian foundations. Dreams and other manifestations of the unconscious 'tend also to express a general and common viewpoint, a kind of perennial philosophy of the unconscious which seems to have a more or less universal validity' (Edinger 1992: 199). In this view Jung's psychology at one and the same time undermines traditional metaphysical positions and reconstitutes an equivalent, which takes over their function as sources of meaning. After metaphysics has become defunct, psychology takes its place.

This would then have to be seen as a psychological equivalent to Berdyaev's 'existential metaphysics'. Psychology, by withdrawing the projections inherent in metaphysical conceptions, reconnects them to their existentially real and alive meaning for the experiencing subject. 'It is possible,' writes Jung in *Aion*, 'to relate so called metaphysical concepts, which have lost their root and connection with natural experience, to living, universal psychic process, so that they can recover their true and original meaning' (Jung 1951: para. 65). And Edinger comments: 'It might be added that a projected metaphysical content, when withdrawn from projection, may still retain its metaphysical quality' (Edinger 1992: 199). We will want to explore how this new 'empirical metaphysics' of the unconscious in Jung's psychology (Edinger 1992: 197) relates to Berdyaev's existential metaphysics of freedom.

Kant and existential metaphysics: The loss of original participation and the awakening of the existential subject

Berdyaev sees in the 'old' pre-Kantian metaphysics an increasing loss of 'original participation' (Barfield 1988)[1], which becomes fully evident in Kant. Initially, Berdyaev interprets this development of the rational consciousness, culminating in Kant, as a mainly negative progression, saying that 'Kant was the ingenious formulator of a serious illness of human beings . . . Kant's philosophy confronts man with an empty abysmal void' (cited in Dietrich 1979: 110, trans.).

Later on, though, as his focus on the person increased, the positive aspect of this development came to prominence: Berdyaev now believes that it liberates man from the 'great mother' (Neumann 1989), the overwhelming power of cosmic forces. But what initially is liberation for man hardens into an ever increasing enslavement to 'objectivity'. The static and rationalized world of ontologism crushes the person. It is at this point that Kant's 'great discovery, which makes a sharp cut in the history of human thought' becomes at one and the same time both possible and necessary. Kant's thought is both a culmination of rationalism and a potential turning point. His discovery 'consists in this, that what refers merely to appearances and phenomena must not be transferred to what is *noumenal*, to things-in-themselves' (Berdyaev 1976: 9).

What makes this discovery all important for Berdyaev? It is the discovery of the dimension of existence itself, because the sphere of the *noumenal* is the sphere of freedom and 'the order of freedom is indeed *Existenz*' (ibid.: 9). Its discovery results, in Hegelian terms, from the 'negation of a negation': increasing objectification negates a state of original participation mystique, and seeing through objectification itself negates the subjection of the existential subject to the sphere of objectified phenomena. As a result the human person, or existential subject, awakens to itself, and thus no longer transfers to its authentic existential sphere that which it now has recognized as being a product of its own objectifying rational consciousness. A new capacity for conscious participatory knowledge becomes possible.

Kant instigated a dramatic 'paradigm shift' by understanding the whole of ontology not as a study of the fundamental structures of *being*, but of the fundamental structures of *consciousness*. Ontology therefore became transcendental philosophy. This Kantian insight is formulated by Berdyaev as follows:

> Pure being is an abstraction and it is in an abstraction that men seek to lay hold upon primary reality, primary life. Human thought is engaged in the pursuit of its own product. It is in this that the tragedy of philosophical learning lies, the tragedy, that is, of all abstract philosophy.
> (Berdyaev 1976: 92)

That human thought, inasmuch as it has become abstracted from its spiritual roots, is engaged in the pursuit of its own product and does not penetrate into primary reality is demonstrated by Kant in his doctrine of transcendental illusion, which Berdyaev considered to be his most ingenious achievement. In this doctrine he shows that while reason cannot but conceive of 'the world', 'the soul' and 'God' as real objects of knowledge, doing so leads reason into irresolvable contradictions. This is a theme that returns in a more existential form again and again in Berdyaev's philosophy. In particular, his 'paradoxical ethics' focuses on contradictions that cannot be resolved as long as one posits 'this world' as being the final and real world. For Berdyaev, the process of becoming conscious of transcendental illusion is a profoundly liberating one, because it destroys the naïve assumption about the *ultimate* reality of the objective world, and frees us from the circle of immanence.

The step that Kant took, of overcoming the deeply ingrained unconsciousness underlying the whole tradition of western European thought, was as dramatic as the step which the Greeks had taken in discovering the rational mind, thereby growing out of mythological consciousness. For Berdyaev, this step 'unlocks' in the sphere of philosophical thought the liberating potential for personalization contained within Christianity, which had remained obscured by Greek ontology, particularly in its Aristotelian form.

Berdyaev characterizes mythological consciousness as an unconscious immersion in the immediacy of still unreflected experience, in which there is not yet any clear differentiation between subject and object. The awakening of rational thought slowly dissolves this identity, but retains for a long time the 'metaphysical projection' of a 'true being' of reality that can be rationally apprehended. Gradually, however, the centre of gravity shifts from a contemplative understanding of truth as a kind of self-revelation of true being to a new conception of truth as certainty. The conscious subject seeks to get a firm grip on reality and elevates the subjective criterion of certainty to the status of an absolute norm. This subjective certainty can place emphasis on either one of the two dimensions of conscious experience: either on conscious thought, as is the case with rationalism, or on sense experience, as is the case with empiricism. Kant ingeniously synthesises both of these lines of modern philosophy into a form which may be characterized as the awakening of the modern subject to full self-consciousness. This self-consciousness has eliminated the last vestiges of *participation mystique*.

Transcendental and existential subject

At this point a more thorough elaboration of the distinction between the transcendental or epistemological and the existential subject is in place. The unity of self-consciousness is, for Kant, the most fundamental precondition of objective knowledge, from which all the others that he uncovers in his analysis of experience must ultimately be seen to derive. And it is evidently an ineradicable and necessary precondition of conscious experience, because every possible object given in experience has to be capable of being subsumed under the unity of this subject, otherwise it cannot even be experienced by me, or by any other subject at all. What has happened in Kant's philosophy, therefore, is that the 'I think' has emerged as the transcendental subject of all subjects and as such as the basis of all objectivity while that which in previous philosophy was called *subjectum* now becomes the object, i.e. the representation of the subject.

Paradoxically, the true objectivity of the object has its root in the subject itself. Abstracted from the subject, the content of experience is nothing but a chaotic jumble of sense-impressions. The rational, objective order of these impressions – their objectivity – stems from the transcendental subject. Through this 'Copernican revolution' Kant, in Berdyaev's view, 'overcomes the power of the object over the subject by bringing to light the fact that the object is the offspring of the subject' (Berdyaev 1976: 9).

It would be a mistake to identify Kant's 'I think' with the ego of Jung's psychology. Empirical self-consciousness is a complex web of actual and potential representations, which form a unity at whose centre there is the 'ego', which is nothing but the sum total of acquired memories and representations (Jung's ego-complex), whereas the 'I think' as pure self-consciousness (or apperception) is the transcendental condition for the possibility of such an empirical self-consciousness. But precisely because it is the condition of empirical self-consciousness, it cannot itself be made into an object of knowledge. This is what the term 'transcendental' means:

> By this I or he or it (the thing) which thinks, nothing else but a transcendental subject of thoughts is represented = x, which is known only through the thoughts which are its predicates, and of which, separately, we cannot have the slightest idea.
>
> (Kant 1971: B 404; A 346, trans.)

This unknowable x makes itself known in or as an act of spontaneity. This means that it makes itself known as freedom, because spontaneity is free, and it is at this point that an opening appears into the realm of the *noumenal*. The unknowable I makes itself known through its free, spontaneous acts. It therefore appears in Kant's practical philosophy as the *noumenal* subject, which is free and morally responsible, even though empirically it necessarily has to understand itself to be a part of nature, and is thus determined by necessary laws, which admit of no freedom. Thus Berdyaev can say: 'The *noumenal* world was revealed to him [Kant] as the world of freedom. He knows what the thing-in-itself is and it is only in respect of method that he gives the impression of knowing absolutely nothing about it' (Berdyaev 1976: 15). Just as Kant's transcendental philosophy tries to understand, through philosophical analysis, what happens 'behind the back' of our normal rational consciousness (which is concerned with rational explanations of 'objective reality'), so Berdyaev's existential philosophy tries to divine intuitively what happens 'behind the back' of transcendental consciousness.

One has to move from the concept of 'transcendental consciousness' to that of 'transcendental man', Berdyaev claims, otherwise the whole benefit of Kant's insight, its true existential import, is lost. Transcendental consciousness remains alien to the actually existing person and as a result the chance to overcome existential alienation slips away. At this very point, therefore, Berdyaev decisively moves beyond Kant. By freeing transcendental consciousness from its abstracted status, it acquires for Berdyaev a mobile, changeable character:

> The transcendental mind cannot be regarded as immobile; it is mobile and depends upon the social conditions, which obtain among human

> beings. But social relations among human beings do not belong to the world of phenomena; they belong to the world of *noumena*, to primary life, to *Existenz*.
>
> (Berdyaev 1976: 17)

Integral epistemology and Berdyaev's 'sociology of knowledge'

For Berdyaev, 'the very necessity of subjecting thought to the laws of logic is a social necessity; for thought is originally founded upon intuition, which is a personal and anthropocentric revelation of the mystery of Being' (Berdyaev 1938: 80). The full implications of the expression 'social necessity' have to be grasped if we are to understand what Berdyaev means here. Objectification is a movement towards disintegration and fragmentation. It is primarily a process in 'primary life' itself, and only secondarily an epistemological process. Expressed in religious terms it signifies a 'state of sin', i.e. of separateness and disintegration. It constitutes a degradation of being itself. To consider it only as the result of rationalization would be 'to propagate a serious error. The state of sin, of deficiency and of degradation should be attributed to Being rather than to knowledge' (Berdyaev 1938: 62). Under these ontological conditions, objective knowledge 'is in fact a unifying force in a disintegrated world' (Berdyaev 1938: 62).

This unifying force operates socially, inasmuch as objective knowledge enables universal social communication, and also in relation to the natural world, by helping us to orient ourselves in this world and to control it technologically. In a world governed by external necessity, scientific and technological knowledge play – to an extent – a positive, emancipating role. But viewed existentially, this is the most objectified expression of spirituality as it extends and attenuates into the alienated sphere of objective processes, Kant's world of phenomena. In this sphere, knowledge takes on a partial, fragmented character. It becomes specialist knowledge for purely pragmatic, utilitarian purposes. Logic is the dim reflection of the unifying force of the *Logos* within this sphere. The *Logos* is to be sought beyond the sphere of differentiated forms of rationality in a dimension of intuitive insight, which strikes like lightning into the existential core of the person and changes its whole existence for good. It is closer to Pascal's 'reasons of the heart', which are not to be confused with sentimental reveries but seen as a spiritual capacity to intuitively apprehend the moral–spiritual order of existence beyond subjective conjecture and sentiment.

Berdyaev creates a sociology of knowledge,[2] in which knowledge is characterized by different degrees of general validity and social communication on the one hand, and intuitive participation in the mystery of existence and existential communion on the other. These two poles of the spectrum are in inverse proportion to one another. At one end of the spectrum there are the natural and mathematical sciences, which entail a maximum of social communication and a minimum of existential communion, and at the other end there is living spirituality, which involves a maximum of existential communion and a minimum of objectified social communication. From the natural sciences follow the social and human sciences, then philosophy and finally religious knowledge (which, in its distortions, may nevertheless be highly subjected to the sphere of social communication, and show only a small degree of existential communion). The more existential a form of knowledge is, the less objectifiable and capable of 'proof', and the smaller the group of people who share this knowledge in existential communion. But on both sides of the spectrum, the element of relationship, either in the form of social communication or of existential communion, belongs inseparably to the inner structure of knowledge.

For Berdyaev, knowledge is somehow ultimately about the depth of relationship or absence of relationship between persons – i.e. existential centres with an interiority – not about the relation of subject and object. Full existential reality is known in communion while objectivity and objective processes are directly related to a degeneration of communion: 'For me objectivity can never be synonymous with truth . . . on the contrary, the term will connote the dependence of objectivity on subjective states, and on human relationships' (Berdyaev 1938: 41). Just as being *qua* object is already secondary, alienated being, so the subject which stands in relation to this 'objective being' is already alienated from its own existentiality and characterized by a loss of communion.

Berdyaev's sociology of knowledge has to be placed in the context of the conception of *sobornost* and 'integral knowledge' in Russian religious thought (see Chapter 3). Communion in freedom and love, in a shared intuitive realization of fundamental existential import, belongs as much to integral knowledge as social communication within the context of the shared logical rules of a 'language-game' (see Wittgenstein 1958) as it does to technical scientific knowledge and to what we would call today the social construction of reality. As Buber writes in *I and Thou*: 'The fundamental word [*Grundwort*] I-Thou can only be spoken with the whole being. The fundamental word I-It can never be spoken with the whole being' (Buber 1979: 9, trans.). Buber here expresses the same fundamental intuition as Berdyaev. The two fundamental words, I-Thou and I-It, signify the two fundamentally different spheres: existential communion and integral knowing of the whole person on the one hand, and social communication and rational knowing of the abstracted, rationalized, epistemological subject on the other.

Rational knowing operates with concepts, and presupposes the intentional abstraction of the knower from his subjectivity, whereas the participatory knowledge of existential philosophy presupposes a basis in metaphor and symbol, and can only come about where the whole person as thinking, feeling and willing subject is totally involved. 'The mystery of existence can only be interpreted by means of symbol and metaphor. . . . The existential sphere is also the personal sphere. There is nothing general, nothing abstract in it' (Berdyaev 1938: 64). But it does not therefore become for Berdyaev a purely subjective, intra-psychic sphere.

Existential philosophy, as Berdyaev understands it, accepts the results of Kantian philosophy with respect to its Copernican revolution, which overcomes traditional ontology and naturalism but rejects Kantian agnosticism in relation to the *noumenal* realm of freedom. It discloses the existential subject as more fundamental than the transcendental subject. The existential subject, as existent, *participates* directly in primary reality in a pre-reflexive manner. By the intensity of its presence and through the concentration of its inner forces, it has the capacity to come to a clear, intuitive awareness of its own existentiality, and thereby, by participation, of primary reality itself. In this way Berdyaev's existentialism moves beyond constructivism and relativism, while at the same time acknowledging its relevance in the sphere of social communication. Against Kant, Berdyaev maintains that 'non-conceptual, spiritual, existential apprehension of a *noumenon* is a possibility' (Berdyaev 1976: 14), but that if such an intuitive apprehension is possible, it cannot be a purely 'intellectual intuition', as the German idealists maintained, 'it can only be integral, concrete, that is to say it must also be emotional and volitional' (ibid.). This 'heightened awareness' is what Berdyaev means by superconsciousness.

This greater alertness for the mystery of existence does not lead to the construction of an intellectual 'absolute system' but is a mostly unnoticed dimension of the complex tapestry of our actual experience. Waking up to it means gathering the scattered sparks of insight and being more fully present to the reality of actual existence in all its complexity so that it becomes transparent for the authentic meanings disclosed in it. It does not mean superimposing some system of thought, even one based on 'intellectual intuition' of the absolute. We can think back here to Jung's notion of a life lived with total devotion leading to individuation, i.e. the disclosing of a meaning which is not imposed but unfolds out of the very life-process itself. But the *pointe* in Berdyaev's conception is that such devotion leads us beyond the immanentism of the psychic dimension towards the existential apprehension of the noumenon, the sphere of existence beyond objectification.

The primary reality of real existence is not some remote *Hinterwelt* in which the intuition of the existential subject is immersed, but the existential depth of the real world of real, flesh and blood persons. We ought to beware of reading into Berdyaev's distinction of primary and secondary reality a Platonic world of ideas and shadows of ideas.

> The particular is more deeply rooted in Being than the general. The world of eternal Ideas is not the image of existence, as the Platonic tradition would have us believe; this image is more truly reflected in

> human nostalgia, despair, unrest and dissatisfaction. Thus contradiction is more fruitful than identity.
>
> (Berdyaev 1938: 54)

The innermost essence of the concreteness of knowledge that Berdyaev seeks is to be found in the 'vertical' dimension of communion. Knowledge is Divine–human, and as such it is creative. Within the person, the act of transcendence is experienced:

> The function of knowledge is not to reflect, but to create. Beyond any given stratum of Being there lies a still deeper stratum; and transcendence is the only means of attaining this deeper stratum of Being. The static notion of the transcendental should be replaced by the dynamic notion of transcendence.
>
> (Berdyaev 1938: 59)

Through this active transcendence, the freedom of the person becomes illuminated freedom. Creative knowledge of this kind is 'dialogic'. It activates its creative potential for a 'transfiguring knowledge' out of its communion with a transcendent source of meaning.

Thus 'subjective freedom allies itself with the *Logos*. But the *Logos* is divinely inspired, whereas subjective freedom originates from the irrational abyss prior to any Being' (Berdyaev 1938: 75). Knowledge, in its Divine–human dimension, shows itself to be fundamentally creative, even 'essentially cosmogonic' (ibid.). If existential philosophy is concerned with the overcoming of objectification, and if objectification is a process in being, this ought to be so. The overcoming of objectification means the overcoming of the disintegrated, alienated condition of being by the force of love and communion illuminated by the *Logos*. 'Existential philosophy marks a transition from the interpretation of knowledge as objectification, to understanding it as participation, union with the subject matter and entering into cooperation with it' (Berdyaev 1976: 61). This is no longer the original 'participation mystique', but what Barfield calls 'final participation', which imposes on us 'the acceptance and conscious ensuing of that directionally creator relation to the phenomenal world' (Barfield 1988: 159).

In Berdyaev the Kantian dualism of the world of phenomena and the thing-in-itself becomes radicalized and dynamized (Dietrich 1975b: 9). It becomes radicalized because the 'thing-in-itself' is not a thing at all, but the opposite of all 'thingness' or objectivity (like Buber's Thou). It is not-yet-rationalized primary being as freedom, spirit, subject and personal existence, whereas the world of phenomena is interpreted as the alienated, fallen sphere of objectified secondary being. In this way human knowledge is interpreted as a dialectical dynamic that is ultimately rooted in the existential dialectics of the Divine and the human.

Human existence happens in the field of tension between these two modes of existence. They are not hermetically sealed off against each other (as they are in Kant's philosophy) but dynamically and dialectically related to each other, so that one can transform into the other, can irrupt into the other. The authentic existence of the person can become objectified, and conversely the objectified condition can be transformed and illuminated, the spiritual dimension can break into it, so that the person awakens to existence.

Esse in anima: Towards psychological religion

Kant's philosophy becomes for Berdyaev a means of providing a foundation for his existential philosophy, which 'marks a transition from the interpretation of knowledge as objectification, to understanding it as *participation*' (Berdyaev 1976: 61) or a transition from the cognitive mode of the 'I-It' to that of the 'I-Thou'.

Jung for his part uses Kant to establish the status of his psychology as an empirical science, which highlights the role of the *esse in anima* as the new post-metaphysical point of gravity, which mediates between philosophical/religious (*esse in intellectu*) and scientific (*esse in re*) discourses. Jung's reading of Kant is a Neo-Kantian one that is very different from that of Berdyaev, who reads Kant as a metaphysician of freedom. While Berdyaev shifts the point of gravity towards the spirit, Jung shifts it on the basis of his neo-Kantianism towards the psyche. This shift does not just concern a methodological basis for psychology; it also paves the way for psychological religion.

Psychology as an 'empirical science from the phenomenological standpoint'

Psychology is for Jung an empirical science from a 'purely empirical or phenomenological standpoint' (Jung 1947/1954: para. 343). To study the psyche empirically from the phenomenological point of view means to let it reveal itself to the investigator, who is called upon to suspend all preconceived philosophical, metaphysical and religious notions as to its 'real nature'. It is not enough for empirical psychologists to do research in the laboratory, because the conditions of the laboratory experiment limit and predetermine what the psyche may reveal about itself.

Such a phenomenological attitude will first of all have to clear out the prejudice that conceptual constructs concern the 'nature' of the psyche and instead look at them as descriptive tools which refer to the actual phenomenology of psychic life, not its presumed 'essential nature'. Here Kant's philosophy is important, because it denies to conceptual knowledge the capacity to penetrate beyond phenomena into their 'true nature'.

A good example is the relativization of the purely causal point of view. Kant has already demonstrated that the two viewpoints of causality and finality 'are not antagonistic if they are regarded as regulative principles of thought and not as constituent principles of the process of nature itself' (Jung 1916/1917: para. 690). A purely causal description of psychic process under laboratory conditions, or as it is practised in Freudian analysis, may obscure the reality of the psyche, because it changes regulative principles of thought into constituent principles of the process of nature itself, thereby neglecting the teleological viewpoint.

A phenomenological approach must find ways to 'see' everything that escapes a point of view that is locked into such a Newtonian framework of causality. In Jung's reading of Kant, by 'denying knowledge in order to make room for faith' (cf. Kant 1971: B xxx), i.e. by limiting knowledge to the sphere of phenomena, Kant potentially already made room for a psychological way of seeing which pays attention to all that escapes the net of causal reasoning. But it is only through the revolution of modern physics that the post-Newtonian paradigm became, at least in principle, fully established (see Jung 1950: para. 967).

The explicitly (or implicitly) materialistic outlook which often underlies experimental research is, for Jung, only 'an exaggerated reaction against medieval idealism and has nothing to do with the empirical method as such' (Jung 1926/1946: para. 127). Psychology had to struggle very hard to emancipate itself from traditional (i.e. pre-Kantian) philosophy. Jung thinks of traditional philosophy as being, in one way or another, the manifestation of a 'medieval idealism', which posited that speculative insight into supposed metaphysical principles could form the basis for an accurate understanding of reality. But materialism as a reaction against idealism is just as metaphysical as idealism. The 'matter' of the materialist is just as much a transcendent metaphysical principle as the 'spirit' of the idealist. Any metaphysical positions – indeed, all expressions of the human spirit – ultimately have to be understood as 'symptoms of certain psychic conditions' (Jung 1947/1954: para. 344).

This, for Jung, is the crucial point: the Kantian limitation of knowledge lays bare the psychic nature of all knowledge, by locating the foundations of all claims to truth in the subject, whose range of cognition is limited to the sphere of phenomena. 'Every science is a function of the psyche, and all knowledge is rooted in it. The psyche is the greatest of cosmic wonders and the *sine qua non* of the world as an object' (ibid.: para. 357). This is the central and fundamental insight which, so Jung believes, ought to have dawned on all those who took the route of the natural sciences, which have emancipated themselves, one after the other, from metaphysical philosophy. This emancipation meant a break with any speculatively predetermined metaphysical framework in favour of a gradual process of careful, evidence-based research, which remains tentative, hypothetical and always open to new and unexpected results. If there is anything to fall back upon 'outside' objective sense-experience, it is only the soul itself, as the locus of all conceivable experience, and no longer any metaphysical realm into which the soul is 'fitted'. In Jung's Kantian mind the advance of science is thus linked with the rise of psychology to the status of the new *prima philosophia*. Philosophy itself has become *ancilla psychologiae*. The 'subjectivist turn' of Kant's philosophy, when its implications are fully understood, turns out to be a 'psychological turn'.

The fact that the 'cosmic wonder' of the soul nevertheless remains (notoriously) unnoticed does itself have a psychological explanation. Western man, being predominantly rationalistic and oriented towards the object, is driven by his conscious attitude to grant the right of existence only to those parts which 'accord with the prevailing trend of consciousness' (Jung 1947/1954: para. 347). In this situation, the soul – and therefore a psychology that is truly serious about letting the soul itself speak, instead of dogmatically pronouncing what it ought to be – constitutes the inferior, rejected content. But this content, like the philosopher's stone, while being rejected, is really the greatest cosmic wonder, the hidden treasure lying under everyone's nose, but recognized only by very few.

On the philosophical level, or on the level of the development of consciousness, the reason for this is that few people have assimilated the full consequences of the implications of Kant's philosophy. When pressed to defend his psychological approach, Jung again and again referred to Kant. I have already quoted Jung's statement, in relation to his controversy with Buber, that Kant's theory of knowledge represents a 'threshold which separates two epochs . . . On this threshold minds go separate ways: those who can follow Kant and those who can't' (Jung 1973: 375).

Buber criticizes Jung for blurring the boundaries between psychology and philosophy/theology. Jung, he says, by claiming that all statements are statements of the soul – which is an inevitable conclusion 'if they are not considered according to their meaning and intention in regard to their content but in regard to the process of their psychological genesis' (Buber 1994: 86, trans.) – extends the boundaries of psychology beyond their proper limit. In contradistinction to Jung's own repeated claims, 'psychology here becomes the only admissible form of metaphysics' (ibid.). Thus Jung's psychology becomes 'the only religion which can still be true, the religion of pure psychic immanence' (ibid.: 89). Buber's critique has more substance than Jung was happy to admit.

Jung responded to Buber's critique with some irritation, insisting that the fundamental issue was that Buber was one of those people who could not understand his psychological approach, because he could not follow Kant. Buber was obviously perfectly capable of understanding Kant's philosophy. Jung's argument therefore is a psychological one, diagnosing a condition of psychological immaturity, a still 'medieval' psychology in Buber. Buber's critique, it seems, hit Jung in a vulnerable place and he hit back. In his response to Buber, Jung emphasizes that he is first and foremost an empirical scientist who studies psychological facts. He feels best understood by descriptions of his psychology that emphasize its scientific nature, such as the one that appeared in a British medical journal: ' "Facts first and theories later is the key-note of Jung's work. He is an empiricist first and last". This view finds my approval' (Jung's response in Buber 1994: 137, trans.). John Dourley rightly comments that 'Jung might have been more open in simply admitting that indeed such philosophical and theological implications were there' (Dourley in Ryce-Menuhin 1994: 136).

As a way of understanding better how Jung's reading of Kant becomes pregnant with philosophical and theological implications (to which Jung often does not own up as frankly as one might find desirable) it is worth considering a passage from the *Critique of Pure Reason* concerning the 'Land of Understanding', which is

> an island, and enclosed in unalterable boundaries by nature itself. It is the land of truth . . . surrounded by a broad and stormy ocean, the true seat of illusion, where many a fog bank and rapidly melting iceberg pretend to be new lands and, ceaselessly deceiving with empty hopes the voyager looking around for discoveries, entwine him in adventures from which he can never escape and yet also never bring to an end.
>
> (Kant 1971: B 294ff., trans.)

This is how Kant describes the precarious condition of all attempts at introducing metaphysics into theoretical philosophy. As long as we remain on the safe ground of empirical science, each concept has to be related to a product of perception in order to yield valid insight into (phenomenal) reality. Kant's theory of knowledge has, so he believes, managed to substantiate the validity claim of such empirical/scientific knowledge. Such knowledge is both possible and valid because it can be demonstrated that consciousness cannot but employ certain a priori structures to order the material given to sensation, and these structures are therefore universally valid and necessary (for any conscious subject). Truth can only come about by interpreting the data of sense-experience in terms of these structures that are inherent in consciousness, i.e. by thus offering an account of phenomena which is both necessary and universally valid. Thus the 'Land of Understanding' goes only as far as sense-experience goes, while beyond it, the wide, stormy sea of metaphysics begins.

The mere fact that there have always been different schools of philosophy, such as materialism and idealism, whose advocates have never been able to resolve their differences, demonstrates the elusiveness of all metaphysical adventures, an elusiveness to which Kant hoped to put a final end.

And yet, at the same time, Kant acknowledged the inevitability of these adventures, because even in our scientific pursuits the activities of understanding rely on the regulative, guiding principles of reason. For example, we inevitably have to presuppose the idea of a world, even though we never have 'the world' present as a datum of experience. It is 'nothing but' an idea of reason, but one which we cannot do without. Little wonder that we feel seduced into asking metaphysical questions about 'the world' as a whole – whether it has a beginning, is created or is eternal, for example – especially because it is always in these questions, which concern the whole, that truly existential issues are at stake for us. Such questions have to do with our need for meaning.

Thus we may reason further with Jung that, in addition to a certain 'inbuilt' structural property of the mind (i.e. understanding cannot function without reason, which, due to its inherent nature, transgresses the 'bounds of sense'), there is also a psychological factor at work here (i.e. the need for meaning) which 'entwines' the 'voyager' in adventures in the stormy ocean (i.e. the unconscious) and makes its presence felt in ever returning and ever renewed 'metaphysical' projections. This happens wherever we treat the idea as a real, hypostatized object of knowledge[3]. For Jung, the idea is an a priori psychic factor which has as its precursor 'the primordial, symbolic image' (Jung 1921: para. 736) i.e. the archetypal image which is 'an inherited organization of psychic energy' (ibid.: para. 754).

Whatever the metaphysical truth of different religious and metaphysical positions may be, one thing is certain: they constitute a formidable psychological reality based in the inherent vitality, numinous power and dynamism of archetypal images. Whether the representatives of different religious and metaphysical doctrines are talking about anything 'metaphysically real' nobody will ever know (according to Kant's epistemology), but one thing is for sure: they are talking about their own psyches. Yet to say 'their own' psyches is actually wrong, because it introduces the notorious prejudice of our consciousness-centred culture that the psyche is either identical to consciousness, or that the unconscious is, as it was for Freud, purely a sort of appendix of consciousness.

As an empirical science, psychology does away with metaphysics but, on this Kantian basis, it collects the facts of the varieties of statements of the psyche about itself and tries to describe them faithfully. Thus it seeks to provide a scientifically based phenomenology of the archetypal structures of the psyche. It becomes an *empirical* metaphysics of the unconscious. Religions, myths and philosophies are revealed as statements of the psyche about itself. And if anybody should be concerned that mystery has been extinguished in psychologistic reductionism, Jung would retort that they do not have the capacity to appreciate the profound mystery of the psyche.

Esse in anima

In a letter to Paul Maag dated 1 June 1933, Jung makes one of his many references to Kant in the context of responding to accusations of atheism and continues by dropping the following hint: 'If you would submit the epistemological statements of psychological types to a well-disposed examination [paras 59–67], you could clearly discern my philosophical position' (Jung 1976: 123). In this passage, to which Jung refers as defining his 'philosophical position', he develops the very ideas that we have just seen in relation to the passage from Kant.

The context of the discussion is the dispute between nominalists and realists. Jung is interested in the ontological proof for the existence of God, going back to the writings of the realist, Anselm of Canterbury. This ontological argument for the existence of God brings the issue at stake into the sharpest possible focus, because in it the existence in rational consciousness of a concept of God as the highest and most perfect being is taken as a proof of God's existence, because a perfect being which did not exist would evidently be distinctly lacking in perfection: 'So, then, there truly is a being than which a greater cannot be thought – so truly that it cannot even be thought of as not existing. And thou art this being, O Lord our God' (Jung 1921: para. 59).

Jung asks how is it possible that so many philosophers could take such an evidently flawed argument so seriously? There must be, he concludes, a psychological reason for this, a psychological factor of numinous force, which lends some archaic 'magical power' (Jung 1921: para. 65) to concepts in a way that clearly resonates with archaic, primitive beliefs in the magical power of words. Kant, in his criticism of the ontological argument, precisely deflates this 'magical power' of the concept: he criticizes the 'concept of God', but he still retains a belief in God by justifying it within his practical philosophy, as a postulate of practical reason.

By criticizing the ontological argument, Kant draws a sharp distinction between *esse in re* and *esse in intellectu*. Once this distinction is drawn, any knowledge that can claim objective truth depends on the combination of the purely abstract concept and the data provided by sensation. But in his practical philosophy, Kant gives a place to the whole human, existential dimensions of value and meaning. Jung reinterprets this psychologically:

> But between *intellectus* and *res* there is still *anima*, and this *esse in anima* makes the whole ontological argument superfluous. Kant himself, in his *Critique of Practical Reason*, made an attempt on a grand scale to evaluate the *esse in anima* in philosophical terms.
>
> (Jung 1921: para. 66)

What Jung illustrates here, in relation to the ontological argument for the existence of God, applies to all metaphysical and religious statements: they all are still caught up in some remnant of magical thinking, in which concepts and images are believed to give us access to metaphysical realities. Once this illusion is dissolved by means of 'the theory of knowledge', *esse in anima* can be identified as the only appropriate context in which all such statements are to be located and validated.

The statement 'God exists' now becomes a statement by the psyche about itself: 'In the language of analytical psychology the God-concept coincides with the particular ideational complex which . . . concentrates in itself the maximum amount of libido, or psychic energy' (Jung 1921: para. 67). Kant's moral postulate of practical reason has become a self-manifestation of the deepest core of the psyche – the Self – in the sphere of consciousness. Jung's psychological reinterpretation of Kant is well formulated by M. Nagy when she writes:

> Jung substituted 'inner experience' for Kant's concept of a priori reason . . . Knowledge which is of crucial importance for the human individual is won at the moment when we acknowledge a priori inner experience, experience which is not dictated by the perceptual and sensual power of the outer object. For Kant this was the experience of the categorical imperative. For Jung it was the experience of the self.
>
> (Nagy 1991: 37)

This reinterpretation of Kant, Nagy further claims, has been made possible because Jung applies a specific neo-Kantian reading of Kant's first Critique to Kant's own moral writings, 'thus conflating what Kant had most carefully differentiated, namely moral and phenomenal knowledge' (Nagy 1991: 21).

Moral judgements are value judgements, and as such are connected to the feeling function. With ideas, the primordial or archetypal image 'comes to the surface indirectly . . . Only the development of the counter-function can take the idea further – that is to say, once the idea has been grasped intellectually, it strives to become effective in life. It therefore calls upon feeling' (Jung 1921: para. 751). Thus, for any form of knowledge, religious or philosophical, which is of crucial importance for the human individual and thus compels it to venture out onto the stormy ocean, what really happens is that the realm of psychological experience, beyond the sharply defined boundaries of rational–empirical knowledge, is entered.

For Jung, Kant's philosophy becomes a way to validate psychological experience – *esse in anima* – and to conceive of psychology as an empirical science. The Kantian a priori becomes for Jung the priority of the unconscious psyche. The closer to its original manifestations, not yet modified by consciousness, the more appropriate it becomes to use the term 'a priori'. Thus, for Jung, 'the idea is not something absolutely *a priori*, but must also be regarded as secondary and derived [from the primordial image]' (Jung 1921: para. 751). Not surprisingly, for Jung, Kant's categorical imperative now no longer derives its a priori quality from the inherent nature of pure practical reason but from a much more dynamic, unconscious, psychic factor.

Jung interprets it as being 'unquestionably a manifestation of the anima' (Jung 1973: 305).

Just like Kant, Jung performs a 'transcendental' turning around to the subject and its way of knowing the object, but the subject is in his case the psyche, and the object is 'life' in the broadest sense, i.e. human existence. The very same issues which confront patients in clinical practice in countless different forms are the ones which have been addressed in mythology, religion etc. This opens up a vast field for comparative study and the amplification of those images produced by the psyche. In this way the phenomenology of psychic experience can be developed beyond the highly subjective sphere of introspection and achieve the greatest possible objectivity, given the ineradicable problem posed by the fact that in psychology the psyche is at the same time both the subject and the object of the study.

Just as for Kant, for Jung the objects intended in the three fundamental transcendental ideas of the soul, the world and God are unknowable to us. Strictly speaking, then, psychology does not study the soul as an object. The psychic totality is, like Kant's *Ding an sich*, a borderline concept:

> By 'self' we mean psychic wholeness, but what realities underlie this concept we do not know, because psychic contents cannot be observed in their unconscious state, and moreover the psyche cannot know itself . . . The concept of psychic wholeness necessarily implies an element of transcendence on account of the existence of unconscious components. Transcendence in this sense is not equivalent to a metaphysical postulate or hypostasis; it claims to be no more than a borderline concept, to quote Kant.
>
> (Jung 1958a: para. 779)

In the same passage, Jung goes on to speculate that this transcendent dimension may be ultimately something akin to the *unus mundus* of the alchemists. 'In that case all reality would be grounded on an as yet unknown substrate possessing material and at the same time psychic qualities' (Jung 1958a: para. 780). At the deepest layer of the unconscious there may be a unified layer of the *ununs mundus* 'in which the multiple archetypes appear to be united or integrated into one *single* center' (von Franz 1980b: 81). Thus we can see how Jung's psychological notion of transcendence leads him towards a monistic conception.

This can be further elucidated by once more returning to Jung's use of Schiller. In *Psychological Types* (1921), the *esse in anima*, which Jung proposes (with reference to Kant) as occupying a third, mediating position between the *esse in intellectu* and the *esse in re*, is explored in greater depth in his discussion of Schiller's *Aesthetic Education of Man*. Schiller proceeds rationally, Jung thought, and so falls victim to his own conclusions. 'Had he been acquainted with Indian literature, he would have seen that the primordial image which floated before his mind's eye had a very different character from an "aesthetic" one' (Jung 1921: para. 188). This primordial image is expressed much more accurately in 'that particular configuration of eastern ideas which is condensed in the *brahman–atman* teaching of India and whose philosophical spokesman in China is Lao-Tzu' (ibid.). The experience of the *brahman–atman* or Tao follows 'the withdrawal of libido from all contents', which results in a state of 'complete identity of inside and outside' (ibid.: para. 189). Something similar is to be found 'in the fundamental ideas of Meister Eckhart and also, in some respects, of Kant, which display a quite astonishing affinity with those of the Upanishads' (ibid.: para. 193).

The eastern practice of *tapas*, or meditation, which results in the withdrawal of libido from all contents and its concentration in the self, in some respects has as its psychological equivalent the withdrawing of projections (see von Franz 1980b: Ch. 8). Kant's philosophy, by unmasking metaphysical projections, has fostered this process immensely. It has, in Jung's view, paved the way for the recognition of psychic interiority, a recognition that has for a long time been much further advanced in the east.

Jung's Kantianism thus opens a door to allow him to validate the psychological experience, *esse in anima*, as the locus of the profoundest values for modern man. At the same time it allows him to claim a scientific status for his phenomenology of psychological experience. While remaining scientific, in this 'Kantian' perspective psychology becomes, as Buber says, the only admissible form of metaphysics, and one that finally touches upon the transcendent dimension of the *unus mundus*: 'Here was the empirical field common to biological and spiritual facts, which I had everywhere sought and nowhere found. Here at last was the place where the collision of nature and spirit became a reality' (Jung 1995: 130).

Psychological idealism and existential intuition

Earlier, in Chapter 3, I pointed out Kant's role in the emergence of modern philosophical anthropology, and placed both Jung's psychology and Berdyaev's existential philosophy in this anthropological context by using the terms 'anthropological and psychological reduction'. We can now understand better how their different appropriation of Kant's philosophy defines the different direction which Jung's and Berdyaev's thought takes, beginning from a similar starting point, which had been defined by the modern, post-metaphysical predicament.

Kant's 'Copernican revolution', his decisive turn towards the subject, is founded by both Berdyaev and Jung in a deeper, more fundamental dimension of subjectivity. For Berdyaev, this is the dimension of 'transcendental man' given in existential/spiritual experience, while for Jung it is the objective psyche given in psychological experience.

Up to this point, a clear structural analogy appears to be discernible between Jung's and Berdyaev's approach to Kant. But there is a decisive difference between their evaluations of Kant's limitation of legitimate knowledge claims to the sphere of empirical science. Whereas Jung clearly affirms the inaccessibility and unknowability of the 'archetype as such', which constitutes an analogy to the Kantian 'thing-in-itself', Berdyaev affirms the accessibility of the *noumenon* through integral, existential intuition. 'Things-in-themselves,' he affirms, 'are entities and their existence . . . the thing-in-itself . . . is freedom, not a cause; and as a result of a certain line of direction taken by freedom it gives rise to the world of appearances' (Berdyaev 1976: 16).

While for Berdyaev the psychological becomes integrated into the spiritual as apprehended in existential intuition, for Jung the spiritual becomes integrated into the psychological. Kant demonstrates that any metaphysical claims are unfounded. This demonstration paves the way for psychology, for the insight into the objective reality of the psyche, which is initially only experienced indirectly, in religious and metaphysical projections. Modern man has finally 'become conscious of his *empirical* psyche, which has loosened itself from the embrace of the spirit' (Jung 1955/1956: para. 775).

Responding to Buber's criticism that he transgresses the legitimate boundaries of psychology and ends up proclaiming 'the religion of pure psychic immanence' as the 'only one which still can be true' (Buber 1994: 89, trans.), Jung affirms that he is just an empirical scientist whose approach is not properly understood. I have tried to show how Jung thinks he can give this claim legitimacy by founding his understanding of psychology as a science on his version of Kantian epistemology.

But if, on this Kantian basis, anything we can ever know is only psychic, psychology does indeed appear to become an all-encompassing viewpoint which suffers – as far as its scientific status is concerned – from a lack of boundaries. By extending its field of 'research' indefinitely, psychology inevitably takes on a 'philosophical' character, inasmuch as philosophy is always concerned with the whole while any particular science limits itself to a clearly defined 'field'. In this way, 'analytical psychology is a position-taking on philosophical issues of the nineteenth century' in the form of 'a *psychological* format for idealism' (Nagy 1991: 265). And in this sense we can also say that we find in Jung's psychology a new 'empirical metaphysics of the unconscious', built on a Kantian foundation.

It would nevertheless be inaccurate to accuse Jung of focusing exclusively on psychic immanentism, especially if we take his late studies on synchronicity (Jung 1952) and his reflections on the *psychoid* and the *unus mundus* (Jung 1947/1954, Jung 1955/1956) into account. For Jung, just as for Berdyaev, Kant's philosophy becomes a turning point, where the alienated objectifying rational consciousness returns to a higher, participatory form of knowing. Individuation is a process, which resolves the 'collision of nature and spirit within the person' in a new state of wholeness. For 'nature and spirit' we could also write 'instinct and archetype', because the archetype is 'a formative principle of instinctive power' (Jung 1947/1954: para. 416), and represents 'the authentic element of spirit' (ibid.: para. 406). The realization of wholeness leads towards a *coniunctio* of these opposites, which ultimately tends towards the realization of the *unus mundus*: 'We may safely interpret this world as the one which the unconscious sees and seeks to produce' (Meier 2001: 129).

Jung's statement that 'personality is Tao' gains a deeper meaning in this context. The realization of a new unitary centre of the total personality, of the Tao, means the realization of '[t]he state in which ego and non-ego are no longer opposed [and which] is called the pivot of Tao' (Chuang-tzu, quoted in Jung 1952: para. 923). The *Tao* concept thus corresponds to the traditional idea of man as a *microcosm* in inner correspondence to the *macrocosm*. The 'self-man as he is and the indescribable and supraempirical totality of that same man' (Jung 1955/1956: para. 765) is 'the microcosm', i.e. in the language of Berdyaev's philosophy, the person who has overcome the condition of objectification and entered into a condition of existential, participatory knowing. The *unus mundus* is the 'potential world' that was called *mundus archetypus* in philosophical tradition (Jung 1955/1956: para. 761), and in which the psychic inner world and the physical outer world are united. Within this unknowable, transcendental, unitary dimension, matter and spirit – which are experienced within the psychic sphere as physiological drive and archetypal image – are united (see Jung 1934: para. 420). And this sphere, although unknowable in itself, can be the source of synchronistic events as well as the content of experiences, a fact to which mystics in both the east and the west can testify (see Jung 1955/1956: para. 771).

But in all this, there is a distinct dissimilarity with the type of spiritual experience that both Berdyaev and Buber describe: it is the experience of the Divine in an impersonal and cosmic form to which Jung's process of individuation seems ultimately to lead. This is the experience of the 'alchemical Sophia' (cf. von Franz 1995; Raff 2003). With 'Sophia as his consort [the spirit] also has a feminine aspect, which emerges more clearly *the closer one gets to the unconscious. In this matriarchal sphere, the spirit is the son of the mother*' (Meier 2001: 126, emphasis mine). The spirit is here the result of a process within the 'matriarchal sphere' of the unconscious, and the matriarchal darkness of this sphere supervenes over any 'superconsciousness', which can always only be relative to it.

For Berdyaev, on the other hand, the personal spirit is not born from matriarchal darkness, but is, in its relationship to the personal, trihypostatic God, *ab initio* the prime actor in the Divine–human drama, which is a drama of the interaction of divine and human freedom. What stands behind Jung's 'psychological reduction', based on 'the theory of knowledge', is ultimately what one could call his implicit 'religious' orientation towards the 'matriarchal sphere of the alchemical Sophia'. What stands behind Berdyaev's 'anthropological reduction', based on Kant (interpreted as the creator of a new existential metaphysics), is his religious orientation towards the mystery of the Trinity, the mystery of Divine-humanity. It is to the ways that both men interpreted these central Christian symbols as forming the 'archetypal basis' of the person that we will now turn. Kant provides the basis for Jung's new 'psychological religion' while for Berdyaev he enables a philosophically reflected formulation of a purified, spiritual Christianity in line with its mystical tradition but with a distinct anthropological emphasis. Berdyaev does not want to promote a new religion. He believes that he only unfolds more clearly the full meaning of the dogma of Chalcedon: a spiritual, inward, liberating union of the divine and the human without separation, without confusion.

Appendix 6

Person and God-image

I want to set this chapter in the context of the vision of the three ages of the Calabrian abbot Joachim of Fiore (ca. 1132–1202). This vision presents us with an understanding of Christianity as a religion that is inherently destined to go through radical transformations. For this reason it influenced many radical minds, from the Franciscan vision of an 'ecclesia spiritualis' (see Benz 1934), to the idea of the 'friendship with God' in German mysticism, the reformation and revolutionary social and political movements, and the philosophies of Hegel and Schelling. For Jung and Berdyaev, too, it provides a template for their creative appropriation of Christian symbols. The Trinity, according to Joachim 'manifests itself progressively in three successive periods of the history of salvation' (ibid: 37): those of the Father, the Son and the Spirit. Joachim writes that

> in the first period learning prevails, in the second one partly completed wisdom, but in the third one the fullness of knowledge . . . The first one has the servitude of slaves; the second one the servitude of sons; the third one will bring freedom.
>
> (ibid.: 39)

Both Jung and Berdyaev look forward to this third age of the Spirit, beyond the servitude of traditional religion, which will be the new dawn after the 'death of God'. Jung writes to Victor White that

> The state of the Holy Spirit means a restitution of the original oneness of the unconscious on the level of consciousness. This is alluded to . . . in Christ's logion 'Ye are gods'. This state is not quite understandable yet, it is a mere anticipation. . . . The later development from the Christian aeon to the one of S. Spiritus has been called 'evangelium aeternum' by Goachino da Fiori when the great tearing apart [the absolute opposition expressed by the symbol of Christ and Satan] had just begun. Such vision seems to be granted by divine grace as a sort of 'consolamentum' . . .
>
> (Lammers and Cunningham 2007: 220)

Jung's psychological interpretation of Christianity understands itself as such a 'consolamentum' for modern man, an anticipation of a new (post-confessional) religion of the 'Holy Ghost and the *Sapientia Dei*' (Jung 1955/1956: para. 531) for which psychology paves the way.

Berdyaev's rendering of Joachim's vision points similarly in the direction of a new spirituality:

> The three epochs of divine revelation in the world are three epochs of revelation about man. In the first epoch man's sin is brought to light and natural divine force is revealed; in the second epoch man is made a son of God and redemption from sin appears; in the third epoch the divinity of man's creative nature is finally revealed and divine power becomes human power. The revelation about man is the final revelation about the Trinity . . . The anthropological revelation of the creative epoch is at once fully human and fully divine; in it humanity is deepened to the point of divinity and divinity is made visible to the point of humanity.
>
> (Berdyaev 1962: 295ff.)

For both men the third epoch brings with it a form of *coniunctio oppositorum*. For Jung that of the dark and light halves of the Self, while for Berdyaev that of the divine and the human in a way which, although foreshadowed by the formulation of Chalcedon, has never before been realized in historical Christianity in its full import. It is a mystery that can only be revealed in the Spirit. Implicit in Berdyaev's understanding of this union is a theology of the 'kenotic Christ'[1], a Christ that was fully human, identified with our darkness to the utmost on the cross, while being without sin. This is the basis for Berdyaev's notion of an interpenetration of the human and the divine in which the human is not obliterated but fully revealed. And this revelation of man is at the same time the final revelation about the mystery of the Trinity. It is not a new, but a fuller revelation of the central mystery of Christianity. For Jung, on the other hand, if Christianity is not going to remain a religion for well brought up children, the dark side has to be integrated into the God-image in an even more radical way, which takes his thinking beyond the Christian tradition altogether.

This chapter prepares the ground for the exploration of the ethical implications of these divergent understandings of revelation. It proceeds in two steps: first it will explore their approach to the content of Christian revelation, and second it will explore how both attempt a further development of Christian symbols in the direction of the new aeon of the spirit.

Trinity and Divine-humanity in Berdyaev

Berdyaev attempts a philosophical critique of revelation, which is based on his existential understanding of philosophy as both an awakening and a purification of the spiritual element in man that is open to the Divine–human truth of revelation. On this basis he shows how 'the revelation about man is the final revelation about the Trinity' (Berdyaev 1962: 295ff.).

A philosophical critique of revelation: There is no religion higher than the truth

Berdyaev tells us that, after his philosophical 'conversion', he was henceforth convinced 'that there is no religion above the Truth . . . and the awareness of the supremacy of Truth put a lasting stamp on my spiritual and philosophical development' (Berdyaev 1950: 78–79).[2] Truth is revealed only in the spirit, and 'everything spiritual emanates from within, from the inner depths' (Berdyaev 1946: 49). Berdyaev was 'shaken to the depths' by his 'philosophical' insight in a way that changed his whole life forever. So, for Berdyaev, any genuine insight of such existential import already has within itself the seeds of a 'trans-subjective' mystical experience. There is no impenetrable boundary between philosophical and mystical experience. The former finds its fulfilment in the latter. At the root of discursive thought lies the simple intuitive insight, which emanates from the inner depths of the heart and only later becomes objectified in reflection. Existential thought by its very nature gives primary importance to this type of insight.

As a mode of knowledge, mysticism is therefore inherent to Berdyaev's specific type of existentialism, which he understands as 'a philosophy which does not accept objectifying knowledge' (Berdyaev 1998: 166). This form of existential philosophy stands within the context of an intuitive awareness of existence as rooted in a deeper existential ground than the reality accessible under the conditions of the subject/object division of consciousness. Mysticism, in this broadest sense, can simply be considered as 'life at its deepest' (Berdyaev 1935a: 251). It is on this basis that Berdyaev forges his interpretation of Christianity as the religion of freedom and personality. Such an interpretation accepts nothing on the basis of purely external authority. The knowledge of God 'can only be given in an experimental and symbolic theology' which 'rests upon spiritual experience and its symbolic expression' (ibid.: 68) and therefore 'the truth of dogmas is the truth of religious life and experience . . . they mark out the way of the spirit . . . [and] are mystical facts belonging to spiritual life' (ibid.: 75ff.).

In his book *Truth and Revelation* (1953a), Berdyaev intends to offer a 'critique of revelation' analogous to a Kant's *Critique of Pure Reason*. Just like Kant wanted to liberate reason from its dependence on outer authority, so Berdyaev wants to liberate Christian spirituality from all forms of objectification. Such a project raises questions: in the *Critique of Pure Reason*, reason criticizes itself, but how should we conceive of a critique of revelation, which does not result in a rationalistic distortion of its content?

From all that has been said it will be clear that such a critique can only be 'a Critique through the spirit which stands in relationship to the revelation and not a critique through reason, which is alien to revelation' (Berdyaev 1998: 160ff., trans.). If there were no such spirit in human beings, there would be no revelation at all. Insight into revelation requires the opening of the 'eye of the spirit'[3]. A critique of revelation therefore has to be based on the conviction that 'revelation should be interpreted as the agency of the spirit on spirit, as the agency of Divine spirit on human spirit, on human freedom, on human consciousness and conscience, all of which are themselves agents' (Berdyaev 1946: 53). Berdyaev focuses his attention on the anthropological dimension of revelation: 'Revelation presupposes the existence of a divine element in man and that there is a commensurability of the Divine and the human. Revelation is Divine–human' (Berdyaev 1998: 162). Just as there is no strictly impenetrable boundary between philosophy and mysticism, so there is, for Berdyaev, no impenetrable boundary between a purely 'natural' mysticism based on the capacities of the human spirit, and a mysticism which depends on the interpenetration and inward union of the divine and the human through the agency of the Holy Spirit. Ultimately, a critique of revelation can only be issued by its original author: the Holy Spirit that acts within the human spirit. This can never be an individualistic enterprise, because the Holy Spirit is one and engenders communion in the one truth, but is nevertheless not dependent on external authority.

From this perspective it becomes evident that, insofar as revelation does always imply some measure of adjustment to the human condition, which is more or less objectified, '[r]evelation is always at the same time some measure of concealment' (Berdyaev 1953a: 48). Revelation has to be understood as the *convergence* of two movements, a descending divine movement and an ascending human movement. If these two movements are separated, it cannot be understood. Berdyaev thus opposes the idea of an absolutely transcendent God that is entirely cut off from the human, just as much as he opposes a monistic/pantheistic conception of God in which the human is merged with the Divine.

A philosophical critique of revelation therefore has to start from an understanding of revelation in which neither the human nor the Divine is taken in isolation, but both are seen in dynamic interaction:

> The basic and original phenomenon of religious life is the meeting and mutual interaction between God and man, the movement of God towards man and man towards God. This fact finds its most concrete and fullest expression in Christianity, in which the humanity of God is revealed. The humanisation of God is the fundamental process of the inner consciousness of humanity.
>
> (Berdyaev 1935a: 189)

Divine-humanity is, for Berdyaev, the *Urphaenomen* of spiritual experience. The degree of humanization of God is dependent on the degree of the actualization of this original phenomenon in spiritual experience. This actualization happens in Berdyaev's view to a larger extent in the typically prophetic experience rather than in the conservative type of spirituality which is bound up with the ecclesiastic hierarchy. Inasmuch as his philosophy has a mystical dimension, it is of a 'gnostic–prophetic' rather than a 'monastic–ecclesial' type. It is this former type of mysticism which in Berdyaev's view continues the eschatological trajectory of sophiological Russian religious thought most clearly. It is dynamic–creative rather than conservative. The mystery of Divine-humanity is known in the spirit. Human spirit in its highest quality freely receives the *hagion pneuma*, the Holy Spirit, in which the divine and the human find communion:

> Prophetic mysticism is that of the Holy Spirit. It is Russian mysticism par excellence. It is inherent in the Russian people and it springs from the spiritual soil of Orthodoxy though the official hierarchy may be hostile to it . . . Orthodox mysticism seeks to acquire the grace of the Holy Spirit and we find human nature transfigured, illuminated and deified from within. It is the mysticism of the heart which is the centre of life. Therefore the heart must be united to the mind if there is to be any spiritual unity within. Christ enters the human heart and changes the whole nature of man. Man becomes another creature.
>
> (Berdyaev 1935a: 254)

Berdyaev sees in this form of prophetic mysticism a form of humanizing spirituality which can organically integrate a stronger focus on wholeness (instead of 'angelism', a striving for one-sided spiritualization and perfection) and on human creativity in the world: 'If there is ever to be a revival of Christian mysticism in the world, it will not be exclusively monastic. It will rather be a renewal and a deepening of life in the world and a fresh understanding of it' (ibid.: 260). Such a fresh understanding depends on a full blossoming of free human creativity, which at the same time becomes progressively transformed and illumined from within.

Berdyaev's existential–anthropological focus culminates in the attainment of an intuitively apprehended wisdom: 'Philosophy seeks the truth, not truths . . . At the summit of philosophic consciousness, Sophia enters into man' (Berdyaev 1962: 29). This Wisdom reveals the existential import of the mysteries of the Trinity and of Divine-humanity. It is a transformative truth, which – inspired by revelation – unfolds an understanding of human existence within an encompassing vision of the meaning of history.

If Berdyaev makes claims about the supremacy of Truth over revelation, and affirms that 'there is no higher religion than the Truth', what has to be kept in mind is that, for him, Truth *is* Divine-humanity. Based on John 14: 6,

Berdyaev offers this formulation: 'Truth is not that which exists; it is *the meaning of that which exists*, the *Logos* of it, but this meaning is . . . *He who* exists' (Berdyaev 1976: 43, emphasis mine). Such meaning can only be apprehended by being lived out so that it encompasses and transforms the totality of one's existence. In this process of the unfoldment of integral knowledge, therefore, there is an intimate interaction between the Divine and the human that finds its orienting 'archetype' in Christ, in whom there 'is a perfect union of these two movements, the realization of unity in duality of the Divine–human mystery' (Berdyaev 1935a: 189). It is on this basis that Berdyaev suggests a philosophical critique of revelation. Because philosophy is a much more personal, much less socialized endeavour than theology, it is, given this existential/theosophical understanding, predestined to bring about the purification and spiritualization of the *human* aspect of revelation.

Forms of objectification of revelation

The way in which revelation is presented in collectively determined historic Christianity is more or less distorted by a twofold process of objectification, which the existential philosophical approach ought to overcome. First, there is the objectification related to 'the primitive stage of tribal socialization'. This initial 'primitive layer' is then further objectified by 'the objectivization which arises in theological systems in more developed ecclesiastical thought' (Berdyaev 1953a: 51). The primitive, tribal level of objectification is not simply some insignificant remnant of the past. It constitutes an active, unconscious factor that shapes much of ecclesiastical thought, often in significant ways. With respect to these sorts of distortions, the scientific criticism offered, for example by the historical critical method, sociology and depth psychology, can be of great use. With regard to the critical usefulness of depth psychology, Berdyaev refers to Jung's *Symbols of Transformation* (1956a), his only reference to the concept of the collective unconscious:

> The psychoanalytical method is of importance for sociology, history of culture and the study of myths. Jung in particular insists upon the existence of the collective as well as the individual unconscious. The collective unconscious shows the presence of an archaic layer in man. The human soul is sick and tormented by atavistic false moral ideas and by the tyranny of society, which goes back to times immemorial. Myths are rooted in the collective unconscious. This is Jung's main contention, though he does not see all its implications.
>
> (Berdyaev 1945a: 73)

What interests Berdyaev about the concept of the collective unconscious (which he apparently knew only through Jung's early writings) is its critical potential. In his view it primarily helps to elucidate the distorting character of archaic layers of the psyche, related to tribal socialization. He seems to imply that Jung himself does not sufficiently recognize this critical potential of his own ideas. The psychology of the collective unconscious is for Berdyaev primarily a mass psychology, which shows the tremendous power that atavistic elements in the psyche hold over each one of us inasmuch as we are not yet persons but still caught up in collective dynamics.

The history of revelation is, from one angle, a history of successive spiritualizations of originally archaic and atavistically distorted experiences of the Divine. The collective unconscious is not so much the source of revelation as the source of its distortions. The old biblical conceptions of God can

> hardly harmonise with our religious thought. Already the prophets broke through the boundaries of the biblical understanding of God which was adopted to the old nomadic tribe. Our contemporary God is not an anthropomorphic and sociomorphic tribal Deity, a God of battles, a revengeful and murderous God. In the revelation He gave through His Son, he shows Himself very differently.
>
> (Berdyaev 1998: 224)

But even in the Gospels, divine Truth appears distorted as long as one does not penetrate into its spiritual meaning. God is represented in the parables as 'Lord, emperor and governor, man as his subject and slave. The master–slave relation is fundamental. God is insulted like men. He is revengeful and asks for ransom. He instigates punishments against disobedient men' (Berdyaev 1998: 225). In the idea of eternal damnation and hell Berdyaev detects

> the force of the primitive instincts of Sadism and Masochism, which have played no small part in religious life . . . perhaps the most distressing aspect of the whole matter is that the idea of hell is connected with a notion of justice which is derived from the instinct of revenge.
>
> (Berdyaev 1953a: 128)

Berdyaev interprets Boehme's ambivalent God-image from this perspective, arguing that it has to do not with how God is in himself, but with the condition of human consciousness in the act of receiving Divine revelation.

> The light of revelation only spreads in proportion to the capacity of consciousness and to the degree of receptivity which the natural man possesses for the spiritual world. Jacob Boehme said that the divine love suffers distortion through the darker elements of existence and appears as Divine wrath and as a consuming fire. God in Himself, in the divine Trinity, is absolute love, but it is possible to regard Him as the wrath of, as it were 'an element separated from God' and devoid of love.
>
> (Berdyaev 1935a: 111)

Berdyaev does not subscribe to the traditional distinction between natural and revealed religion. To his mind, it is more appropriate to treat natural and spiritual religion as *different phases* of revelation. 'God is revealed in nature and in spirit, and he is revealed in man as a natural and spiritual being' (Berdyaev 1935a: 89). The 'darker elements of existence' are those elements in man and in the cosmos which are subject to objectification, and thus God is revealed through them, in part at least, as dark and terrifying. In this view it is divine love itself that is experienced as terrifying because of the subjective condition of the one undergoing the experience.

While there are some points of resemblance to Jung's characterization of the God-image in *Answer to Job* (1952/1967), we can see here the consequences of the divergent epistemologies becoming evident. For Jung there is *only* the God-image and the unconscious within the psychological sphere as the *source* of revelation, while for Berdyaev these are primarily *obscuring* factors pertaining to natural man, while God as he is in himself is revealed only in the deep heart, the superconscious spirit. Berdyaev would of course acknowledge that this spiritual revelation is ultimately apophatic because God is always infinitely transcending our heart's knowledge but the Divine darkness is not the unconscious in Jung's sense, but a dark intuition, dark due to a superabundance of light.

If the unconscious plays a distorting role, human rational consciousness no less often ends up just cementing these distortions of anthropomorphism, sociomorphism and cosmomorphism. On top of the anthropomorphic, sociomorphic and cosmomorphic God-images ecclesiastical thought erects its theological edifices, which are based on a philosophical foundation that is thoroughly pre-Kantian, and therefore incapable of a genuine spiritual purification. Instead, they become compounded into 'infallible truths' through sophisticated rational elaborations. The three 'categories of objectification' of revelation – anthropomorphism, sociomorphism and cosmomorphism – have their origins in the fundamental condition of the objectification of human existence, and therefore in what is not truly human in man.

The humanization of God, which Berdyaev asserts to be the fundamental process in the inner consciousness of humanity, is therefore essentially the awakening of the transcendental man, resulting from the gradual overcoming of man's own inhumanity. Berdyaev often repeats the paradox that it is God who is truly human while man is inhuman, to the extent that the transcendental man, the true image of God in man, is obscured in him.

> The real humanity of revelation, the humanity of God, comes to light precisely from the awakening of transcendental man . . . The *critique* of revelation consists in bringing into view as far as may be possible the transcendental man who is also the humanized man.
>
> (Berdyaev 1953a: 19)

Within this process of the humanization of God, even atheism can under certain conditions have a positive role to play as 'a dialectical moment in the process of theological purification, spiritualization and humanization' (Berdyaev 1946: 172). There is a form of atheism which is, unknown to itself, actually spiritually motivated.

> When we make judgements about God or when we pass judgement on him we can do this only from the point of view of the highest, or the divine within ourselves. *And the very revolt against God may be the action of God within us.* The highest humanity is the divine in man and the human in God, this is the mystery of God-manhood. It is the deep-down mystery of Christianity when it is set free from false anthropomorphism and layers of sociomorphism.
>
> (Berdyaev 1953a: 116, emphasis mine)

This mystery is to be sought entirely outside of the sphere of objectification. 'In speaking of God we cannot even say that he is an objective reality' (Berdyaev 1953a: 110). To 'God as object', all the naturalistic, anthropomorphic and sociomorphic categories (such as causality, ideas of domination and might and so on) become transferred, and it is against this 'objective God' that atheist criticism is justly directed. And yet, the rational mode of thought underlying it cuts itself off from the possibility of attaining to an existential experience of God as spirit.

Apophaticism, symbolic philosophy and mythological creativity: Revelation as an interior experience of the spirit

In the last chapter we saw that Berdyaev simultaneously acknowledges and refutes the limitations that Kant imposes on reason. Precisely by recognizing its own limitations, reason can transcend its objectified state and can become integral intuition of the *noumenal* realm of freedom that lies beyond the subject–object division of rational consciousness. This happens to the degree that there is an integration of mind and heart.

The naturalism of a large portion of traditional theology (particularly in the west) 'projects' onto God rationally elaborated categories, and extends them far beyond the boundaries that Kant has (rightly) drawn. At the same time it invokes the notion of 'mystery' whenever anyone criticizes doctrines such as predestination or eternal damnation as being insults to more refined ethical sensibilities.

> Positive theology goes too far in rationalizing the mystery and at the same time it does not go far enough, for it puts limits to knowledge and lays down prohibitions. When we pass to negative theology we begin to breathe more freely as though coming out of a prison-house. Mystery,

> *docta ignorantia* has a profound significance. The whole meaning and value and importance of life is determined by the Mystery behind it, by an infinity which cannot be rationalized but can only be expressed in myths and symbols. God is the mystery which underlies existence.
>
> (Berdyaev 1945a: 24)

The category of infinity is, for Berdyaev, a symbol of the mystery of existence that refuses to be locked into any closed and finite form, however perfect. Berdyaev's mysticism is a mysticism of freedom. The Boehmean symbol of the *Ungrund*, which is eternal freedom itself, is a symbol of that infinity which transcends all finite forms, and as such it is the presupposition of all symbolism. Symbolism is not subjective, but a deeper kind of realism, inasmuch as an existential perspective places freedom at the heart of reality, while the naturalism of the objectifying mind can only grasp its elusive surface.

Symbolism is, for Berdyaev, the means by which the static Kantian agnosticism, which seals off the unknowable 'thing-in-itself' from the phenomenon known to consciousness, is transformed into a dynamic apophaticism in which the spiritual–existential dimension of freedom interacts dialectically with the secondary reality of objectified existence. The fact that Kant, while postulating the existence of these two dimensions, hermetically sealed them off from each other, produced disastrous results, which can only be avoided by affirming a symbolism that constitutes the mediating 'third way', which allows a continual 'osmosis' between these two dimensions.

> By affirming a dualism between the two worlds Kant attempted to defend the sphere of faith and religion, by transferring it to the knowing subject. But along this line faith soon comes to an end . . . Symbolism alone, by a delimitation of the spheres of spirit and nature, by putting a barrier to the competence of rational knowledge, and by opening up new ways of knowledge, safeguards the inalienable rights and the eternal truths of religious life.
>
> (Berdyaev 1935a: 66)

The barrier is one that limits the competence of rational knowledge to the interpretation of the world of phenomena. But because this dualism is not an ontological one but one of two different existential conditions of the subject, a 'drastic revolution in our consciousness which brings with it a spiritual illumination transforming the very nature of reason itself' (Berdyaev 1935a: 73) is a real possibility. For Berdyaev, 'reason thus illuminated is now a reason of another kind . . . God is immanent in reason when it is illuminated and spiritually integrated, but He remains transcendent and inaccessible so far as the old reason of the natural man and the first Adam is concerned' (ibid.: 73). Symbolism, then, becomes the creative expression of the 'supra-conceptual' spiritual experience of the transcendental man. The move from concepts to symbols is the move from the unredeemed, limited, fallen reason of the 'old Adam' to the spiritually integrated reason of transcendental man, the 'new Adam'.

On the conceptual level, contradiction, antinomy and paradox gain central importance for such religious knowledge. They belong together with symbolism as the constitutive elements of apophatic knowledge. All of them are, so to speak, 'liminal phenomena', belonging to the cognitive process on the threshold of mystery; on this threshold, reason either shrinks back, as it does in Kant, or gains greater acuteness and intensity and undergoes a qualitative transformation.

Inasmuch as it both separates and unites the objective and the existential order of reality, symbolism is an ambivalent phenomenon. While on the one hand it serves as a bridge to spiritual reality it can, on the other hand, also lead to its objectification whenever the symbol becomes a substitute for the reality. Berdyaev thus sees a close link between symbolism and objectification. In the 'idolatrous' use of symbols the personal is subjected to the objectified and therefore dead idol of the once living spirit. Much of religious life is characterized by this tendency. It is not a life of faith but of superstition. Jung would say that such symbols have lost their connection to the living psychic process.

True faith is of a different nature. It dissolves such 'religious positivism'. At a deep, existential level a primitive spiritual will operates within the person, which determines its fundamental orientation in crossing the symbolic threshold: either towards the spiritual or towards the objectified condition of being. Inspired faith is that liberating force within the person that makes it capable of crossing the 'paradoxical–symbolic' threshold towards an intuitive apprehension of reality in spiritual experience that can only be expressed antinomically. True faith therefore depends on a 'redirection of the primitive will latent in the original life of the spirit towards another world, involving an extension of experience to an unprecedented degree' (Berdyaev 1935a: 104). This primitive will is a spiritual not a psychological force, and thus 'the direction of consciousness and the extent of experience are not determined in the sphere of the soul, but in that of the spirit' (ibid.).

The Kantian, agnostic dividing line is, for Berdyaev, the end not the precondition of faith. It denies the possibility of spiritual experience and leaves us with nothing but the dead corpse of moral postulates. But faith, for Berdyaev, is precisely a 'fact of spiritual experience' (Berdyaev 1935a: 103) without which revelation would be impossible, just as faith itself would be impossible 'without that fact of spiritual experience which we call revelation' (ibid.). Faith is a creative, spiritual force that opens up the way to a spiritual experience in which a meeting and *synergy* of the human and the divine in the spirit becomes possible, and which thereby also enters into the mythopoeic creativity of the one who lives this experience. Faith leads us towards realizing the spirit as the primary reality and in this way it is a force to be employed in the 'fight against the power of necessity' (Berdyaev 1976: 177).

Berdyaev's grounding of revelation in the existential dimension of actual lived experience means that, for him, the 'process of mythological creation in the life of the Church is a continuous movement which marches irresistibly forward' (Berdyaev 1935a: 81). Our mythological creations, if they achieve true profundity, are expressions of 'a creative life which proceeds without interruption, at once individual and supra-individual, a life in *sobornost* in which the past and the future, tradition and creation are bound together in eternity' (ibid.). This life forms the superconscious counterpole to the distorting role of the collective unconscious, however difficult it may be to separate them in practice.

The full manifestation of the transcendental man requires a breakthrough from symbolism to the reality symbolized. It runs counter to a superstitious literalization of symbols. Myth, for Berdyaev, remains the most accurate expression of concrete, existential reality. But while the mythological creations of the ancients happened in a state of 'original participation', the new mythological creation can only come from 'final participation', which follows from the awakening of the transcendental man or the 'supraconscious'. A simple return to the older form of mythic consciousness would only lead to further distortions. One could even say that it is the remnants of original participation that lead to the false idolatry of symbols. The spiritual situation of modern man demands a renewal of mythopoeic imagination in the service of a living spirituality that is not regressive, but dynamic enough to overcome false objectifications:

> A new system of symbols must . . . be established and a moment arrives when a return to reality, the transfiguration of life, and the attaining of true being, becomes possible . . . The coming of . . . [the] new era of spirituality and fresh realism will demand a symbolism which will deliver the human spirit from a false realism and from its subjection by means of symbols to the natural world.
>
> (Berdyaev 1935a: 86)

For Berdyaev, this new symbolism is a symbolism of the spiritual experience of freedom. In this way Berdyaev wants to prepare the way for the new 'anthropological revelation of the creative epoch [which] is at once fully human and fully divine' (Berdyaev 1962: 295ff.).

Meta-history: Dynamic movement in God

What today is called 'process theology' may perhaps be considered as one of the creative developments of Christian symbolism with which Berdyaev's and Jung's thought share a significant affinity[4]. But in Berdyaev's case this affinity takes a specific shape, different from the one it takes in Jung. This difference will turn out to be significant for us. Berdyaev's 'process theology' is shaped by the emerging 'love paradigm in modern theology'[5]. This paradigm 'emerged within Russian Philosophy and theology as the result of a rethinking of the eastern patristic tradition in the light of both eastern Patristic tradition and western love mysticism and modern philosophy' (Meerson 1998: xiv). The influence of modern philosophy means that the love paradigm has been 'enriched by anthropocentric premises of modern philosophy' (xiv).

Berdyaev's version of the love paradigm furthermore owes much to his major source of inspiration, Boehme, who

> maybe was the first one in the history of human thought to see that the foundation of being and preceding being is the groundless freedom, the passionate desire of nothing to become something . . . i.e. he was the founder of an original metaphysical voluntarism which was as yet unknown to medieval and Greek thought.
>
> (Berdyaev 1932a: 11)

Boehme's metaphysical voluntarism offered Berdyaev a dynamic understanding of God which admits a genesis, a birth within God:

> If there would be no genesis in the self-consciousness of God, divine self-consciousness would not be life and process. The dynamic understanding of God does also imply that God is for us living, ensouled, that the tragedy common to all life inheres also the divine life.
>
> (Berdyaev 1932a: 17)

A personal God is a God that is living, ensouled and experiences tragedy.

> Personalism is, so to speak, incomprehensible by means of abstract metaphysics. God and man are living personalities whose relationship is intimate to the highest degree and constitutes a concrete drama of love and freedom. Such a living personalism is always mythological.
>
> (Berdyaev 1935a: 195)

For the mythological–symbolic account of the concrete drama of love and freedom in which God and man interact in concrete history Berdyaev coined the term 'meta-history', which 'etymologically comprehends both metaphysics and history' (Bonner-Richardson 1968: 32). Existential philosophy is a 'dramatic philosophy of destiny', and as such it 'admits of only one possible metaphysics, and that is meta-history' (Berdyaev 1949a: v). Human historical destiny within time is not closed, but open to the transcendent, which may at any point enter into time. Nowhere is this eruption more dramatic than in the incarnation of the God-man.

According to Friedrich Christoph Oetinger (1702–1782), a disciple of Boehme, God is the *ens manifestativum sui*, a creative force striving 'towards his own realization and corporealization' (Benz 1967: 196). What Berdyaev calls meta-history can be understood as the inner creative dynamic of divine life flowing out into manifestation, erupting into history. Even more: history is in truth a 'moment' in eternal divine life itself.

Berdyaev distinguishes the cosmic time of natural cycles from linear historic time which is 'placed within cosmic time . . . but every event is unrepeatable' (Berdyaev 1976: 206) and existential time whose 'flow depends on the intensity of experience' (ibid.). 'Eternity' simply means the greatest conceivable intensity of experience, not an endless extension of cosmic or historical time. 'Existential time, which is known to everyone by experience . . . is evidence of the fact that time is in man and not man in time, and that time depends on changes in man. At a greater depth we know that temporal life is consummated in eternity' (ibid.).

Existential time constitutes an opening of the historical and evolutionary process towards the dynamic that is the innermost driving force of these processes: the process of divine self-manifestation. A philosophy of history based on such a meta-historical foundation

> studies man in the concrete fullness of his spiritual being; psychology, physiology and the other spheres of human knowledge study him incompletely in one or other of his aspects. The philosophy of history examines man in relation to the world forces which act upon him, that is, in his greatest fullness and concreteness. By comparison all other ways of studying him are abstract.
>
> (Berdyaev 1945b: 14)

All these 'world-forces' have their ultimate root in the meta-historical dimension of the dynamic life of the Trinity. In the mystical experience, the 'point' of existential time, symbolizing movement into the depth of total silence and presence, ultimately touches upon this deepest mystery of existence, the mystery of the Trinity. The movement into depth, into existential time, uncovers the deepest stratum of the world-forces acting upon man. 'Heaven', i.e. the interior spiritual life, 'is not a remote transcendental and unattainable sphere; it is a part of the inmost depths of our spiritual life' (Berdyaev 1945b: 44).

Trinity and Divine-humanity: Meta-history as the Divine–human drama

The mystery of the Trinity is the deepest foundation of the person in its Divine–human nature. The Son, the second hypostasis of the Trinity, is eternally the God-man, and this means that the 'eternal face of man abides in the very heart of the Divine Trinity itself. The Second Hypostasis of the Trinity is Divine-humanity itself' (Berdyaev 1935a: 207).

Berdyaev's criticism of humanism is that there 'has not been enough emphasis on man: there has not been emphasis on man to the point of affirming him in God' (Berdyaev 1950: 180). The mystery of the Trinity is, for Berdyaev, above all the mystery of the 'humanity of God', which is the deepest foundation of a 'more extreme and consistent kind of humanism' (ibid.).

Basing it on Soloviev's and Boehme's Sophiology, Berdyaev develops a 'Christology of man' to give expression to this humanism. 'Christ is the second Hypostasis of the Holy Trinity but in the second Hypostasis heavenly humanity is present' (Berdyaev 1932b: 8). Just as for Boehme, so for Berdyaev 'the first-man Adam precedes the world process and is not derived from it' (Berdyaev 1962: 257), and 'the androgynous sophianic image of Adam is the heavenly pre-existence of man' (Berdyaev 1932b: 4). Sophia is thus for him not so much the 'eternal feminine', but primarily the androgynous image of man which symbolizes the eternal in man, the image of wholeness which was restored to humanity in the incarnation of Christ.

In orthodox theology shaped by the 'love paradigm' the Trinity is the mystery of love, understood not as a psychological condition, but as the most fundamental 'ontological' reality, because the unity of the three Divine hypostases is love, and God *is* this unity: He is not three 'Gods'. God not only has love, but, above all, God is Love, '*ho theos agape estin*' (1 John 4: 8, 16). That is, love is God's essence, His own nature, and not only His providential relationship, which is proper to him. In other words, 'God is love (more precisely, He is "Love") and not only "the Loving One", even if the "perfectly Loving One" ' (Florensky 2004: 54).

The hypostases of the Trinity are not 'similar' (*homoiousios*), but one (*homoousios*). They are *homoousios* precisely because they are unique. Love is the ontological condition of personal identity in this vision. Things or objects are identical to themselves and similar to each other inasmuch as they belong to the same genus. Persons, on the other hand, are *unique* in the sense that they fall under no genus or concept. '[I]n contrast to a thing which is subordinate to a concept, a "person" is "unconceptualizable", [he] transcends all concepts' (Florensky 2004: 61), just as the hypostases of the Trinity 'have' their divine nature or *ousia* as their common genus, and are not subordinate to it.

For the orthodox theologian Christos Yannaras, this represents a revolutionary and radical break with Greek ontologism, a break that has repercussions that persist into modernity:

> What does this radical break lie [in]? In one phrase we would say: in the identification of hypostasis and person[6]. Person, for the Fathers, was the hypostasis of being; personal existence makes being into a reality. For the first time in history, being, existence in general, is considered neither

> something self-evidently given, nor something subject to a predetermined ground or mode of actualisation (a substance). What exists is not pre-determined in its hypostasis by its given essence.
>
> (Yannaras 1991: 33)

In analogy to the distinction of hypostasis and nature in the Trinity, in the human sphere there is one single, common human nature, and a plurality of persons who all 'have' this common human nature in their own unique way, i.e. as potentially free beings, who choose how to actualize their human nature. After the pattern of the Trinity, free communion in love enables the most complete actualization of our common humanity. This is the Trinitarian foundation of *sobornost*, as the mode of existence proper to persons. The Russian philosopher Fedorov therefore can say that 'the Trinity is our social project' (cited from Sakharov 2002: 124).

This mystery of love in which personal existence is rooted is, for Berdyaev, inseparably bound up with the mystery of irrational freedom, to which he gives 'such an immense significance as may probably be unique in the whole spiritual history of humanity' (Klein 1976: 107, trans.). Love presupposes freedom. To exist as a person means to be free. Existentially, freedom and existence are synonymous.

The 'radical break with Greek ontologism' implicit in Trinitarian theology provides Berdyaev with the point of departure from which he can appropriate Boehme's theosophical ideas about the *Ungrund*. The lack of predetermination by substance/*ousia* implies the priority of the irrational will over rational categories, Platonic ideas or any other ordering patterns conceived as ontological structures. All existence is personal and free. Being is, in relation to it, secondary. While classical metaphysical philosophy sees in the category of 'being' an ultimate primary unity, from this perspective being becomes only hypostatized, i.e. actualized in and through personal centres of will (cf. Segundo 1963: 368).

This is the basis on which Berdyaev unfolds his theogony, which is at the same time a cosmogony and an anthropogony: Deeper than being is the *Ungrund*, the Divine Darkness of the *Gottheit*: 'Out of the Divine Nothing, the *Gottheit* or the *Ungrund*, the Holy Trinity, God the Creator is born' (Berdyaev 1945a: 25). God eternally gives birth to himself out of the Divine Nothing, i.e. out of His own divine freedom. He becomes manifest as the creative Holy Trinity; as Creator-God he calls forth his self-manifestation through both the cosmos and man out of the *me-on*, the potential being of freedom.

The birth of God out of the *Ungrund*, which is at the same time the birth of the cosmos and man, does *not* mean, for Berdyaev 'the birth of a previously non-existent God, but a divine mystery-play going on in the eternal hidden life of the Deity' (Berdyaev 1945a: 29). What Berdyaev seeks to offer here is a symbolic account of an intuition of the hidden mystery of existence as the infinite, eternal dynamism of divine life at the root of existence. God is like the eternal, infinite, ever newly born wellspring of life, all life.

Berdyaev does not accept the notion that God created the world out of nothing in the sense of *ouk on*, or *absolute* nothing. The 'nothing' out of which God creates the world is freedom, *me on*, or *potential being*.

> Freedom is not determined by God; it is part of the nothing out of which God created the world. The opposition between God the Creator and freedom is secondary; in the primeval mystery of the divine Nothing this opposition is transcended, for both God and freedom are manifested out of the *Ungrund*.
>
> (Berdyaev 1945a: 25)

For created beings therefore the apophatic mystery of the *Ungrund* is the origin of two kinds of freedom, *meontic* or irrational freedom and 'final' freedom in God. These, while distinct for created beings, are mysteriously one in the apophatic mystery of the infinite Godhead. These two forms of freedom stand in profound tension to each other. While final freedom depends on the positive contents of goodness and virtue, the initial, irrational freedom is purely negative and contains all the potentialities not only for good but also for evil and destructiveness. The best 'amplification' of this thought of Berdyaev's is the notion of the *Sod ha Tsimtsum* in the Lurianic Cabbala:

> According to Luria, God was compelled to make room for the world by, as it were, abandoning a region within Himself, a kind of mystical primordial space from which He withdrew in order to return to it in the act of creation and revelation. The first act of *En-Sof*, the infinite Being, is therefore not a step outside but a step inside, a movement of recoil, of falling back upon oneself, of withdrawing into oneself. Instead of emanation we have the opposite, contraction.
>
> (Scholem 1974: 261)

The God of the Bible is not the impersonal Absolute of philosophy. The personal God of revelation is love, that is: relation to His other. Berdyaev formulates this paradox: 'The perfection of God is the perfection of relation' (Berdyaev 1976: 102). The perfection of relation is love, which leaves its other totally free and yet longs for the free response of that other. More than this, the other is free in such a way that the Creator God is *entirely powerless* in the face of this freedom: freedom is not determined by God. God is *not* omnipotent. He is powerless over the freedom of the creature, because this freedom is not created by God but uncreated, manifested out of the *Ungrund* by an act of divine self-limitation.

This notion of uncreated freedom has garnered Berdyaev a great deal of criticism, because it seems to imply a fundamental dualism. It clearly deviates from the common theological notion of the *creatio ex nihilo*, in which *nihil* is understood to be equivalent to *ouk on* and therefore God is omnipotent. Berdyaev passionately rejects this notion, which amounts – he believes – to an absurdity: an omnipotent and omniscient God endows his creatures with freedom and foresees that they will abuse it, so that countless numbers of them will end up in 'eternal damnation'. Such a God would not be the God of love.

True divine 'omnipotence' is entirely paradoxical; it resides entirely in the sacrificial power of infinite divine love which is utterly powerless. It is thus a very different kind of 'omnipotence', which is diametrically opposed to the idea of absolute power. From this point of view, the world-creation is not finished once and for all, but is continuous. This is the 'divine mystery-play'. It proceeds in stages, in aeons that are rooted in the inner life of the Trinity itself. The historical Incarnation of the God-man is a further phase in the world-creative process itself, which in its totality consists in the illumination of the dark *Ungrund*: 'God, in the Aspect of God-the-Son, descends into the abyss, into the *Ungrund*, into the depths of freedom out of which springs evil and every kind of good' (Berdyaev 1945a: 25). Christ is thus the true bringer of freedom, because in the unique historical event of the crucifixion he transmutes the irrational power of man's original freedom in such a way that it is illuminated and transfigured from within, by love, without being obliterated.

The 'perfection of relation' is the perfection of love, which is the divine creative force. Love is the invincible power of utter powerlessness. Love calls forth its other, which is *truly* other in that it is entirely free and undetermined by God, and overcomes the irrational chaotic forces of the abyss of freedom through a total and unconditional sacrificial outpouring of itself. 'The Divine sacrifice, the Divine self-crucifixion must conquer evil *meontic* freedom by enlightening it from within without forcing it, without depriving the created world of freedom' (Berdyaev 1945a: 26). Without this divine drama, without this tragic, existential dialectic, God would not be a personal God. God-in-Trinity is thus 'the God of love and sacrifice' (Berdyaev 1945a: 27).

One could say, therefore, that the cross is the deepest foundation of both creation and free personal existence, which unites in itself the opposites of irrational freedom and divinely illuminated freedom. The cross transmutes the evil that arises from *meontic* freedom from within. Christ crucified is the source of true freedom, by uniting irrational freedom and divine freedom through love. As in Jung's thought, he appears in Berdyaev's thought as a symbol uniting the opposites.

The eternal, infinite Godhead itself is entirely beyond all comprehension. Where symbolic apprehension of the mystery begins, the tension between the Creator-God and the *Ungrund* as the abyss of irrational freedom opens up. In between lies what the Cabbalists call the *Sod ha Tsimtsum*, the act of divine self-limitation, the cross at the foundation of the world. The mystical

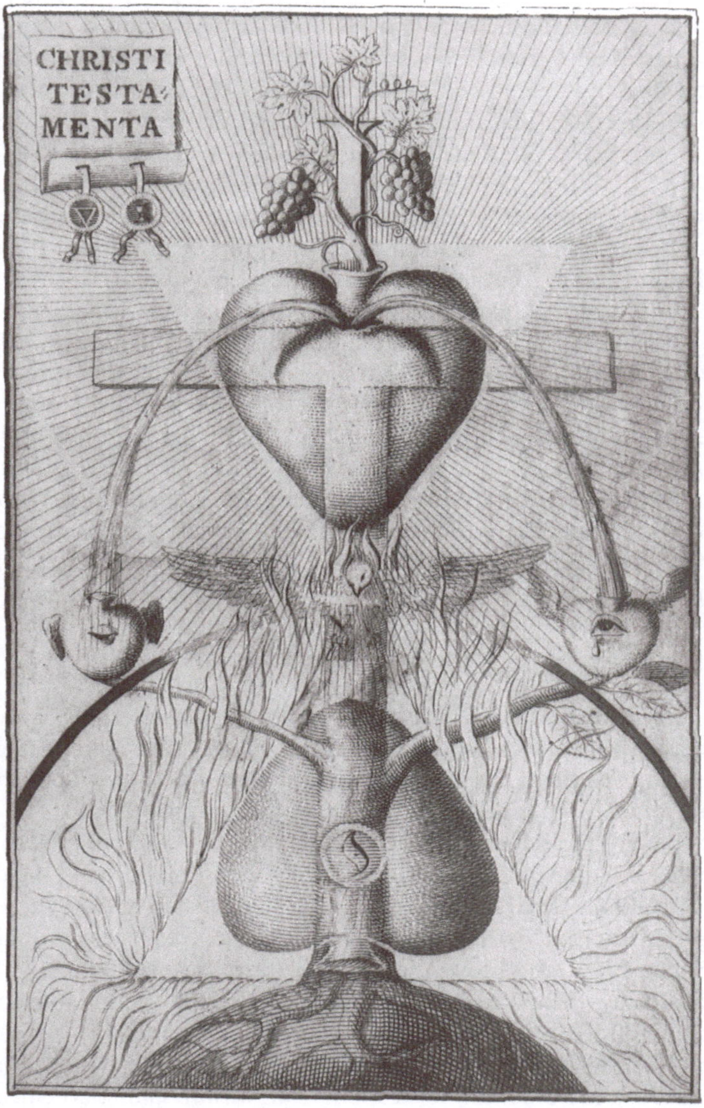

Figure 6.1 The symbol of the cross as uniting the opposites and at the same time transforming the dark fire of passion into light. Title print for Boehme's *Christi Testamenta.*

intuition of the *Ungrund* in this second sense states that 'the primal foundation of being rests upon a certain irrational and wilful principle, and that the whole significance and essence of the world process consists in the illumination of this dark, irrational principle in cosmogony and theogony'

(Berdyaev 1945b: 56). German mysticism has focused on this primal intuition, but, according to Berdyaev, it has not yet fully developed the process of anthropogony which is for him supremely important as representing the deepest foundation of his personalism.

The mystical intuition of Divine-humanity, which inscribes the eternal face of man into the heart of the inner life of the Trinity itself, completes that of the *Ungrund.* In fact, it is the anthropogonic process which constitutes the true heart of the theogonic and cosmogonic process. In God 'there is a passionate and anguished longing for man. In God there is a tragic deficiency which is satisfied by the great gain of man's birth in Him' (Berdyaev 1962: 121). This 'tragic deficiency' is that God lacks His 'other', which is truly and entirely other, i.e. absolutely free in relation to God, capable of both responding to God with love and turning away from Him. It is the tragic deficiency of superabundant Love. If God were 'omnipotent', no such other could ever exist. If this other does exist, then, there is inevitably a tragic element to God, because God is then truly powerless against evil. He has to suffer it because He longs for His other, and His omnipotence resides only in the infinite patience of sacrificial love. By drawing from the notion that God is Love, the most radical consequences Berdyaev provides, I believe, the most promising Christian counterpoint to Jung's interpretation of the Christian God-image:

> The mystics taught the mystery of God's birth in man. But there is another mystery, that of man's birth in God. There is a summons, a call in man, for God to be born in him. But there is also God's call for man to be born in Him. This is the mystery of Christianity, the mystery of Christ . . . The substantial and multinomial being revealed in One, is greater than a One undifferentiated. Only the myth of God's longing for man and man's love can bring us near to the final mystery.
>
> (Berdyaev 1962: 121)

This is how Jung's vision of the transformation of the God-image as he presents it in *Answer to Job* appears in the light of the love paradigm. It is as if we were to look at Jung's psychological myth as a veil having become transparent for the very depths that can have no place in psychology.

The 'substantial and multinomial being revealed in One' (ibid.) is humanity, which participates in the life of the Trinity both in and through the Holy Spirit. The Holy Spirit is the agent of a unity within a maximal differentiation of individuated beings, a unity of freedom and love: *sobornost.* This unity is the actualization of the Church in its cosmic dimension as the Christed cosmos. We have seen that redemption through Christ is the 'second act' of the world-creative process. Man's birth in God through the active, creative realization of his sophianic image is the final act of the world-creative process. Christ is the 'firstborn among many brothers' (Rom. 8: 29).

The Divine–human mystery is the mystery of 'unity in duality'. God and man are distinct and yet one, one and yet distinct. But this divine mystery of unity in Duality is fulfilled only in the fullness of their life, which is the Third Person of the Holy Spirit. Only the Holy Spirit fully reveals the sophianic element in man and therefore man/woman in his/her full dignity as God's other. This is the final revelation about man, or man's birth in God.

A Christianity of the Spirit which recognizes the sophianic dimension in man and in all of creation is oriented more towards wholeness than perfection and avoids the danger of a more traditional ascetic mysticism which 'may take the form of the extinction instead of the illumination of man's *psyche*, that is to say, of the concrete multiplicity of human personalities . . . Multiplicity is lost in unity and soul in spirit' (Berdyaev 1935a: 260ff.). The new type of mysticism under the inspiration of Sophia will show 'a different attitude towards the world, which will unite detachment and contemplation to an enlightened love of the whole divine creation and every human personality' (ibid.: 262). It is the sophianic element in man/woman, which enables such a *coincidentia oppositorum*.

To reach this sophianic element, we have to face the abysmal darkness of irrational freedom within ourselves from which arises the spirit of rebellion in countless forms, which is hidden and active in the dark recesses of the heart. We have to suffer through this confrontation with our own darkness and allow it to be transmuted by sheer unmerited grace through our continuously deepening union with Christ crucified. Here much of what Jung has to say about the assimilation of the shadow in the process of individuation becomes relevant. It is out of this darkness that the sophianic light is born. 'The Kingdom of God (the kingdom of an enlightened humanity and an enlightened cosmos) is only realised through the Holy Spirit in Whom the Drama is complete and the circle closed' (ibid.: 199). The Kingdom of God is therefore humanity and the cosmos as the body of Christ in which the divine Life of Love pulsates as the perfect realization of *sobornost*. It is the sophianic or divine element in man which makes such a transformation possible, because only if there is in man an element which can mediate between the 'above' and the 'below' is such a transfiguration through man's creative activity possible. Sophia is 'a third mediating principle between Creator and creation . . . The transfiguration of the earth is possible only through the Sophianic. A total exclusion of all Sophiology leads to a dead dualistic theism and finally to deism' (Berdyaev 1932b: 24). Thus we have, at the deepest level of Berdyaev's personalism, something akin to 'a religion of the Holy Ghost and of the *Sapientia Dei*' (Jung 1955/1956: para. 531), which Jung believed was anticipated in alchemy. As a further development of the as yet projected insights of alchemy into the workings of the psyche on the level of modern scientific consciousness, Jung believes his psychology to be a further step in the fulfilment of this anticipation. We will want to gain a deeper understanding of what this means and how Jung's religious vision differs from Berdyaev's.

Jung's psychological interpretation of the Christian God-image

Jung's psychology leads to its own form of 'process-theology', which is informed by the notion of the numinous taken from Rudolf Otto[7]. For Jung's psychological approach to religion, it is not love, but libido, psychic energy, which lies at the root of religious life. This is of course psychologically correct: psychology as such cannot base itself on a 'theology of love'. But if all we can ever know is psychological reality then the psychological perspective inevitably gravitates towards becoming a new psychological religion, which appears now as the only (or at least the most evolved and enlightened) option left. Psychological religion is more exactly post-religious, it is *sublated* religion. Jung, on the basis of his epistemology, offers a psychological interpretation of Christianity of this sort. What we will explore therefore is the move from Christianity to psychological religion.

The alchemists gradually tended to project 'even the highest value – God – into matter' (Jung 1944: para. 432). Jung shows that the unconscious in its unknowability is the psychological origin of this projection. From this notion of an unconscious ground, religiously a *theos annoetos*, an unconscious God, Jung develops his views on the relativity of the God-image, which constitute the psychological analogy to Berdyaev's notion of the Divine–human character of revelation. The psyche is the 'vessel' in which the *prima materia* undergoes a series of transformations, leading to the philosophical gold of the Self. Jung relates his psychology to revelation by founding revelation itself in a psychological–alchemical myth, the myth of individuation.

The relativity of the God-image: Soul as sacred vessel

From his psychological point of view, Jung identifies the God-image as that factor in the psychic economy which establishes wholeness. The Self is the unifying centre of the person, and is as such indistinguishable from the God-image, which represents the highest unifying factor. The God-image changes and transforms at particular crisis points in the psychic development of the individual and the collective, when it has lost its unifying, balancing capacity. 'The psychological point of departure for God-renewal is an increasing split in the development of psychic energy, or libido' (Jung 1921: para. 326). The God-image therefore cannot be understood in abstraction from the psyche. This leads Jung to develop his psychological notion of the relativity of the God-image, which he sets out in a chapter of *Psychological Types* entitled 'The relativity of the Symbol'.

This chapter opens with the following sentence: 'The Christian principle which unites the opposites is the *worship of God*, in Buddhism it is the *worship of the self* (self-development), while in Spitteler and Goethe it is the *worship of the soul*, symbolised by the *worship of woman*' (Jung 1921: para. 375).

Jung lists here different forms of spirituality, related to different psychological structures. But, inasmuch as these different structures can be seen to designate degrees of psychological maturity, it could also be read as charting a progression. This progression leads from devotion to an external God to devotion to the impersonal Self, and from the impersonal eastern form to the western one, which is more immersed in the particulars of individual differentiations because it has soul, not spirit, as its point of gravity. Whereas spirit aspires upwards, towards the transcendent One, soul 'sticks to the realm of experience' (Hillman 1992: 69). In this way, the 'service of soul' links us back, on a higher level of individuation, to 'primitive poly-daemonism' (Jung 1921: para. 375). To individuate means to follow one's *daimon*. Service of the soul is therefore oriented towards the *daimonic*, mediating realm ruled by *eros*, and partakes of its ambiguities.[8]

The erotic–religious passion and intensity in the medieval devotion to woman contained both an earthly and a spiritual dimension. By diverting this energy towards the purified, one-sidedly spiritual and idealized image of the Virgin Mary, the Church lost this potentially integrating dimension. Through its assimilation with the Christian universal symbol, the anima 'lost its individual form of expression . . . [and consequently] any possibility of an individual differentiation of the soul was lost when it became repressed in the collective worship' (Jung 1921: para. 399). Thus something significant was left out in the formation of the Christian God-image, which, from the very beginnings of the formation of the Church, nevertheless sought expression in 'heretic' compensatory counter currents, from Gnosticism through to the Grail legend, various other heresies, and alchemy. What was left out was 'service of the soul', the quest for the '*Grail*-vessel', which can be the vessel 'in which the "soul-substance" of the God remains held' (E. Jung and von Franz 1980: 163, trans.) and which therefore is the condition for an individual and (in Jung's meaning of the term) 'psychological' experience of the Divine. Jung sees in early Gnosticism a Promethean and creative element 'which will bow only to the individual soul, and to no collective ruling' (Jung 1921: para. 409).

Two points are to be noted here: the element of uniqueness which Berdyaev locates in the spiritual is for Jung to be found in a decisive focus on the psychological. The spiritual in itself detracts by its one-sided idealism from the task of individuation. Second, this psychological focus has its embattled origins precisely in those heretical movements which the collectively oriented Church had to fend off. Psychological religion champions the ancient 'heretic' cause for the rights of the individual soul against the collective tyranny of religion. In its fight it is now supported by the newly established science of psychology, which finally managed to free itself from the clutches of religion and metaphysics.

In order to deepen this theme of the 'worship of the soul', and its significance for Jung's approach to the contents of Christian revelation, it will be useful to explore the image of the 'Grail-vessel' in greater depth. I will use a statement by W. Giegerich as a starting point: 'In the account Jung gives of the prehistory of his psychology, it primordially appears as the mixing vessel sent by the higher god' (Giegerich 1999: 11). In this statement Giegerich identifies the Gnostic *krater*, which later became the *Grail* and the alchemical *vas*, with Jung's psychology itself as a later metamorphosis of the same archetypal image. The soul/anima is a 'vessel for the unconscious' (Jung 1921: para. 425).

Following E. Neumann, it might be better for our purposes to speak not of the anima, but of what he called the 'psyche–archetype'. Neumann wrote:

> It is no accident that we speak of the 'soul' in men as well as in women, and it is no accident that analytical psychology defines the totality of consciousness and the unconscious as the 'psyche'. This psyche as the whole of the personality must be characterised in man as well as in woman as feminine . . . For this reason the mandala figure which appears in man and in woman as the totality of the psyche, is feminine in its symbolism as circle and round, or *uroboric*, as that which contains the opposites.
>
> (Neumann 1971: 141)

Psychology, as Jung understands it, is meant to be a kind of healing vessel, characterized as comprehension or receptivity of understanding (*Auffassung*) 'which is not brought from consciousness to the unconscious but which develops with careful observation of the unconscious from the latter one itself. It is in this sense *theoria* in which the unconscious explains itself' (E. Jung and von Franz 1980: 149, trans.). Psychology as 'soul-making' (Keats) is the 'forming of the vessel', the *vas hermeticum* that no longer leaks so that 'all God is outside', i.e. psychic energy is dispersed in projections.

Both in alchemy and in the Grail legends, the vessel is equated with its content. In terms of analytical psychology the same idea appears, inasmuch as psychology 'is the coming to consciousness of the psychic process, but it is not, in the deeper sense, an explanation of this process, for no explanation of the psychic can be anything other than the living process of the psyche itself' (Jung 1947/1954: para. 429). All of this has to be kept in mind when one considers Jung's 'psychological, empirical' approach to Christian revelation.

In *Memories, Dreams, Reflections*, Jung makes it very clear that, like Berdyaev, he is not intending to negate the importance of the Christian myth; on the contrary, 'not only do I leave a door open for the Christian message, but it belongs in the centre of western man. It needs, however, to be seen in a new light, in accordance with the secular changes wrought by the *Zeitgeist*. Otherwise, it stands apart from the times and man's wholeness stands apart from it' (Jung 1992: 213, trans.). The Christian message belongs at the centre of western man, i.e. it is concerned with western man's living experience of the Self. It needs to be seen in a new light, but this does not mean a cheap adaptation to the *Zeitgeist*, it means penetrating more deeply into the psychological meaning of the changes the *Zeitgeist* has brought about, because time and the 'spirit of the times' (*Zeitgeist*) are deeply bound up with 'the process of archetypal transformation which has gone on through the centuries' (Jung 1992: 210, trans.). Man's wholeness is, in one sense, this process itself, it is not a static 'entity', and psychology is thus the self-portrayal of this 'life process of the psyche'. If the Christian message loses touch with the 'life process of the psyche' in modern western man, then by standing apart from 'time' (which, psychologically/synchronistically speaking *is* this life process) it stands apart from man's wholeness, when in fact it should really address itself to this very wholeness as belonging to its innermost core. Jung recognizes the vital *psychological* function that the Christian symbols still potentially hold, even if their religious value as a means of promoting the worship of an external, institutionally defined collective God-image is essentially bankrupt.

On his travels in India, Jung had a very 'western' dream about the *Grail*. 'It was', he says,

> as though the dream were asking me, 'What are you doing in India? Rather seek for yourself and your fellows the healing vessel, the *servator mundi*, which you urgently need. For your state is perilous; you are in imminent danger of destroying all that centuries have built up'.
>
> (Jung 1995: 313)

The *Grail*, like the *krater*, and like the soul as the vessel of the unconscious, is the healing vessel needed to contain all that the centuries have built up, and so save from destruction the Christian message, which belongs at the centre of western man. Without this containing vessel, the healing soul-substance of the God disappears into the unconscious, and then resurfaces in the form of destructive symptoms: the ideologies and the vast plethora of destructive manifestations of inhumanity which have swamped the twentieth century. Psychology is called to provide the only remedy left for the potentially catastrophic consequences of the decline of religion.

'God is gotten of the soul'

With all this in mind, we can now turn to Jung's understanding of the 'relativity of the God-image', which he developed in *Psychological Types*, with reference to German mysticism in general and Eckhart in particular. Emma Jung, in her book on the *Grail*, points out that in the language of German mysticism the word *vaz* (vessel) refers to man himself, who in modern psychological terms has developed, through the cultivation of the transcendent function, a conscious attitude which is

> willing to take account of the contents of the unconscious, to understand them as far as possible and build them into real life, so that man himself becomes so to speak the vessel for the contents that flow from the unconscious.
>
> (E. Jung and von Franz 1980: 150, trans.)

In this sense, Jung says that we find in Eckhart an 'extraordinary enhancement of the value of the soul i.e. of his own inner being, that enabled him to rise to a purely psychological and relativistic conception of God and his relation to man' (Jung 1921: para. 411).

Let me quote Berdyaev at this point, as a contrast to Jung. For Berdyaev, mysticism is 'essentially a spiritual *as distinct from a psychic state* and implies a spiritual penetration of the soul' (Berdyaev 1946: 119, emphasis mine). Whereas for Jung Eckhart's mysticism is indicative of an extraordinary heightening of the soul-value, for Berdyaev it is precisely the transcendence of the natural man, i.e. the 'creature compounded of body and soul' (ibid.) which is characteristic of mysticism.

For Jung, the spiritual can exist for us only as a 'psychic factor' because, according to his 'theory of knowledge', it is *unknowable* in itself. A spiritual state distinct from a psychic state would therefore quite simply be an impossibility for Jung: there can only be a psychic state in which the spiritual manifests itself as a psychic factor. For Jung, the more central and transformative a 'spiritual experience' is, the more it is an experience that wells up from the primitive archetypal foundations of the unconscious. It is an experience of the 'numinous', the 'extraordinarily affective', something closely connected to the primitive notion of *mana*, or, in modern psychological language, 'psychic energy'.

Religious renewal requires a return to the primitive, the maternal ground of the unconscious – to 'Mother Earth, the prime source of all power' (Jung 1921: para. 415). At its deepest, most impenetrable level, this maternal ground becomes identical to the *Ungrund* and to Eckhart's *Gottheit*. The *Gottheit* 'is obviously all pervading creative power or, in psychological terms, self-generating creative instinct, that neither knows nor possesses itself, comparable to Schopenhauer's universal Will' (ibid.: para. 429).

For psychology, libido and the unconscious replace love and the freedom of the *Ungrund*. As a consequence, the language of mysticism and religion takes on a different meaning by being transcribed into the psychological idiom. This transcription requires a suspension of the 'theological' perspective while at the same time inclining towards its own 'metaphysics of the unconscious': the unconscious at its deepest, most unknowable level is hypothetically postulated as a sort of infinite repository of psychic energy, which is akin to the Schopenhauerian Will.

It is only within the soul as a 'vessel of the unconscious' that the God-image is born, an image which, like the soul, is a personification 'of an unconscious content' (ibid.: para. 421). Here Jung quotes Eckhart: 'God is gotten of the soul, his *Gottheit* He has of himself' (ibid.: para. 428). This phrase would lend itself to be interpreted according to the 'love paradigm'. The psychological interpretation gives it quite a different meaning: the soul as a 'vessel of the unconscious', as a sort of mediating, daimonic entity, mediates between the impersonal, unconscious 'pleroma' and the conscious ego.

> The determining force (God) operating from these depths is reflected by the soul, that is, it creates symbols and images, and is itself only an image. By means of these images the soul conveys the forces of the unconscious to consciousness . . . what it perceives are symbols. But symbols are shaped energies, determining ideas whose affective value is just as great as their spiritual value.
>
> (ibid.: para. 425)

'God', i.e. the God-image, is created by the soul in its imaginative capacity, the 'transcendent function'; therefore, an experience of 'God' is the result of the operation of this transcendent function.

To Jung's mind, nothing is taken away from the reality of 'God' in this psychological conception, inasmuch as 'God' is the name for the highest value, the highest concentration of libido, which therefore determines the psychic process (not only of the individual but of whole nations and epochs) in an absolutely decisive way. It makes no sense for him to speak of 'God' apart from the soul. Apart from the soul God is *Gottheit*, something perhaps akin to the Schopenhauerian Will, a sort of world-creating energy which – strictly speaking – defies any definition. It is simply the 'Unconscious' reaching down into finally unknowable dimensions, known and symbolized by the soul in countless symbolic formations of archetypal images. What is possible is the empirical, psychological study of these products of the soul's imagination, and with that a living connection to the psychic process, which is consequently in a significant sense the 'becoming of God'. The psychic process is, after all, at its deepest level determined by a series of transformations of the God-image, which periodically 'dies' and becomes renewed through a reconnection to the living sources of the unconscious.

Psychology and religion: The 'death of God' and the religious function of psychology

Jung begins his lecture *Psychology and Religion* by emphasizing that he approaches religion from a psychological, empirical and 'exclusively phenomenological' point of view (Jung 1938: para. 4). We can now understand better what he means by this. If psychology really is 'soul-making' in the sense in which we have explored it, then Jung's use of the terms 'empirical' and 'phenomenological' will be deceptive if we do not take into account the specific meaning of these terms in the context of his psychology.

This psychological aspect of religion is apparently at first presented as just one among several (i.e. the theological, metaphysical and philosophical aspects), even though it is a 'very important' one (ibid.: para. 2). But in light of Jung's 'Kantianism', it becomes evident that, for Jung, these other, non-psychological aspects are in reality, by definition, of the order of secondary elaborations of the 'original phenomenon', which is the authentic religious experience in the *psychological* sphere. Of themselves they do not provide religious contents, but only elaborate upon them within the sphere of consciousness.

In a precise parallel to Berdyaev's emphasis on 'spiritual experience', Jung's definition of religion focuses on 'psychological experience'. This crucial distinction has already been raised repeatedly. At this point it interests us in relation to Jung's prioritization of the notion of the numinous. To give priority to the dimension of psychological experience entails such a prioritization. For Jung therefore the word *religere* means 'a careful and scrupulous observance of what Rudolf Otto aptly termed the *numinosum*, that is, a dynamic agency or effect not caused by an arbitrary act of will' (ibid.: para. 6). According to Otto, the *numinosum* is experienced in two forms, *mysterium tremendum* and *fascinans*.[9]

One of the things that makes Otto's definition so appealing to Jung is its broadness, and in particular its ability to capture the character of the 'primitive' religious experience which, for Jung, is the most authentic one. Furthermore, it squares perfectly with Jung's expanded conception of libido or psychic energy. The experience of the *numinosum* as *mysterium tremendum* and as *fascinans* can easily be understood as the experience of a particularly high 'charge' of psychic energy, which therefore becomes the central determining factor in the psychology of an individual, around which everything else revolves. Religion, then, in whatever form, becomes the 'attitude peculiar to a consciousness which has been changed by experience of the *numinosum*' (ibid.: para. 9). Not truth but intensity is the important criterion.

What appears to be absent from this definition of religion therefore is precisely what is most essential for Berdyaev: the dimension of truth. It follows logically from Jung's 'energetic' or 'dynamic' definition of religion that a (religious) idea 'is psychologically true inasmuch as it exists' (ibid.: para. 4). Beyond this, what makes a religious idea 'true' is simply the fact that it is shared by a social group. It is 'true' because it is 'objective', i.e. it is 'shared by a society – by a consensus *gentium*' (ibid.). This problematic aspect of Jung's conception of religion has been pointed out by, among others, Victor White:

> Yet among these [psychological] facts [of religious experience] must surely be counted the psyche's deep yearning for true judgement concerning facts, whether attributed to faith or to reason . . . The 'truth' of

> religion does indeed lie outside the competence of the empirical psychologist as such, and the practising psychotherapist must necessarily confine himself to the manner in which it works . . . Yet it must always be found itself a psychological fact that a religion which is not 'true' – or at least apprehended as true – does not even work.
>
> (White 1960b: 87–88)

Jung would probably have responded to this by saying that religious ideas – in fact, all speculative, philosophical ideas which trespass across the boundaries of the 'theory of knowledge' – are 'apprehended as true' precisely because of the energetic charge which has led to their formation. That a particular religious idea needs to be subjectively *perceived* as true by those who entertain it, in order for it to be effective, is obvious. It's just that 'we know' that, as 'the theory of knowledge' has demonstrated, this is a 'transcendental illusion'. On this basis, then, Jung interprets all religious experience in terms of the objective reality of the psyche, and thus sees it not as 'literally' but as 'psychologically' true.

Considering the fact that Jung, due to his Kantianism, when considering religious contents excludes truth as a function of judgement relating to extra-psychic realities and instead takes them as being 'only' psychologically true, it would seem that, if we accept his psychological interpretation, we could speak of the 'truth of revelation' only in a very limited way. On the basis of his Kantian epistemology Jung has to postulate that psychology 'deals with ideas and other mental contents as zoology, for instance, deals with the different species of animals. An elephant is "true" because it exists' (Jung 1938: para. 5). Along with White, we may wonder, then, how Jung could have believed that his psychological understanding of the Christian message was going to place it once again into the heart of western man where it rightfully belonged. How could such a psychologistically reduced view of Christian revelation – i.e. one that disregards the trans-psychic truth of revelation as irrelevant, and sees it *exclusively* as a psychological event – achieve this? It may be granted that truth cannot exclusively be seen as a function of judgement, but is also a function of spiritual intuition. But all mystics caution against confusing this form of knowing with intuition as a purely psychological function.

Jung's first answer would probably be that this is not at all 'psychologism' in the sense of reducing everything to my personal issues. The offence that his opponents take is due to their underrating of the reality of the psyche by reducing it in this Freudian manner to a 'nothing but'. But, we will want to respond, we still cannot help but thirst for some form of truth reaching beyond the confines even of the archetypal psyche in all this. Such an act of transcendence is inherent to spirituality, which cannot take intensity and overwhelming numinous force as its standard of truth. The 'still small voice' of the spirit may lack these attributes entirely. It may go unnoticed most of the time precisely because of this. At the very least we want to know in what sense, on the basis of what epistemology this reality of the psyche is affirmed.

To answer this question we must turn to Jung's discussion of the Paracelsian term of the *lumen naturae* as 'the paradigm of true knowledge' (cf. Nagy 1991: 79ff.). Nagy sees in this Paracelsian idea a paradigm for *another epistemology* (besides the Kantian one) that is present in Jung's work. This 'other epistemology' seems at first glance to be surprisingly close to Berdyaev's conception of integral epistemology. It suggests the possibility of knowledge through sympathy, which represents 'a type of identity theory associated with the doctrine of the microcosm and the macrocosm' (ibid.: 82). What are the implications of this epistemological paradigm for Jung's understanding of revelation and the sort of truth it contains?

The *lumen naturae* is a 'second, independent source of knowledge' (Jung 1942: para. 148) set against the light of revelation, which is received through faith. It is 'the *quinta essentia*, extracted by God himself from the four elements, and dwelling "in our hearts" . . . The light of nature is an intuitive apprehension of the facts, a kind of illumination' (ibid.). It is the highest treasure of nature, and has a twofold source: both a 'mortal and an immortal' one. It is the light of the *scintilla animae*, 'the divine spark buried in the darkness' (Jung 1942: para. 197). The heart, where this divine spark is hidden, is also the 'seat of the imagination' (Jung 1942: para. 201), so that the *lumen naturae* is the source of the alchemical *vera imaginatio*, the key to the opus.

As a 'light in the darkness' the *lumen naturae* is a source of true knowledge in the unconscious. Nature, too, has spirit within itself: 'Nature is not matter only, she is also spirit. Were that not so, the only source of spirit would be human reason' (Jung 1942: para. 229). The *lumen naturae* in the unconscious is responsible for the fact that the unconscious is not only nature, but also a source of genuine spirituality which 'anticipates in its symbols future conscious processes. It [i.e. the unconscious] is therefore quite as much a "supra-consciousness" ' (ibid.).

The *lumen naturae* turns out to be a second source of 'revelation', one which dangerously competes with the supernatural 'light of faith' even though, according to Paracelsus, both lights in the end have the same source: 'the unity of God' (ibid.: para. 150). In fact, as the 'Enlightenment' and the rise of modern science later showed, this union of the two lights is anything but unproblematic: the potential conflict between the two lights goes to the heart of the problem of the 'death of God' in modernity.

> What still maintained the balance in the case of Paracelsus and Angelus Silesius – 'I under God and God under me' – was lost in the twentieth century, and the scale sinks lower and lower under the weight of an ego that fancies itself more and more godlike.
>
> (ibid.: para. 154)

Jung's psychology seeks to redress this balance in two steps: first, by returning the modern, over-rationalized consciousness to the *lumen naturae* as a source of spirit in the unconscious that can compensate for the one-sided 'spirituality' of consciousness; second, by approaching the contents of Christian revelation through this light in such a way that modern consciousness can reconnect with them, so to speak, from 'below'.

The emergence of the *lumen naturae* as an independent source of knowledge – even as a second source of revelation – is, from this perspective, itself part of the ongoing process of revelation. The awakening of the 'divine spark' in man is destined to instigate a new phase in the process of revelation itself. This is necessary because 'the light from above made the darkness still darker; but the *lumen naturae* is the light of darkness itself, which illuminates its own darkness and this light the darkness comprehends' (ibid.: para. 197); that is, it leads finally to a 'hierosgamos of light and darkness in the shape of Sol and Luna' (ibid.: para. 198).[10] For Jung the 'divine spark' is not the spirit in man but rather the inherent instinctive wisdom of the soul itself, where its inherent spontaneous life is not extinguished by the 'great light which shines in the darkness and which the darkness comprehended not' (ibid.: para. 197), i.e. by the one-sided spirituality of consciousness modelled after the figure of the dogmatic Christ.

The psychological understanding of revelation, which is the only one still open to us, in Jung's view, is symbolically the transition from the unconscious condition of the fishes that swim in the water – i.e. the unconscious psyche experienced in projection – to the condition of the 'water-bearer' – i.e. the one who holds the vessel.

The hermetic *krater* is the vessel that contains the *nous*, and those who were baptized in it 'got a share of *gnosis*; they received *nous* and so became complete men' (Scott 1993: 61). The *nous* is, for Jung, closely related to the *lumen naturae*, and the production of this light as true *sapientia* is 'the central mystery of philosophical alchemy . . . [It is] almost always . . . personified as the *filius* . . . it is a *δαιμονιον* pure and simple' (Jung 1942: para. 162).

The *krater* or alchemical *vas* that gathers up the *nous* or *pneuma*, which was previously held in religious projections, becomes the saving vessel at a time in which 'the stars have fallen from heaven and our highest symbols have paled' so that now 'a secret life reigns in the unconscious . . . Our unconscious . . . hides living water, spirit that has become nature, and that is why it is disturbed' (Jung 1936: para. 50). In this situation it becomes necessary to approach Christian revelation 'from below', in a new light – the *lumen naturae* – i.e. as it appears when the unity of the light of revelation and the light of nature itself is reconstituted from below. What appeared as height now appears as depth: 'Revelation is an "unveiling" of the depths of the human soul first and foremost, a "laying bare"; hence it is an essentially psychological event' (Jung 1938: para. 127). In this way, so G. Wehr maintains, Jung 'becomes the inaugurator of a "depth-theology", a theology that . . . is open to the dimension of spiritual depth, to esoteric Christianity' (Faivre and Needleman 1995: 394).

Do we need to revise our critical assessment of Jung's 'psychologism' after what has been said? Does Jung's psychology not suddenly seem surprisingly close to Berdyaev's position? Does the *lumen naturae* not hold all the characteristics of the *nous* in the heart?

It would appear to me that Wehr goes more than a step too far here. For Jung the psychologist, the *filius* as *lumen naturae* receives decisively greater emphasis than the transcendent God, because the soul itself makes this religious statement. And for Jung, the *lumen naturae* is a conjunction of light and darkness, not the 'eye of the spirit' of tradition. Thus the soul itself proclaims the new psychological (post-religious) religion. The 'Death of God' is, while being a universal archetype, also centrally a Christian mystery inasmuch as Christ 'always dies, and always he is born' (Jung 1938: para. 149), and is therefore the 'transforming God' who is now proclaimed by the soul of modern man as the psychological Self.

For a 'depth-theology', the concept of psychological experience would have to be modified in the light of faith (i.e. the light of revelation of Paracelsus) through a conceptualization of spiritual experience as 'a spiritual *as distinct from a psychic state* . . . [which] implies a spiritual penetration of the soul' (Berdyaev 1946: 119). The *scintilla*, the divine spark buried in the heart, would then be understood as the deep centre in which this penetration is experienced, the 'door' to transcendence: 'Behold, I stand at the door, and knock: if any man hear my voice, and open the door, I will come in to him, and will sup with him, and he with me' (Rev. 3: 20).

Trinity and Quaternity: Jung's psychological myth

Jung considers Christianity not theologically but only in terms of its function as a therapeutic system that helps to restore wholeness, i.e. psychological health. From this perspective, what interests him about religious symbols is that they have the capacity to bring about a structural change in those depths of the psyche which can only be affected by the experience of the numinous. Jung's psychological myth then seeks to elaborate the Christian symbols in the light of the modern experience of individuation.

For Jung, a symbol is the best possible representation of an unknown content. The content is the archetype, which is mediated to consciousness through the symbol/archetypal image. We have seen that it is the soul/anima that mediates these archetypal contents. It stands between the unconscious, in its opaque unknowability, and the conscious ego. Here, in these depths of the soul, the transcendent function is rooted: it is the soul's *imaginatio vera*.

In this way, the archetype, which exists in the unconscious as a potentiality, is 'crystallized' into an archetypal image. The Trinitarian God-image and the suffering God-man represent such crystallizations, which 'may be at least five thousand years old and the Trinity is probably even older' (Jung 1938: para. 81). This gradual, imaginal crystallization of fundamental archetypal structures in the collective psyche of western humanity, dating back at least to Babylonian and Egyptian times, has an unsurpassable significance as a supreme central ordering factor, which reaches down into the deepest foundations of the psyche.

The psyche is the 'mother' of this God-image, which has been born into human consciousness through her. She is the true *Mater Dei*, and it is from her that the symbol of the Quaternity stems. The unknown mystery of the unconscious becomes the fourfold maternal womb of all archetypal images, including that of the Trinity. The Quaternity in this light appears as the '*sine qua non* of divine birth and, consequently, of the inner life of the Trinity' (ibid.: para. 125). The psyche is both the *Mater Dei* and the humble stable housing the animals (i.e. instincts), in which the God-image is born and renewed.

This gives depth psychology a momentous significance:

> As Origen understands Holy Scripture as the body of the *Logos*, so the psychology of the unconscious is also to be interpreted as a manifestation of reception. Here, however, the Christ image which was formerly known has not made an appearance through human mediation, but the transcendental ('total') Christ has made itself a new, more specific body.
>
> (Jung cited from Faivre and Needleman 1995: 389)

For Jung, the 'transcendental, total Christ' is the archetype of the Self, of which the historical Jesus became the carrier.

> That the Christological projection remained attached to the 'historical' Jesus is of the greatest symbolical significance, it seems to me. Attachment to the concrete man was necessary, because otherwise the incarnation of God – most important! – could never have come about. The conception, already growing up of the Osiris tradition, of an Osiris belonging to the individual is continued in the Judeao-Christian idea of the *imago Dei* and in the Christian idea of the *huiotes* (sonship).
>
> (Jung 1976: 6ff.)

Jung's psychological interpretation of revelation stands in the context of his ideas about the continual incarnation of God in man. What religiously is called ' "incarnation" . . . [appears] on the human level . . . as "individuation" ' (Jung 1938: para. 233). The psyche is the matrix, or womb, through which this process of Divine incarnation happens, a process which, psychologically speaking, is the process of individuation, the 'process going on through the centuries'. Through the 'Christological projection' onto the historical Jesus, a significant incarnation of the God-image came about, which from then on was carried by the individual human being. But now the Self seeks a 'new and more specific body', provided by the human psyche itself.

We see here the contours of the psychological myth elaborated by Jung in order to symbolically formulate certain fundamental insights about the process of individuation in western man, in its collective, historical dimension. This 'monotheistic' myth lays out an 'archetypal psychology' of the person, just as the Greek polytheistic myths laid out the archetypal psychology of the soul on the anima/animus level: 'Just as we have to remember the gods of antiquity in order to appreciate the psychological value of the anima/animus archetype, so Christ is our nearest analogy of the self and its meaning' (Jung 1951: para. 79).

The many gods first become one God (a movement from the anima/animus stage to that of the Self), then the one God becomes man (the birth of the human person in 'seed-form'), and finally man himself becomes the carrier of the *opus Christi* (i.e. individuation as realization of personhood, the unfolding of the seed). Inasmuch as this myth is psychological, it nevertheless places the monotheistic myth into the 'vessel' of anima-consciousness. Consequently there is a peculiar return to the 'polydaemonistic stage' during individuation, because the *lapis* includes all those psychic factors which temporarily had to be excluded and which make for plurality, separation from and opposition to the 'one God'. It symbolizes wholeness, not perfection, and thus it reintroduces the 'pagan', polydaemonistic sphere of the psyche. It represents a therapeutically contained 'return of the repressed', so to speak, which, without this containment, would lead to the unleashing of destructive forces.

If we keep this psychological focus in mind, Jung's essay on the Trinity, with its claim that the Trinity has to be completed through transformation into a Quaternity by including a fourth, dark aspect, becomes understandable.[11] Edinger points out that both symbols, threefoldness and fourfoldness,

> refer to two different aspects of the psyche, each valid, appropriate and complete in its own realm. The quaternity image expresses the totality of the psyche in its structural, static or eternal sense, whereas the Trinity image expresses the totality of psychological experience in its dynamic, developmental, temporal aspect.
>
> (Edinger 1992: 182)

In Jung's psychological myth there is no more room for any other interpretation of the Trinity than a dialectical one. The Trinity becomes a fundamental developmental pattern, as it already had done in Joachim de Fiore's teaching of the 'three ages' and, later, Hegel's and Schelling's idealism. Jung therefore speaks of the three ages or three stages of development in human history in relation to the Self. We found the same figure of thought in

Berdyaev, but without the total idealistic immanentism, which, in Jung, takes the form of a psychological idealism.

In the age of the Father an unconscious unity predominates. The Self operates unconsciously (and therefore morally ambiguously) as a 'natural' fact. In the age of the Son discrimination and duality predominate. The necessity for conscious discrimination generates the dualism of Christ and Satan. The ego differentiates itself from the Self and enters into a phase of experiencing conflicting opposites. It struggles to align itself to the exclusively good side and finds itself increasingly crucified between the poles of the opposites. This creates the condition for the third stage of the Spirit, in which a reconnection to the Self happens. More precisely, only in this last stage does the Self as the synthesis of the conscious and the unconscious, to which the ego now submits, come into existence as a factor in the individual (i.e. no longer as part of the collective projection). By surrendering, in this third phase, to the 'inspiration' of the 'Holy Spirit' (i.e. the transcendent function, psychologically speaking) the experience of the 'Christ within' is opened up (see Jung 1938: paras. 268–279). But this is now no longer the entirely good dogmatic Christ, a fabrication of the one-sidedly spiritualized consciousness, but the total, transcendental Christ.

Christ as a symbol of the self

The German Romantic philosopher Franz von Baader compared God to an alchemist 'who uses a receptacle (the creature) to prepare the Tincture that he needs (His Son) . . . the alchemist does not dispose of the receptacle once the work is finished . . . he confers upon his receptacle the Tincture of eternal life' (cited from Faivre 1994: 141). Baader's description squares well with Jung's conception of the incarnation, if we add in the 'psychological turn' whereby God the alchemist becomes the Self on a collective level, which needs the 'Tincture' to relieve itself from unconsciousness. This unconscious condition of the Self thus implies that the role of the alchemist is increasingly transferred to man: 'God' seeks incarnation as a result of his confrontation with Job. The relationship of the conscious human ego to the 'unconscious' becomes the decisive factor in this development.

Jung's transcription of revelation into this psychological idiom leads inevitably to the gradual 'apotheosis' of man the alchemist/depth psychologist who, through his 'confrontation with the unconscious', assists in the transformation of the 'God-image'. In the Yahweh stage of the Self it manifests its omnipotence in an ambivalent, amoral way. Psychologically this implies the early developmental stages. The Self transforms because of the attitude of the ego towards it. The ego develops a capacity to discriminate between opposites. As a result of his confrontation with Job, Yahweh recognizes that

> It just could not be that Yahweh's dual nature should become public

property and remain hidden from himself alone. Whoever knows God has an effect on him. The failure of the attempt to corrupt Job has changed Yahweh's nature.

(Jung 1952/1967: para. 617).

God now seeks to become man so as to become conscious of Himself, and this process of incarnation means individuation for man: the 'Tincture' is conferred upon the receptacle. But for Jung, once again, man is both receptacle and alchemist. Humanity is engaged in the age-old struggle for consciousness, which means (to pursue the alchemical metaphor) a struggle to transform the *prima materia* (humanity's unconscious condition) into the tincture or *lapis* (the conscious realization of the Self). The contents seeking transformation appear in projection, and in the historical figure of the Rabbi, Jesus of Nazareth, these projections of the Self coalesce in a dramatic way: for the first time the Self manifests itself in a fully humanized form; God has become man.

What causes the projection (which is by definition not 'made' by the ego but 'happens' due to some factor in the unconscious) is the operation of the Self on a collective level. Christ, therefore, is a symbol of the Self in which the archetype of the God-man 'crystallizes' into the image of the historical man, Jesus, in whom the human, historical and mythological–archetypal dimensions coalesce in a unique way. Christ as God-man – one person with two natures, human and divine, according to the Dogma of Chalcedon – equates 'as man to the ego, as God to the self', so that he is 'ego and self, part and whole at the same time' (Jung 1951: para. 171). Christ restores the *imago Dei* to man, which psychologically means that he restores wholeness to man, or rather that he 'reforms' the archetype of wholeness, which is a priori present in man. Jung absorbs the Christ-figure into his more general psychological conception of the Self as the archetype of wholeness.[12] The incarnation of the God-man in Jesus means, for humanity, a new dimension of individuation: man now potentially becomes a *person*. By individuating he unfolds these as yet latent symbolic potentials within the psychological reality of the Christ-figure as a symbol of the Self, as opposed to the dogmatic representation of Christ. Psychology restores to Christianity its true psychological meaning, which has become obscured by ecclesiastic thought.

Koepgen's Gnosis des Christentums

To clarify this point further it will be useful to turn to the work of the Catholic theologian Georg Koepgen, *Die Gnosis des Christentums* (The Gnosis of Christianity), to which Jung refers repeatedly. He interprets Koepgen's standpoint as one of 'creative mysticism', which betrays itself indirectly in 'the living content of his book, which consistently presses for a deepening and broadening of the dogmatic ideas' (Jung 1955/1956: para. 531).

The direction in which this movement heads in Koepgen's book parallels, in Jung's view, that of the alchemists. The logical consequence of Koepgen's work is thus that

> the *opus Christi* is transferred to the individual. He then becomes the bearer of the mystery, and this development was unconsciously prefigured and anticipated in alchemy, which showed clear signs of becoming a religion of the Holy Ghost and of the *Sapientia Dei*.
>
> (ibid.)

Jung evidently sees in Koepgen's ideas a certain living spiritual insight at work, which is well translatable into his psychological idiom.

For Koepgen, 'the Trinitarian conception of God is logically incomprehensible, it presupposes a mystical-more precisely: a mystic–gnostic attitude in the believer' (Koepgen 1978: 75, trans.). We have seen that Berdyaev seeks to develop such a mystic–gnostic attitude centred on the experience of the breath of the *pneuma* in the depth of the soul. Koepgen does in fact refer extensively to Berdyaev and recognizes in him the thinker who 'of all living Gnostics . . . has thought through the essence of the spiritual pneuma most profoundly' (ibid.: 131). While Koepgen does see Berdyaev as representing something quintessential about the Christian spiritual experience – 'he is the quintessential homo religiosus et christianus [*homo religiosus et christianus schlechthin*]' (ibid.: 133) – he is worried that Berdyaev unduly neglects the rational formulation of dogma and undermines the authority of the institutional Church: 'Does not the gnostic with his deeper knowledge stand above law and dogma?' (ibid.: 133). Nevertheless, for Koepgen, Berdyaev gives expression to the profound insight into the Trinitarian mystery contained in the eastern orthodox tradition, which requires a gnostic, circular mode of thought as opposed to a rational one, which can only comprehend monotheism. For Jung this circular mode of thought is equally fundamental to alchemical thought (see Jung 1955/1956: para. 123ff.).

In Kopegen's view two orders collide in Christian gnosis: 'the monotheistic and hierarchically constructed gnosis of "ascent" and the Trinitarian gnosis of "generation" [*Zeugung*]' (Koepgen 1978: 101). While in monotheistic gnosis 'man ascends to God as "angel", in Trinitarian mysticism God descends from heaven to earth as "God-man" ' (ibid.: 99). Monotheistic gnosis thus has a tendency towards one-sided spiritualization, while Trinitarian gnosis tends towards humanization.

The path of Trinitarian mysticism 'rests on the co-enactment (*Mitvollzug*) of the Incarnation. In Christ the unification (*Verbindung*) of God and world happens: divinization of creation. This *theosis* passes also on to the mystic' (ibid.: 84). *Theosis* is not an ecstatic union with the Divine at some remote, transcendent altitude: 'The secret of Christian mysticism does not lie in union but in the parallelism of the Divine and the human life-process' (ibid.: 86).

What does the existential realization of this parallelism entail? It means that man comes into a new and fundamentally different relationship to God, that of 'sonship'. 'The becoming of a child of God is the repetition of what takes place within the Trinity. God has given birth to the Son in an eternal generation. Parallel to this stands the generation of man as a child of God through the Father' (ibid.: 93).

The generation of man as the child of God is the birth of the human person. Christian revelation, which can only be absorbed existentially in a process whereby the mystery of divine generation is experienced internally, requires a completely different and new self-consciousness of man. 'Whoever wants to comprehend Christ has to have had first of all the experience of the revelation of his own "I" in his soul. Without this "gnostic self-consciousness" . . . we still remain "under the law", in the insubstantialness of pre-Christian monotheism' (ibid.: 166). Therefore,

> the revelation of personality belongs to the knowledge of the Trinity. Personality rests on the fact that an I stands over against a Thou. This is the meaning of the Trinity, in which within the Godhead itself an I encounters a Thou; which is why the Son so often turns to the Father.
>
> (ibid.: 195)

In conclusion, then, for Koepgen 'the Gospels imply a totally new anthropology, a new doctrine of the essence of man. The Trinity shows the "I" in the Godhead; parallel to this "I" is the personal I within man' (Koepgen 1978: 196).

Koepgen's paralleling of the human and the divine life-processes to Jung's mind will have squared very well with his paralleling of individual psychology and archetypal process. The archetypal process is the transformation of the God-image understood not from the point of view of individual psychology, but as a process on the archetypal level itself. Thus, for example, in his essay 'Transformation Symbolism in the Mass' Jung claims that 'the Mass functions to reach out to the congregation, to include the people in the process of God's transformation, which is being enacted on the divine plane' (Stein 1986: 137). Through participation in the mystery of the Mass, the congregation shares in the process whereby the ambivalent Father–God is transformed into the good Son–God, which re-enacts the ancient, archetypal image of the renewal of the Old King, so important in alchemy.

Man himself enters within the sphere of Christian Trinitarianism, into the relation of sonship, through the parallel 'generation of man as a child of God through the Father' (op. cit.: 93). This generation happens through the action of the Holy Spirit in the womb of the human psyche. Through the Holy Spirit

> man as a spiritual force is surreptitiously included in the mystery of the Trinity . . . The Trinity therefore, discloses itself as a symbol that

comprehends the essence of the divine *and* the human. It is, as Koepgen says, 'a revelation not only of God but at the same time of man'.

(Jung 1942/1948: para. 239)

The opus Christi transferred to the individual

Psychologically this means a new relation to the Self, expressed in the Pauline 'I live; yet not I, but Christ liveth in me' (Gal. 2: 20). But this also means that increasingly 'the *opus Christi* is transferred to the individual' (Jung 1955/1956: para. 531), which, in the course of individuation, enters into the relation of sonship to the Father through the Holy Spirit. Man now becomes the bearer of the Spirit with a personal 'I', which encounters a divine 'Thou' in a new way. In the religion of the Holy Spirit and of the *Sapientia Dei*, man becomes the alchemist who takes up the redemptive *opus Christi* from where it has hitherto remained incomplete. What has remained unredeemed is the Divine imprisoned in matter (i.e. the unconscious).

As a consequence of this transferral of sonship to man, which finds its confirmation in the sending of the Holy Spirit, a gradual shift in emphasis takes place during the Christian era. First, the Christ-figure fully 'captures' the projection of the Self. In *Aion*, Jung shows how the Christ-figure is assimilated by the unconscious psyche, emphasizing in particular the image of the fish as a symbol of Christ. The two fishes of the astrological sign of Pisces become a symbol of the opposites, which are constellated in the Christian *aeon*. If Joachim de Fiore foresaw the coming of the Age of the Spirit in the eleventh century, this was an indication, for Jung, that – gradually – the balance would now begin to shift towards a new and immanent experience of the Divine, through the Spirit.

This newly emerging enthusiasm for the Spirit had an ambivalent nature, and it thus happened that 'a confession to the Christian Holy Spirit also helped the emergence of the Spirit archetype with its characteristic ambivalence' (Jung 1951: para. 141). The ambivalent archetype of the spirit is *Mercurius*, the alchemical, transformation substance, which potentially contains the *lapis*. *Mercurius* is, so to speak, the as yet untransformed 'underground god' stirring in human souls. He is the chthonic counterpart of Christ, who is nevertheless not entirely hostile to Christ, but in fact a compensatory completion of the Christ-figure. *Mercurius* is the dangerous trickster spirit rumbling in the depths of newly liberated and 'enlightened' souls, who can either lead to disaster and destruction or to individuation and a manifestation of the spiritual potential of human creativity. The alchemical transformation of *Mercurius*, leading to the production of the *lapis*, thus becomes the religious–spiritual task of the modern era, a fact that was first darkly intuited by the alchemists.

In Jung's psychological interpretation, the Holy Spirit becomes the energetic manifestation of the unconscious. We already quoted a passage in a letter Jung wrote to White in connection with his *Symbols of Transformation*: 'My personal view of the matter is, that Man's vital energy or libido is the divine *pneuma* alright' (Lammers and Cunningham 2007: 7). The freedom that the spirit brings thus implies a liberation of man's vital energy, which is at one and the same time both creative and destructive. We can see how Jung's psychological interpretation, based on his notion of the numinous, increasingly takes a turn that becomes difficult to assimilate for those who take the Christian spiritual tradition seriously. In Jung's psychological conception the Joachite scheme of the three ages inevitably leads to a new stage beyond the Christ-figure of the Christian tradition. The Spirit brings with it all that has still been missing from this figure. White writes in a letter to Jung about the 'insoluble dilemma' with which he finds himself confronted:

> If Christ is no longer an adequate symbol of the Self, and in fact very inadequate, one-sided, unintegrated and harmful, then must one not choose – at whatever the cost? Faith in him, it seems to me, must be unconditional; once one 'criticizes Christ' one has lost faith in him . . .
>
> (ibid.: 216)

The unconditional faith in Christ which White talks about has a theological basis. But the whole momentum of Jung's interpretation of Christian symbols is in the opposite direction: away from the theological – which posits a reference to the extra-psychic, transcendent dimension (and in this broad sense Berdyaev would also be a theological thinker) – to the psychological – for which wholeness (a purely 'psychological transcendence' towards the unconscious archetype of wholeness as an immanent telos) is the essential reference point. By using alchemy as a sort of 'midway station' leading to his psychology, Jung prepares the ground for a thoroughgoing transliteration of Christian symbols into his psychological idiom to offer a sound foundation for his vision of a new spirituality of individuation.

The Christ-figure was first amalgamated with the *lapis* by the alchemists. Alchemy, as a 'religion of the Holy Ghost and the *Sapientia Dei*', appears 'like a continuation of Christian mysticism carried on in the subterranian darkness of the unconscious – indeed some mystics pressed the materialization of the Christ figure even to the appearance of the stigmata' (Jung 1944: para. 452). In these depths, this continuation is experienced as a painful suspension between opposite poles, a crucifixion that leads to a *coniunctio* or to the manifestation of the transcendent Self as the *pharmacon universalis* of the *lapis*.

The interiorization of the symbol of Christ crucified between the two thieves means the birth of something entirely new out of the suffering that *the archetype of wholeness* imposes on the individual. This 'something new' is a Christed humanity, belonging to a non-institutionalized *ecclesia spiritualis* built out of living stones (*Transmutemini in vivos lapides philosophicos*, wrote the alchemist G. Dorn). To conceive of Christ as a symbol of the Self means, in this context, to state that the *opus Christi* has now shifted decisively to the individual. The God that had been declared dead is resurrected from within the individual. In the psyche of the individual the 'pneumatic Christ' seeks now a 'new, more specific body'. This is so because God now seeks to be incarnated in ordinary men and women. This is a further stage of incarnation, which reaches down even deeper into 'dark matter'. Christ has given the Holy Spirit to humanity, so that the work that He began may be brought to completion by precisely those flawed and broken 'earthen vessels' which have been tinctured by the 'soul substance of the God'. Jung does not mean to say by all this that there is no God any more, only man. Rather 'God wants to unite His opposites in Man . . . Man is no more an end in himself, but becomes an instrument of God and this is *really* so and no joke about it' (Lammers and Cunningham 2007: 264ff.).

Pneuma and psychic energy

We find striking parallels and contrasts between Jung's and Berydaev's understanding of revelation. The most interesting parallel lies in their anthropological focus. Out of human interiority itself, both men expect a renewal and further development of Christianity in the direction of an aeon of the spirit.

Nevertheless, that man moves into the centre means something very different for each of them. For Jung it means that psychology takes on central, even religious, significance, while for Berdyaev it implies the awakening of a new mysticism, which seeks to move beyond the symbolization of spirituality to its co-creative manifestation. Not only is God to be born in man but also man is to be born in God. In this way free human initiative and creativity receive a new religious meaning which allows for an integration of the 'secular' and the 'sacred' beyond the lukewarm compromises of historical Christianity. The secular domain of human creativity itself ought to be given a new religious meaning, not the sacred compromised through secularization.

For Jung, revelation is 'an "unveiling" of the depths of the human soul first and foremost, a "laying bare"; hence it is essentially a psychological event . . .' (Jung 1938: para. 127)[13]. On the other hand, the critique of revelation which Berdyaev proposes depends upon the liberation of the spiritual element in man. Jung's collective unconscious appears to Berdyaev primarily as a distorting factor. Jung, on the other hand, uncovers precisely within these depths the guiding wisdom of nature, the *lumen naturae*, which is closely linked to the ambivalent and elusive *Mercurius* (Jung 1943/1948: para. 256). His emphasis is not on the masculine personal spirit, but on the feminine vessel of the psyche, which is needed to contain the 'living waters' of the unconscious. We belong, Jung thinks, to 'an age in which the spirit is no longer up above but down below, no longer fire, but water' (Jung 1934/1954: para. 32).

Another parallel can be found in Jung's notion of the 'relativity of the God-image', which shows clear affinities with Berdyaev's understanding of revelation as a Divine–human process. In both cases an interaction of the Divine and the human is posited instead of a 'unilateral' action of God. But once again the meaning is quite different: whereas Jung interprets revelation as the psychologically immanent interaction of the impersonal depths of the 'absolute unconscious' with the conscious ego via the psyche/anima, Berdyaev interprets it as the 'immanent–transcendent' interaction between the personal, Trinitarian God and the human person. Consequently, whereas for Jung the numinous and, connected with it, psychic energy become central categories for the interpretation of religious experience, for Berdyaev it is love that is central. Unlike Jung, Berdyaev does not fundamentally depart from Christian premises. The aeon of the Spirit does not usher in a new and different religion of psychic immanence.

Thus, for all the similarities, we are in fact confronted with two fundamentally different perspectives in Jung and Berdyaev. Berdyaev's thought is based on what we called the 'love paradigm', while Jung's psychology of the unconscious aligns itself organically with the scientific theory of evolution. On the psychological level libido, or psychic energy, is the force which drives the process of psychic evolution towards individuation. While Berdyaev does not in any way deny the objective reality of the evolutionary process, which provides the implicit context for Jung's psychological notions, it belongs for him to a secondary order of objectified surface phenomena.

We find in Origen and Pseudo-Dionysius a theory of *eros*, which curiously resonates with our distinction between love and psychic energy/libido (the latter being closely linked to the notion of numinosity) and may help us to establish a way of relating both perspectives:

> If, as Origen believed, *eros* has its source above and has been implanted in us by God–Eros (we could call this EROS I), the motive force powering the soul's ascent must be the transformation of *eros* gone awry (*eros* II) back to its transcendental starting place. Origen's commentary on the *Song of Songs* contains the first Christian theoretical exposition of this transformation.
>
> (McGinn 1991: 120)

Jung's libido could be equated with eros II, while Berdyaev's notion of love would have to be equated with eros I. Both play a role in the total psychological–spiritual existence of the human person but from the psychological perspective the focus will naturally and legitimately be exclusively on eros II. But to the extent that psychology elaborates its own psychological *myth* this focus inevitably leads to a modification of the meaning of all Christian symbols. Psychic energy becomes confused with the energy of Love, the *hagion pneuma*. The latter by definition remain beyond the field of psychology because they are not capable of objectification.

Jung's 'psychological–alchemical myth' provides the foundation for his psychology of individuation by placing it in the context of the historical process of transformation on a collective scale, which finds its most significant expression in the transformations of the God-image. Similar to Berdyaev, with his conception of a concrete understanding of the human being through a philosophy of history, his conception of the archetypal psyche necessarily leads him to such a historical understanding.

Jung establishes a parallel between the archetypal and psychological processes. The continuing incarnation of God (archetypal process) means progressive individuation on the side of human psychology. Through this process, God becomes progressively humanized. 'The humanization of God is the fundamental process in the inner consciousness of humanity' (Berdyaev 1935a: 189). This sentence of Berdyaev's could have been written by Jung, and yet for Jung this process has a very different meaning, one that follows inevitably from his own psychological premises.

God's incarnation means his coming to consciousness within the vessel of the human psyche. 'In the Paraclete, therefore, God is closer to the real man and his darkness than he is in the Son. The light of God bestrides the bridge – Man – from the day side; God's shadow, from the night side' (Jung 1942/1948: para. 267). It is now up to man, the alchemist–psychologist, to produce the *lapis* in which the opposites in God become reconciled: 'Just as man once was revealed out of God, so, when the circle closes, God may be revealed out of man' (ibid.). This is the hour of psychology. The God which now becomes revealed is a God in need of salvation through man. He needs man to reconcile the opposites in himself, which are the source of all psychic energy and numinosity. He needs man to become conscious.

Quite a different, even diametrically opposed, meaning is intended by Berdyaev, who focuses his attention precisely on the non-objectifiable spirit, which inevitably escapes the net of psychological description. For him, God becoming humanized means that the human psychological God-image becomes purified of all naturalistic, inhuman, objectified elements through a process of spiritualization. God is only knowable apophatically, in the spirit, and does not become humanized (or conscious) in the sense that he has ever been 'inhuman' (or unconscious not only for man but in himself). It is man, as a purely natural, psychosomatic entity, who is inhuman by being ignorant of the divine element in himself. Man's existential alienation and subjection to collective tribal atavisms (the 'collective unconscious'!) makes him incapable of comprehending the God of infinite Love which can be known only in the spirit. The God of Berdyaev's pneumatic Trinitarian gnosis is a God of Love, who seeks in man his 'other'.

Only in this sense – that the birth of man in God fulfils the 'lack' of Love seeking its other – does Berdyaev talk of a 'transformation of God'. God empties himself in a divine *kenosis*, the Lurianic *Sod ha Tsimtsum*, to enable the birth of this other who is called forth out of the abyss of irrational freedom by the creative force of self-devastating, sacrificial Love. From beginning to end the world-creative process is a Divine–human drama of Love and freedom. Love progressively illuminates and transfigures the dark irrational freedom that lies at the foundations of all existence without violating or eliminating it. In this process man is increasingly called to become co-creative. It goes without saying that none of this has anything to do with psychology. Nevertheless, man's co-creative participation in this process does imply something very much akin to Jung's process of individuation, a process of confronting and assimilating the shadow.

But is Jung's psychological myth really 'just' psychology? Or do we not have to say, with Wolfgang Giegerich, that '[Psychology] is "sublated religion" *aufgehobene Religion,* just as it is "sublated science", no longer subject to the contradiction of science versus religion, but, by having overcome it, containing this contradiction in itself' (Giegerich 2005: 225)?

I have made the point in this chapter that on reading Jung's writings on Christianity, especially *Answer to Job* (1952/1967), it becomes difficult to avoid the conclusion that, because psychology has become all encompassing for Jung, for the epistemological reasons given in the last chapter, it now becomes much more than 'just' psychology. It becomes the 'sacred vessel' *par excellence* for the new religious content. It thereby threatens to leave no room for any religious perspective transcending the psychological, just like Hegel's philosophy leaves no room for any religion transcending the 'absolute philosophy'. It inevitably inclines towards a psychological idealism while staunchly pretending to remain purely empirical, just as inevitably as Kant has led to Hegel. Giegerich only makes explicit what is already clearly implicit in Jung's writings (see Giegerich 2001). Jung's psychology, not Hegel's 'absolute philosophy', accomplishes the full sublation of religion.

This 'Hegelian' view of Jung's psychology gains further plausibility as one considers the difficulty of disentangling Jung's myth from its origins in von Hartmann's *Philosophy of the Unconscious* (1923) and its Romantic and idealistic predecessors. Berdyaev writes that in this philosophy was 'accomplished the deformation of the theme' outlined by Jacob Boehme. According to Boehme,

> out of the *Ungrund*, which preceded the being of the world, in eternity and not in time takes place the birth of God and the Holy Trinity is unfolded, and the Holy Trinity creates the world. In German metaphysics . . . the ideal succession is altered. Out of the *Ungrund*, out of the depth of the dark unconscious, the world is created, and in this world God is formed . . . The world process is the becoming of God; in man God

> finally becomes conscious. Both a deification of man and a repudiation of man take place.
>
> (Berdyaev 1949a: 31)

Jung himself, of course, keenly seeks to avoid precisely this consequence of the 'idealistic myth' of the 'becoming God' by reconstituting the lost Divine–human relationship through the psychological subordination of the ego to the objective psyche. Psychology has to make sure that the *antimon pneuma* will not 'twist the indwelling Paraclete into a self-deification of man' (Jung 1942/1948: para. 267). Man is the instrument of 'God', i.e. of the psyche's deepest foundation and root. 'Scientific' depth psychology puts a resolute distance between itself and its speculative–metaphysical origins by 'empirically' deconstructing them and retaining only the purified remnant of the 'empirical metaphysics of the unconscious'. But, as Giegerich has shown with regard to Hegel, the implicit conceptual 'deep structure' of Jung's thought nevertheless remains undeniably shaped by the metaphysics of idealism and its development in von Hartmann's *Philosophy of the Unconscious*. Where it deals with the God-image, Jung's psychology is drawn into this gravitational field of idealistic conceptions. The 'unconscious philosopher' Jung is a Hegelian.

Von Hartmann described the unconscious 'as the "all-unity" which embraces the Cosmos, and is at last revealed as that which has formed the core of all great philosophies, the Substance of Spinoza, the Absolute Ego of Fichte, Schelling's absolute Subject–Object, the Absolute Idea of Plato and Hegel, Schopenhauer's Will, etc.' (White 1960b: 55).

It would nevertheless be unfair to claim that, therefore, in Jung's psychology as well 'both a deification and a repudiation of man takes place'. Jung's psychological myth evidently has therapeutic value for many. It is in this sense itself a 'therapeutic tool' that testifies to its own validity on purely pragmatic grounds: it works . . . for some. To individuate certainly means to become more human, more humble, less inflated. Psychological experience shows furthermore that the unconscious is clearly not only a distorting factor; there is also genuine instinctive wisdom to be found in it. Victor White cites C. G. Carus, the Romantic predecessor of Jung, writing that 'the unconscious is the subjective expression for that which we know subjectively under the name of "Nature" ' and continues 'and this in turn is a partial revelation of, a participation in, the divine Mind' (White 1960b: 54ff.).

As has already been pointed out, the divine towards which Jung's psychology implicitly steers the 'religious' devotion of those who cannot any longer find their spiritual home within traditional religion is *Sophia* as *anima mundi* of the alchemists. Like romantic nature, and closely related to it, it is a non-hypostatic, impersonal divinity, which becomes within the framework of depth psychology the 'psyche' as the new locus of the religious/numinous content. She can give birth to the individuated, manifested Self, the new centre of the personality, which might be called the 'personal spirit': 'the spirit is the son of the mother' (Meier 2001: 126). In this sense Jung's psychological myth seeks to give expression to a genuine type of 'religious' experience which does result in a genuine process of becoming more, not less human.

Jung's psychological myth, while fulfilling a therapeutic function for some, cannot strictly be considered to be a part of his psychology as a scientific discipline. But if we consider it as the expression of a particular type of religious experience we can still ask to what extent it can be reconciled with Berdyaev's creative development of Christian symbols, which addresses similar concerns from his existential–philosophical perspective. If we remind ourselves of the 'Sophianic' character of the individuated person in Berdyaev's thought, a degree of reconciliation between both positions seems possible. In the person, according to Berdyaev, both the masculine, personal spirit and the feminine, cosmic, impersonal soul ought to become united in order for its sophianic character to be realized.

The androgynous nature of the *imago dei* in man calls for an integration of the psychology of individuation with the spirituality of creativity. Both conceptions seek to express something similar from different, but perhaps complementary angles. For both Jung and Berdyaev the cross becomes the symbol of the reconciliation of opposites: for Berdyaev, of original and final freedom, for Jung, of the light and the dark side of God. These considerations point us in the direction of the ethical dimensions of individuation and personalization, to which we will now turn.

Chapter 7

Individuation and the ethics of creativity

This chapter will in many respects be drawing conclusions from all that has been said so far. Both Jung's and Berdyaev's understanding of the person refer to a 'larger personality' born in the process of individuation. The way they formulate their understanding of this larger personality has been situated within the context of the breakdown of the traditional God-image and its reconstitution from within human experience. Man now becomes central, but this means different things for Jung and for Berdyaev who envision a 'psychological' and an 'anthropological' reduction respectively, based on different epistemological premises. Their respective interpretations of Christian symbols as the archetypal basis for a deeper understanding of this larger personality show marked contrasts and we will now want to explore how all of this translates into their ethical perspectives.

I want to begin this exploration by some brief reflection on the two orienting ethical ideals of perfection and wholeness. In traditional Christianity, ethics was clearly focused on perfection. Both Jung and Berdyaev's ethical views are in contrast characterized by a shift of emphasis towards an ethics of wholeness. Wholeness itself ought not to be conceived perfectionistically but as also giving a place to 'falling apart' and disintegration, to all that runs counter to a one-sided ideal of perfection.

In reality both dimensions always have to be taken into account. One could envision these ethical dimensions of wholeness and perfection as two coexisting ethical systems within the human person (see Arraj 1986). The interrelation of these two systems could be envisioned under the symbolic image of the vertical and horizontal axes of the cross. The 'vertical' dimension of perfection is oriented towards the transcendent ideal while the 'horizontal' dimension of wholeness emphasizes the kind of integrity which is capable of sustained contact with and assimilation of one's own darkness. There is therefore both a tension and a complementarity between these two systems, well symbolized by the cross.

Jung is especially concerned with the integration of all that has been left in the shadows in the 'Christian aeon'. But he makes clear that 'we are still within the Christian aeon and just beginning to realize the age of darkness where we shall need Christian virtues *to the utmost*' (Lammers and Cunningham 2007: 220). He is well aware that both dimensions are needed. Against Nietzsche he asserts that even 'on the highest peak we shall never be "beyond good and evil" ' (Jung 1942/1948: para. 267).

Berdyaev's ethics of creativity on the other hand unfolds a new understanding of spirituality, which presents itself as a specifically Christian response to Nietzsche's indignant rebellion against traditional Christianity. By seeking to give a new religious significance to human creativity in a way that is oriented not towards the *Uebermensch* but towards an incarnational, kenotic understanding of Divine-humanity, he uncovers precisely the dimension of human spirituality that is most intimately bound up with human wholeness.

Both Jung and Berdyaev contemplate a similar shift in ethical attitudes in which the individuating person appears as the free creator of new values. She/he responds creatively, and in a way that cannot any longer be collectively regulated, to the new, complex challenges of the changing world situation. For these challenges traditional value systems no longer offer any adequate solutions. Such a shift is therefore urgently demanded by the historical situation itself.

Berdyaev, by virtue of his primary focus on spirituality, remains much closer than Jung to the Christian ethics of perfection, rethinking it in terms of wholeness, but not abandoning it, while Jung 'found a system of integrity well beyond anything western culture had previously imagined' (Beebe 1992: 87), transforming ethics through psychological consciousness. This complementarity makes it possible to offer a new perspective on the ethical aspects of Jung's psychology through Berdyaev's ethics of creativity. This perspective opens the possibility of an ethics which harmoniously unites the spiritual and psychological dimensions within the individuating person, who is no longer contained within any of the collective, traditional value systems and collectively organized forms of spirituality.

This chapter will explore how Jung's ethical system of integrity can be made compatible with Christian premises. Also, and especially in the ethical sphere, Berdyaev provides a mediating position between the traditional Christian attitude and Jung's position, which is, as it stands, I believe, incompatible with Christianity.

Berdyaev's ethics of creativity

Berdyaev offers us what we could call a 'spirituality of individuation', which emphasizes the unrepeatable uniqueness of each person's path, which demands creative ethical decisions. Creativity is not to be confused with an 'anything goes' attitude. It demands its own form of sacrifice and asceticism. Instead of demanding subjection to collective norms, it is concerned with finding what it is that I and only I can give to the world. This is a very different but no less demanding form of asceticism.

Such an ethics first of all needs to have its starting point in a 'critique of pure conscience', which aims at transforming the static, normative character of ethics into a dynamic one. We are called to engage creatively in a way uniquely suited to our journey with the existential dialectics of freedom as they play themselves out in our lives. And these dialectics have three principal dimensions: the dialectics between good and evil, male and female and conscious and unconscious. These themes of Jung's psychology of individuation appear in Berdyaev's ethics within an existential context.

Personalistic ethics: A critique of pure conscience

For Berdyaev's existentially oriented philosophy ethical knowledge 'is the final stage of the philosophy of the spirit, the harvest of a philosophical life' (Berdyaev 1945a: 15). Berdyaev attempts a revaluation of values in the light of his philosophy of the person, just as Jung's psychology of individuation leads to a similar kind of revaluation. Both rely for this on a mode of reflection that is rooted in concrete existential (i.e. psychological and spiritual) experience.

Ethics has to be concerned with the lived experience of real persons, not with abstract norms. Personality for Berdyaev is '*the* moral principle and our relation to all other values is determined by reference to it. Hence the idea of personality lies at the basis of ethics . . . Ethics is to a great extent the theory of personality' (Berdyaev 1945a: 55). As a theory of personality ethics considers values not abstractly but existentially, within the dynamic–dialectical context of the existential–spiritual experience of the person. In this way it becomes the very opposite of a static normative theory.

Just as Jung examines ethical issues within the context of *psychological* dynamics, so Berdyaev examines them within the context of *existential* or, more precisely, *spiritual* dynamics. These are, as has been emphasized repeatedly, two complementary perspectives on the same lived experience. One does not cancel out the other. On the contrary, only their juxtaposition gives a complete perspective on the actual phenomenology of lived experience.

The relationship between person and conscience is so close that Berdyaev can even speak of the person 'being a conscience' (Berdyaev 1938: 163). In an analogous way to his 'critique of revelation', Berdyaev conceives of his ethics as a 'critique of pure conscience' (Berdyaev 1945a: 16). This critique seeks to reveal the creative power of the spiritual core of the person, which Berdyaev calls 'pure conscience'. This pure conscience is the 'ontological kernel of the human personality [which] is situated in the heart' (Berdyaev 1938: 169). The notion of conscience that Berdyaev develops shares some significant features with Jung's notion of the Self and departs sharply from the Freudian notion of the superego. Conscience is not understood by Berdyaev as 'the endopsychic authority' which attempts by its reaction to bring about 'agreement with the values of the collective' (Neumann 1969: 37). Agreement with the values of the collective is precisely what *obscures* pure conscience. Conscience is not primarily a psychological function, like the superego, but an inner capacity of the awakened heart to apprehend the spiritual beyond its objectifications in the collective social domain.

Therefore a 'struggle must be waged for the originality, the firsthand character of moral acts' (Berdyaev 1945a: 169). This struggle is directed against the tyranny of 'public opinion' and the power of the collective in all its forms. Yet, on the other hand, '[c]ommunality – *sobornost* – is the immanent quality of the personal conscience as it stands in the presence of God. The individual soul appears before God in a free union with other souls and the soul of the world' (ibid.). Autonomy and heteronomy are both equally inadequate results of the loss of 'theonomy', which implies a spiritual, interior and entirely free acceptance of Divine authority. Psychologically this clearly implies a connection to the Self, which fosters also a new awareness of community and of connection to the *anima mundi*.

The shadow side of conscience is that it can lead to the destruction and disruption of wholeness by fanatical possession by a single supreme idea and supreme value. The fanatic is devoted to *his idea* of God, not to the fullness of the living God. Fanaticism is 'a species of madness due to the incapacity to grasp the whole truth' (Berdyaev 1945a: 170). To counteract this tendency Berdyaev postulates the *whole* person as the supreme value. 'The ideal value of the personality is *the concrete fullness of life*' (Berdyaev 1945a: 56, emphasis mine). The person is only realized as wholeness in the fullness of life, and the elevation of any value, however noble, as an absolute forcibly imposed on this wholeness is a form of possession leading to violence. As an antidote to fanaticism, the most poisonous distortion of conscience, Berdyaev offers therefore the following ethical maxim:

> Strive for the liberation of emotions, but do not allow yourself to be overpowered by feelings or let them become detached from the fullness of life which includes thought and life of the intellect, will and the moral life, relation to God and religious life. Only the spirit synthesises the life of the soul; without it the soul disintegrates into elements of thought, sensations, volitions, emotions, etc.
>
> (Berdyaev 1945a: 173)

Fanaticism implies the violent imposition of a false unity devised by the ego in which true communion with others and with life in its paradoxical fullness cannot be achieved. It has to be counteracted by the virtue of tolerance, which is the 'virtue of humanness and love of freedom, a considerate attitude to human souls and their path in life which is always complex and painful' (ibid.). The spirit as opposed to the literalizing ego is integral, it does not foster narrow, dead moralism but real immersion in the fullness of life that leads to the owning of one's shadow as a basis for genuine tolerance. It is spirit not grasped by the literalism of the ego but received through a living connection to the Self, the archetype of wholeness.

Paradoxical ethics: The existential dialectics of freedom and the overcoming of divisions

Ethics therefore has to start from an in-depth exploration of the dynamics of the objectification of the spirit, which leads to this sort of fanatical intolerance of others, to the destruction of wholeness and to inner division. For this it has to expose the paradoxical character of the most fundamental categories of ethical evaluation itself, which lie at the very root of all violent, inhuman moralism: good and evil.

Ethics has to dissolve the false fixities on which the objectifying ego relies for its hypocrisy. The theory of personality considers values not abstractly and statically but existentially, within the dynamic–dialectical context of the lived experience of the person. And we have seen how for Berdyaev, the human person is deeply characterized by a tension between opposites. It is the dialectical interplay between these opposites that dissolves the normative, static fixities of moralistic ethics into a very different kind of ethics: a 'pneumatology' which stays true to the actual paradoxes of life beyond the false certainties of the rulebook.

This pneumatology is an attempt to reimagine the whole ethical sphere by taking its starting point from 'the highest value, which is a power radiating gracious, regenerating energy' (Berdyaev 1945a: 16). Ethical reflection has to itself be gracious and regenerating, not 'tyrannical'. As a 'theory of the destiny and vocation of man' (ibid.: 22) it brings all fixities into flux. This means that it places them within the dynamic context of the archetypal pattern of human destiny, which is disclosed by spiritual experience. The falling away from an original state of unconscious wholeness into the divided condition of consciousness is the tragic destiny of the human spirit, and the overcoming of this divided condition and a concomitant return to (super)conscious wholeness its vocation. This pattern provides the basis for Berdyaev's approach to the problem of evil.

The division between good and evil and the existential dialectics of freedom

Berdyaev formulates the paradox that it 'is the task of ethics both to provide a basis for morality and to show up its falsity' (Berdyaev 1945a: 17). The falsity of morality has its roots in its *unquestioning* acceptance of a rigidly fixed conventional distinction between good and evil. But however problematic, the distinction itself is nevertheless inevitable. It all depends on the depth or shallowness with which it is made. While on one level it has a social and psychological origin, and is therefore relative, its ultimate roots lie far deeper:

'It is only as a spiritual being that man can know the good as such. As a social being he knows only the changing conceptions about the good' (Berdyaev 1945a: 21). The distinction of good and evil has, we might say, a 'metaphysical sting', which is not extracted by just pointing out its relativity. 'The symbolism of "good" and "evil" is not artificial, accidental, or "wrong"; it tells us . . . about the ultimate reality, but does so "darkly", reflecting it . . . in the mirror of the world' (ibid.: 18). Its falsity appears wherever this symbolic character is overlooked. Within this existential–dialectical conception, Berdyaev therefore asserts that '[t]he origin of good and evil is expressed by a myth, and ethics is bound to have a mythological basis' (ibid.: 39). By providing such a mythological basis the literalizations and fixities of the ego are dissolved and the way is opened for a deeper intuition of the good.

This mythological basis is for Berdyaev to be found in the biblical myth of the fall, which introduced duality (the eating of the fruit from the tree of knowledge) and the subsequent overcoming of this duality through the Kingdom of God. 'It is the fall that has made moralists of us' (ibid.: 36). The suffering of duality leads to consciousness, and in our conscious experience, good and evil become inextricably intertwined. Often 'the struggle against evil can itself degenerate into evil' (Berdyaev 1935a: 167), while on the other hand the experience of evil mysteriously belongs to the path of life, and, once evil is fully overcome by 'the denunciation of its nothingness, [it] can bring us to the highest good' (ibid.: 185). The rationalism of the ego cannot come to grips with such perplexing ambiguities, which social and religious conventions seek to eliminate.

Consciousness mortally wounds living wholeness by inflicting the wound of duality. Duality is finally overcome by a new fullness of life in superconsciousness. This whole process is a drama of freedom. Evil is entirely irrational. If we could assign a meaning to it, it would already no longer be evil. This irrational character of evil reveals its origin in the 'irrational freedom which is grounded in the void' (ibid.: 185), i.e. that irrational freedom which is not itself evil, but the origin of both good and evil. Therefore 'the problem of evil is the problem of liberty' (ibid.: 160). Due to his interpretation of evil as arising from the void of irrational freedom, Berdyaev, unlike Jung, can find profound *existential* meaning in the interpretation of evil as non-being. This 'negative, non-ontological character of evil reveals itself also in our experience of life' (ibid.: 166). Irrational freedom carries within itself the vertiginous attraction to the void from which it arises.

The 'non-ontological' character of evil therefore by no means implies that it lacks power. Just as freedom is spiritual, so evil has a spiritual origin and is thus part of the innermost fabric of existence. It does not originate in 'the flesh', in the material side of life. As free beings we carry within ourselves the spirit of irrational rebellion and intoxicating pride: 'Satan is also an inner reality of the spiritual world of man and he only appears to be something external through the analogy with the natural world' (ibid.: 163). Our rebelliousness sympathizes with this spirit who is 'not the autonomous source of evil in his original being but only the manifestation of irrational freedom at the highest spiritual levels' (ibid.). We are not the victims of evil as an overpowering external force but are probed and tested to the core by our own freedom.

Berdyaev's key point is that because freedom, and not being, is the deepest and most mysterious root of existence, the irrational and the meaningless, although 'non-ontological', are nevertheless terribly 'real'. Due to this reality, any rational monistic system breaks apart, whereas dualism, on the other hand, bestows a false 'metaphysical fixity' on this existential reality. Reason is naturally inclined towards one of these two strategies in its attempt to grasp the phenomenon of evil, but the dynamic existentiality of the phenomenon thereby escapes its grasp. Evil can never be grasped rationally but reveals the irrational foundations of existence, that is, the existential reality of freedom.

The dynamic existentiality of the phenomenon of evil has to be found in the existential dialectic of freedom itself. These existential dialectics are not determined by logical necessity but are the living form of the irrational movements and inner transformations of freedom in the experience of destiny. Freedom, for Berdyaev, therefore has a threefold aspect. First there is the initial, irrational freedom; then there is the final freedom. These two freedoms correspond to St Augustine's *libertas minor* and *libertas maior*. Where the first is irrational and impulsive, the second is 'our final liberty in truth and goodness' (Berdyaev 1935a: 125). The two are finally reconciled only in Christ, the third aspect, who is therefore the *true* bringer of freedom.[1] The inner dialectic of freedom begins with man's actualization of his irrational freedom, which happens 'archetypically' in the myth of the fall, and existentially in every human destiny. According to Berdyaev, the full ethical implications of this dialectic of freedom have not been explored by traditional Christianity. It was Dostoyevsky who opened up these depths.

The dialectics of freedom begin with the stubborn self-affirmation of irrational freedom, which Dostoyevsky portrays in his *Notes from the Underground.* They are situated entirely outside any causal framework of interpretation. The 'subterranean man' rebels against reason, order, harmony and apparent goodness for no other reason than to oppose all reason and meaning and to affirm his own irrational wilfulness:

> Well, gentlemen, how would it be if we would throw all this rationality away once again with a kick into the dust, for the sole purpose to send all these logarithms to the devil and to be able once again to live according to our own free will?
>
> (Dostoyesky cited in Berdyaev 1925: 37–38, trans.)

Why should we always want what is reasonable? It can be much more advantageous to man to want what is most unreasonable and crazy. By no means do we always desire the 'good', as the scholastic philosophers liked to think, because we are first and foremost free, not rational creatures. To protest our freedom we happily go mad.

> It can amongst other things be more advantageous than all advantages, even if it brings obvious harm and contradicts the healthiest intentions of our reason in regard to advantages, because it saves for us what is most important by all standards, what is most precious – our personality and our individuality. . . . [But] if you were to think that all this could be neatly calculated, chaos, darkness and curse, so that the possibility to calculate it all in advance could put a stop to it all and thus reason would come into its rights, man will in this case go crazy intentionally to be without reason and have his will. I believe and I vouch for it because man's whole business, as it appears, consists indeed only in this, that he proves to himself at every moment that he is a human being and not a pencil.
>
> (Dostoyesky cited in Berdyaev 1925: 38–39)

For the subterranean man, 'two plus two is four – that is no longer life, gentlemen, but the beginning of death' (Berdyaev 1925: 40).

What the subterranean man says has its truth, which needs to be given a hearing. Both Dostoyevsky and Berdyaev affirm this truth: the personality is more precious than any norms imposed on it. But left to itself this wilfulness is self-defeating. It does not lead to freedom, but into enslavement to necessity. The empty, irrational and self-centred freedom that is cut off from grace 'is not capable of performing the act of choice, it tends in opposite directions. Through this duplicity is evoked. Two "I's" are formed within man, the personality becomes split' (Berdyaev 1925: 93, trans.). This is a most interesting perspective on the origin of neurosis, which Jung terms a 'disunity with oneself' (Jung 1943: para. 16) which, in some form or other is, more generally also 'the hallmark of civilized man' (ibid.).

The inner division of the personality and the formation of the shadow are, in this existential view, deeply connected to the rebellious self-affirmation of the person, inasmuch as it carries within itself the potentially dark and irrational initial freedom. The divine image, which is the essence of the person, does not operate like a 'natural law' but as a calling from its innermost depths, a calling that can only be accepted freely, but can therefore also be freely rejected. And we all live out this rejection in our destinies. Our self-affirmation, which is directed against our roots in the primary sources of being, condemns us to a phantasmagorical existence. And yet it is engraved as a potentiality in the divine image itself that we carry in our depths as a seal of our inalienable freedom. The inalienable right to rebellion and anarchy is a seal of our humanity; it is a source of both our corruption and our dignity. In all neurosis and psychopathology there is a mysterious core which finally eludes psychological explication and reaches down into these mysterious depths of freedom.

Because we stubbornly and rebelliously seek a total freedom we get caught in the nets of illusion that we spin for ourselves. We create for ourselves a phantasmagorical world. A major element of Berdyaev's understanding of the nature of evil is this idea, which goes back to St Athanasius the Great, that 'evil consists of phantasms' (Berdyaev 1945a: 180). Phantasms are the product of a misguided, distorted imagination. They 'are not produced by the unconscious as such; they are always a product of consciousness severed from the primary sources of being' (Berdyaev 1945a: 183). In other words, they spring from the egocentric self cut off from any deeper reality, and in them nothingness assumes some form of illusory reality. It is at this point that evil comes into existence. Phantasms, as a source of evil, 'come from primeval pre-existential *meontic* freedom which affirms the spirit of non-being within reality. They mean a return to non-being' (ibid.: 183). For Berdyaev there is no question here about dividing humanity into 'sheep' and 'goats': 'This division takes place in each one of us' (ibid.). We all are to some extent creators of a phantasmagorical existence. How then is it overcome?

However unavoidable it may be to try to put limits on evil through law and reason, these forms of 'good' remain ultimately impotent against evil. While evil appears often terribly exciting, good appears often painfully boring, however much our socially adapted personas are drilled to pretend otherwise. In Berdyaev's view this is a significant moral problem to which the ethics of creativity seeks to respond: how to 'make the "good" fiery, creative, capable of active spiritual struggle and prevent it from becoming dull, flat and commonplace' (Berdyaev 1945a: 179).

The other side of this struggle against evil is the task of seeing through it, so that evil is then revealed as the quintessence of impotence, banality and emptiness. 'Man learns the nothingness of evil and the grandeur of goodness not through the operation of a formal law nor by means of prohibitions, but by living experience on the road of life' (Berdyaev 1935a: 185). Evil has to be overcome from within, through genuine existential insight.

Berdyaev posits two theses in relation to evil, which constitute a fundamental antinomy: 'Evil is evil and must be consumed in the flames of Hell, for there can be no reconciliation with it' and 'Evil is the path by which we reach the good, the experience of freedom of the spirit and an inner victory over the temptation of non-being' (Berdyaev 1935a: 184). On the one hand, one has to aspire to fight against it without any hint of compromise; on the other hand, one has to accept it as part of the path of spiritual experience leading to the good. But '[o]nly its ruthless denunciation and destruction in oneself can make it an approach to the good' (Berdyaev 1935a: 186).

Evil becomes an approach to the good only inasmuch as it is overcome

> spiritually and inwardly. Victory over it is linked to the mystery of Redemption and can only be achieved through Christ. We triumph over evil only in communion with Christ . . . For those who employ force

> the conquest of evil is impossible . . . Christ is crucified above the dark abyss . . . The light which shines from the Crucified is a light shining in the darkness.
>
> (Berdyaev 1935a: 187–188)

Christ is therefore the bringer of true freedom, because only through his grace radiating in the dark abyss can the poison be taken out of initial freedom, so that it can become reconciled with final freedom and make manifest the true grandeur of goodness: the all-transforming, creative force of love. In this love the Divine and the human are united 'without confusion and without separation'.

The division between male and female and the alchemy of eros

Berdyaev's ethics is a 'divinely-human ethics' (Berdyaev 1945b: 83), and is therefore based on the overcoming of the separation of the human from the Divine, which alone can free us from our condition of inner dividedness. The war which goes on in each one of us, not only between good and evil, but also between the masculine and the feminine and between consciousness and the unconscious, is the result of the separation of the human from the Divine. We have seen that this separation comes about through the self-affirmation of initial, irrational freedom.

The original void of irrational freedom appears as a chthonic principle. Following Bachofen's theories on the three stages of cultural development (1861)[2], Berdyaev envisions the battle between the masculine and the feminine principles in man as a struggle between cosmic principles. In the light of this, the longing to return to the initial void of non-being appears as a sort of archetypal dimension of the Oedipus complex. The Oedipus myth

> is a profoundly real myth of the ancient struggle going on in man between the solar masculine and the feminine principle of the earth . . . Man rebels against the victory of the logos over the maternal principle and strives to be absorbed in it once more.
>
> (Berdyaev 1945a: 63)

In man's fallen condition, the personal–anthropological masculine principle and the communal–cosmic feminine principle are at war. They 'do not only seek union but wage a war against each other like deadly enemies' (Berdyaev 1945a: 62). Sexual attraction is at one and the same time the attraction between the impersonal cosmic masculine and feminine principles and their mutual hostility. 'Freud was absolutely right in affirming disharmony and conflict of the sexual life', Berdyaev claims (Berdyaev 1943: 232). Sexual conflicts 'go on in the depth, the metaphysical depth of human existence', and 'in man's sexuality we perceive the metaphysical roots of his being' (Berdyaev 1962: 158). But Freud's limitation was that for him 'the problem of eros-love is left hidden . . . due to the limitations of his general view of life' (ibid.).

Personality is positively realizable in eros-love, but not in impersonal sexuality because '[t]he personal can never be realized through the impersonal. The sexual act is always a partial failure of personality and its hopes' (Berdyaev 1962: 180). Even though he feels that the only truly profound metaphysics of sexuality up until now has been developed by the ascetic tradition, his attitude towards sexuality implies not its rejection but its sublimation into eros-love. This is not an ascetic path but a path based on the 'alchemical' dimension in sexuality. The sexual, erotic relationship is transmuted into an 'individuation-marriage' in which each partner helps the other to restore the androgynous *imago dei*.

The erotic union of two human beings that leads to wholeness follows the Quaternary pattern that Jung laid out in *The Psychology of the Transference* (1946). Berdyaev writes about this[3] as early as 1911, when he completed *The Meaning of the Creative Act*:

> The union of the sexes is four membered: It always means the complex union of the male element of the one with the female element of the other and of the female element of the first with the male element of the second. The mystical life of the androgyne is organized not in one bisexual being but rather in the quadripartite union of two beings.
>
> (Berdyaev 1962: 202)

It is in this way that the mystical meaning of marriage as a sacrament, as opposed to a social institution, is realized. A 'sacrament is always connected with the intimate life of the personality' (Berdyaev 1945a: 233). But even though the sacrament exists as a symbol, the 'mystical, sacred meaning of love has not been made manifest in the Church. It is the task of the ethics of creativeness to reveal it' (Berdyaev 1945a: 235). It is clear that this 'mystical meaning' of the sacrament of marriage is intimately linked with what Jung calls individuation and thus the integration of the conscious and the unconscious.

The integration of conscious and unconscious in the superconscious as the existential core of the person

We have already seen that, for Berdyaev, '[t]rue spiritual victories are won in the domain of superconsciousness, i.e. in the spirit, and not in consciousness' (ibid.: 78). The term 'superconsciousness' is potentially misleading, because what is meant is not spiritual abstraction, but the realization of the integrity of the person through its 'heart-centredness'. The awakening of superconsciousness is nothing else but the awakening of the person as the 'hidden man of the heart' (1. Peter: 3, 4).

Following Boehme, this awakening is, for Berdyaev, the fruit of redemption through Christ, who restores the *imago dei* to man. 'If you would find the *lapidem philosophorum* . . . then go and seek the rebirth of Christ' (cited from Wehr 1990: 96), Boehme wrote. The *lapis*, or *androgyne*, is the 'superconscious' spirit, the essential core of the person which, as a receptacle of grace, progressively transmutes both psyche and body into an expression of the divine image – the person as a fully embodied, free, creative individual.

> Ethics in the profound sense of the term must teach the awakening of the human spirit [i.e. the spiritual core of the person] and not of consciousness, of creative spiritual power and not of laws and norms . . . Redemption is only completed through creativeness. This is the fundamental conception of the new ethics.
>
> (Berdyaev 1945a: 78ff.)

Consciousness is essentially 'unhappy consciousness' (Hegel): it is born from conflict and inner division. Superconsciousness does not imply a one-sided, cramped intensification of consciousness, but the realization of the heart-centred, embodied integrity of the person. Maybe J. Gebser's term 'integral consciousness' would have expressed Berdyaev's intended meaning more faithfully (see Gebser 1978, 2003).

The ethics of creativity implies our awakening to our true spiritual stature and calling, which is to participate in the Divine–human process of continued creation. 'Man's weakness and morbid dividedness are overcome through superconsciousness and the ethics of creative energy which continues and completes the spiritual work of redemption' (Berdyaev 1945a: 79).

Ethics of the law, ethics of redemption and ethics of creativity

In order to grasp Berdyaev's ethics of creativity it is important to understand the coexistence of the three levels of ethical consciousness within the person, which imply different ways of engaging the dynamic tensions within the person. The Joachite theme of the three ages reappears in Berdyaev's conception of different stages of ethical consciousness. The ethics of creativity constitutes the third stage of the 'Holy Spirit', which completes the patriarchal stage of the law and its 'personalistic' transformation through the revelation of the Son in the ethics of redemption.

The humanization of God through the different phases of revelation brings about a humanization of ethics. But in the same way that different images of God coexist on different levels of the psyche, so the corresponding levels of ethical consciousness coexist within the same person. This coexistence nevertheless stands within the fundamental context of a process of gradual humanization. Something will have to be said about this process in order to gain a fuller understanding of Berdyaev's revision of ethics.

The ethics of the law

Inasmuch as the rupture between Divine and human freedom took place through the actualization of man's irrational initial freedom, man, as a consequence, inevitably became subjected to natural necessity. Both the virtuous fulfilment of the law and the excess of vice have this in common: that they are forms of subjection to external necessity.

When we talk about ethics, we mostly mean the ethics of the law, which, if elevated to the rank of an absolute standard, becomes a morality that 'strives to make man into an automaton of virtue' (ibid.: 95). The ethics of the law is inevitable – just as inevitable as the moral dualism between good and evil – but it can have a rightful place within the psycho-spiritual economy of man's inner life only if there is a constant striving to overcome its literalness. Yet, in the same way as we are never entirely freed from the existential condition of disunion with the Divine, we are always, in the part of us which is 'subject to necessity', also 'under the law'.

And yet from the perspective of Berdyaev's mysticism of freedom the law is itself only another form of subjection to necessity, and the virtue and goodness that it produces can never get rid of this shadow:

> The law, which has always a social character, demands that the primeval chaos of instincts should be suppressed; but it merely drives that chaos inwards and does not conquer or regenerate it. Chaotic primeval instincts have been preserved in civilised man of the twentieth century.
>
> (ibid.: 89)

The 'good' that the ethics of the law produces is pale, impotent and dull, and 'the intolerable dullness of virtue . . . gives rise to immorality', yet it is even 'inevitable that men should at times rebel against the dull legalistic virtue, and then return to it. Such rebellion is a moral phenomenon and demands careful consideration' (ibid.: 96ff.). In the language of Jung's psychology, such a careful consideration of the need to rebel against dull legalistic virtue, as a moral phenomenon, would be called 'working with the shadow'.

The ethics of the law 'is the expression of herd morality . . . It deals with personality in the abstract; the concrete person does not exist for it' (ibid.: 91). It 'knows nothing of the inner man; it regulates the life of the outer man in relation to society' (ibid.: 93). The law is essentially a social phenomenon: it subsumes the individual person under the general norm. The primitive tribal participation mystique whereby the individual remains entirely dissolved within the group at one end of the spectrum, and the rational, abstract norms of the Kantian categorical imperative at the other, are only two different levels of essentially the same phenomenon. The law is concerned 'with the abstract norm of the good [however this may be conceptualized within a particular sociological context] but does not care about man, the unique individual human person with an intimate inner life' (ibid.: 95).

In its archaic, primitive roots, the ethics of the law springs from a magical mentality. It is based on magical notions of uncleanness and purity and 'the primitive emotion of fear is always at the bottom' (ibid.: 94). The ethics of the law is also based on the instinct of vengeance, and this instinct which leads to the notion of 'vengeance as a religious and moral duty finds its final metaphysical expression in the doctrine of hell' (ibid.: 89). Thus the ethics of the law has a potentially toxic and destructive influence, inasmuch as it is liable to sustain 'atavistic moral instincts of a bygone age' (ibid.: 90). This aspect of the ethics of the law connects it quite clearly to the Freudian superego as its – sometimes exceedingly cruel and sadistic – intra-psychic executioner. From Berdyaev's perspective, this superego must appear, as I have already pointed out, as that component of moral consciousness which is precisely not yet personal, but which is caught up in the primitive, collective, tribal layer of the psyche.

The ethics of redemption

While the ethics of the law 'knows nothing of the inner man', the Gospel, on the other hand, 'appeals to the inner, spiritual man and not to the outer man, a member of society' (ibid.: 123). To turn it into a normative moral system is therefore a complete distortion of its meaning. The ethics of redemption reveals the living reality of the good in the experience of 'gracious radiating energy', not as an abstract principle to which the concrete person is subordinated. 'It is impossible to understand the Gospel as a norm or a law' (ibid.: 122). The Gospel does not prescribe solutions that can be turned into social rules; it is concerned with 'the healing and regenerating of the texture of the human soul' (ibid.). It is then left to 'man himself in his freedom to find a creative solution of the problems that continually confront him' (ibid.).

The Gospel overthrows the law as an absolute and proclaims that: 'The sabbath was made for man, and not man for the sabbath' (Mark 2: 27). In this way the Gospel is the manifesto of a 'personalist revolution' or revaluation of values in which the concretely real person created in the image of God, the inner spiritual man, is elevated to the supreme value to which all abstract values and norms ('the Sabbath') are subordinated.

The Gospel is radically opposed to the 'metaphysical realm of the bourgeois'. The bourgeoisie is, for Berdyaev, 'a certain condition of the spirit . . . the bourgeois is a man of a particular lack of spirituality' (Berdyaev 1947: 35). The roots of this 'metaphysical condition' lie 'in a too strong faith in this visible world and in the lack of faith in the other, invisible world' (Berdyaev

1947: 40). Traditional Christianity has mostly been the systematic attempt to accommodate the disturbing and unsettling character of the Gospel to the realm of the bourgeois.

The Gospel declares love to be the essence of the law: love as a creative, transformative energy, which leads to a total revaluation of values. 'The old legalistic valuations of good and evil apply no more' (Berdyaev 1945a: 112). They are even turned upside down. 'The so-called good are often "wicked" and the apparently "wicked" are often "good" ' (ibid.: 114). Gospel morality is oriented towards the concretely real person as it is revealed in its existentiality. Only love can 'see' this person. But the law 'is inapplicable and its judgement is of no value in the extraordinary, catastrophic situations when alone the depths of life are revealed' (ibid.: 113). It is therefore not Nietzsche who truly reached an ethical standpoint 'beyond good and evil', but the Gospel. It is 'the morality of paradise and is beyond our good and evil, beyond our legalistic distinctions between good and evil' (ibid.: 123).

As a consequence of this radical revaluation of all values which the Gospel brings, Berdyaev comes up with a formulation that closely echoes Jung's statement that each one of us should aspire to be as true to ourselves as Christ has been to himself:

> The Gospel morality of Grace and redemption is the direct opposite of Kant's formula: you must not act so that the principle of your action could become a universal law; you must always act individually, and everyone must act differently. The universal law is that every action should be unique and individual, i.e. that it should have in view the concrete living person and not the abstract good.
>
> (Berdyaev 1945a: 106)

This is not meant as a prescription for individualism, but a call to the creative realization of personality. The most sublimated and dangerous form of individualism is manifested in the

> morality of transcendental, heavenly egoism . . . We must not think about our own salvation; this is a wrong state of mind . . . we must think of the highest values of the Kingdom of God for all creatures – not for men only, but for the whole world.
>
> (Berdyaev 1945a: 114)

It is at this point that we reach the threshold of the ethics of creativity.

The ethics of creativity

For Berdyaev, the essence of the moral crisis of modern man (see Neumann 1969) 'is above all the revolutionary movement from a consciousness for which morality means submission to a general average law, over to a consciousness for which *morality is a creative problem of individuality*' (Berdyaev 1962: 244). Morality or ethics as a 'creative problem of individuality' seems an apt formulation of the sort of ethics that emerge from the 'analytical vessel' as a result of the individuation process.

In fact, Berdyaev's ethics of creativity may be perhaps even better suited than Jung's 'treatment of Christianity' (M. Stein 1986) itself to address Jung's therapeutic concerns with the religious crisis of contemporary man because it does not lead to a break with Christianity. We have seen that for Berdyaev the ethics of redemption itself already overcomes the dualism of good and evil that is characteristic of the law. And yet, at the same time, while man 'owes to Christianity his loftiest moral consciousness and emotions', it may paradoxically be said that 'on the other hand . . . Christianity has made man morally worse by creating an intolerable conflict between consciousness and the unconscious. The man of the pagan world was more whole, more serene and harmonious, less overwhelmed by the loftiness of his creed' (Berdyaev 1945a: 114). Berdyaev characterizes here the problem that Jung sought to solve through his 'psychological myth'. Similarly to Jung he asserts that 'a religion of thirst for salvation and terror of perdition is only a temporary passage through a dualistic division' (Berdyaev 1962: 99). Paradoxically, while Christianity overcomes the dualism of the law, it simultaneously provokes an even more dramatic 'dualistic division' within the psyche. If this psychological/spiritual condition of the Christian psyche is seen by Berdyaev only as a 'temporary passage', does he not in the end inevitably imply a similar discontinuity with traditional Christianity to Jung?

In his autobiography, Berdyaev describes how he experienced 'moments of acute awareness of the sinfulness of man' (Berdyaev 1950: 207). During one such moment of dark depression he was

> suddenly seized by a tumultuous force which seemed to wrench me away from the oppressive spell of my despondent condition and a light invaded my whole being. I knew then that this was the exalting call to creativity: henceforth I would create out of the freedom of my soul like the great artificer whose image I bear.
>
> (ibid.: 210)

This experience gave him the courage to trust in his creative-prophetic calling, and to speak out for a new spirituality and a new ethics of creativeness. He was convinced that he had to give expression to the realization that he had received, not for himself but for the world. Like Jung, he was confident that what had touched him and what he had to give expression to was something reaching beyond the limits of his private universe:

> I may have a larger revelation not because I am a better man . . . less

> sinful than one who lived 2000 years ago but rather because I live in another time and season. . . . To make the degree of revelation exclusively dependent on the individual's upward progress would be confessing religious individualism. But individualism is in conflict with the very idea of the Church as a universal organism which has its own super-personal life. There is a religious growth not only of man as an individual organism but of the Church as a universal organism.
>
> (Berdyaev 1962: 156ff.)

We have seen how the ethics of the law is a socially oriented ethics appropriate to man's fallen condition. It is addressed to the outer man. The ethics of redemption is the ethics of man's spiritual rebirth. It is addressed to the inner man. And the ethics of creativeness is the ethics of the creative unfoldment of the latent spiritual potentials of the inner man. Both are essentially different from the ethics of the law through their focus on the inner man, the person.

This process of spiritual rebirth always implies a profound, shattering awareness of one's own darkness. Jung talks of the importance of the confrontation with one's shadow. No deeper transformation can happen without this suffering of the 'nigredo'. Pre-modern man's consciousness of sin 'was an expression of his deeper feeling for life' (Berdyaev 1946: 69) while modern man's loss of it implies also 'that he has lost his spirituality' (ibid.). Berdyaev clearly affirms that 'the spiritual life is unthinkable without the great mystery of repentance', but he adds that 'the whole value of repentance is the birth into a new life' (Berdyaev 1962: 154). This is what he has learned from his own spiritual experience. Repentance and asceticism are not an aim in themselves, but should lead to a new birth. Yet within traditional Christianity, the emphasis on the fallen, sinful condition of man has often made the path of repentance an end in itself, and in this way the mystery of redemption came to conceal that of creativity. In living spiritual experience, both belong together.

This full, living experience of the Divine–*human* nature of Christ, who gradually, over the course of 2000 years of Christian history, 'became immanent in human nature' (Berdyaev 1962: 95) was not yet fully given in the phase of Christianity as a religion of redemption, despite the focus on *theosis* in the eastern tradition. It has often taken on a character which obscured the mystery of creativity, and appeared at times closer to pre-Christian eastern ideals of an ascetical spirituality which suppresses everything human: 'Man becomes divine, but only by suppressing all that is human, by *the disappearance of man* and the appearance of Divinity in his place. The teachers of the Church had the doctrine of the *theosis* of man, but in this *theosis* there is no man at all. The very problem of man is not even put' (Berdyaev 1962: 81, emphasis mine).

Berdyaev is perhaps overstating his point but what he means is clear: if man is only sinful, everything human has to be subdued by asceticism to attain a one-sided spiritualization and divinization. These distorting influences on asceticism stem from an implicit Neo-platonic dualism of spirit and matter in which matter is considered the source of evil. Asceticism then involves man's 'disincarnation and dehumanization' (Berdyaev 1946: 72). Such an ascetic metaphysics 'turns its back on love and charity, on the mystery of personality and of freedom' (ibid.: 72). Berdyaev discerns this to be a tendency of the Christian ascetic tradition, however much Christian theology speaks out against it. And yet the 'Gospel is a Messianic book – a revolutionary –Messianic book if you like – rather than a strict ascetic one' (ibid.: 75). This type of – essentially pre-Christian – asceticism has great difficulty in following the 'dual Gospel commandment of *love God* and *love thy neighbour*' (ibid.: 74). Nor does it realize that

> there is a divine truth not only in love for our neighbours but in love for ourselves. Christ commanded us to love our neighbour as ourselves, that is to love ourselves in the image and likeness of God. Divine love for oneself has nothing in common with egoism. Egoists may regard themselves with revulsion.
>
> (Berdyaev 1962: 249ff.)

Thus there is a shadow side to asceticism which gradually, over the course of the history of Christianity, became more and more marked, and eventually provoked justified rebellion.

> Sadistic and masochistic instincts in idealised form have played an important part in the spiritual life and have often determined the character of asceticism. There was a tendency to transform the struggle against sin into a struggle against humanity. It was against this that humanism very justifiably rebelled.
>
> (Berdyaev 1946: 80)

Severe asceticism had an important function in the initial phases of Christianity. The psychic structure of man was different: it was still much closer to its 'pagan' roots and less deformed. In this situation the

> asceticism of the fathers was . . . a new world, a heroic challenge to the old nature, the old Adam. But today the asceticism of the fathers has . . . become a mortal prison for the new man, for our new times . . . Now the world is moving towards new forms of ascetic discipline.
>
> (Berdyaev 1962: 155)

Berdyaev is therefore not rejecting asceticism as such. He recognizes that 'asceticism is one of the eternal ways of religious experience' (ibid.: 150). Some form of asceticism is indispensable for any form of genuine spirituality.

Rather than rejecting asceticism as such it is a question of finding the new form which is suited to the new world we live in.

What is the nature of this 'new asceticism'? It is a 'positive asceticism', which is in the service of our creative calling in the world. While much of traditional asceticism is an effort directed towards the 'suppressing of all that is human' within the ethics of creativeness, asceticism 'should help the liberation of man's creative forces' (Berdyaev 1946: 88). Negative asceticism works by suppression of human passions. The consequences of such a procedure

> have been studied by Freud and the psychoanalysts. Human nature is deformed, and the value of man's latent spiritual forces is distrusted. . . . But . . . sin is more effectively overcome in a positive than in a negative way – through the awakening of love, knowledge, creation, through an aspiration towards the beautiful, noble and sublime.
>
> (ibid.)

Asceticism within the ethics of creativeness is therefore in the service of an alchemical process of transforming the destructive passions into positive creative energy. The idea that 'from each passion a corresponding virtue must be formed' (Berdyaev 1946: 89) is not foreign to patristic thinking, but Berdyaev gives it a more strongly 'alchemical' meaning through his focus on the liberation of man's creative forces, which would dry out without a passionate and erotic element. Creativeness 'does not assert what asceticism denies' (Berdyaev 1962: 153) but constitutes itself as another way of overcoming the world by 'burning up' the demonic evil latent in human nature in 'creative ecstasy' so that it 'transforms itself into another kind of being' (ibid.). It has to stay closer to the untamed sources of life and passion than traditional spirituality would allow for.

The ethics of creativity is 'one of dynamics and energy' (Berdyaev 1945a: 133), not of laws and prescriptions. It is essentially an erotic ethics. As such, it alone has the power to finally overcome the dualistic split that Christianity has introduced into the human psyche. 'The ethics of creativeness alone can save the human soul from being warped by abstract virtue and abstract ideals transformed into rules and norms' (Berdyaev 1945a: 137). Only an ethics of 'dynamics and energy' is true to the essentially dynamic nature of life, which continuously seeks expression. Evil arises from the passions inasmuch as they are fuelled by a will, which is 'at bottom objectless and can only be overcome by a will directed towards an object, towards the valuable and divine contents of life' (Berdyaev 1945a: 137).

In each passion there is an insatiable craving, a 'dark fire' that is inextinguishable as long as it has not found its true object, which it blindly seeks to realize. The soul is the 'flower of fire' (Deghaye 1985: 128), the lily born from the fires of passion. Jacob Boehme says that the demons are incapable of finding full embodiment, thus they remain in a state of being consumed by craving and hunger. A passion is really an impotent craving for creative expression, for the creation of values that enrich life. Seen in this light, 'passions are the material which may be transformed into a higher qualitative content of life. Without passions, without the unconscious element in life and without creativeness, human virtue is dry and deadly dull' (Berdyaev 1945a: 137). It lacks soul and deadens the spirit.

The ethics of creativity thus overcomes the dualism of 'good' and 'evil' that has been opened up as a gaping wound within the Christian psyche, by seeking 'the transformation of evil into good, rather than the mere destruction of evil' (ibid.: 133). This creative transformation becomes possible through love. 'Love is, as it were, the universal vital energy capable of converting evil passion into creative forces' (ibid.: 138). Love is the 'gracious radiating energy' (ibid.: 134), the highest value beyond 'good' and 'evil'. It is the energy which makes possible the union of opposites, in the sense of a transformation both of evil and of a limited moralistic notion of 'goodness' into true creative aliveness.

Creativity presupposes a close contact with this potentially destructive and chaotic realm of passion, rooted in the irrational freedom of the *meontic Ungrund*. Whereas in the redemptive process there is a descent of the Divine towards the human, in the creative process there is an upsurge of creative human energy towards the Divine. But this upsurge presupposes the 'descent to the mothers': 'In every creative conception there is an element of primeval freedom, fathomless, undetermined by anything, not proceeding from God but ascending towards God' (ibid.: 128). Without this element of freedom there would be no creation of anything genuinely new.

The other element that is involved in the complex fact of human creativeness is the daimonic element: the gift of genius. A creator who expresses the quality of genius 'feels that he acts not of himself but is possessed by God and this means that God works his own ends and designs . . . His work is a manifestation through freedom of gifts bestowed upon him from above' (ibid.: 127). This gift of genius is a quality of grace immanent within the human dimension, which gives man the capacity to transcend 'the world' and effect a creative transformation. This quality of an individually specific 'indwelling of the Divine' is aptly symbolized by the image of the Holy Spirit as a flame which descends on the individual apostles and the members of the Church. The Holy Spirit leads to an experience of the Divine as individualized and immanent in the person. Therefore 'true creativeness is always in the Holy Spirit, for only in the Holy Spirit can there be the union of grace and freedom which we find in creativeness' (ibid.: 131).

Within the 'new spirituality' underpinning this new ethics the Divine is, above all, experienced immanently as the originating source of the wholeness of the person. 'Spirit – the Holy Spirit – is incarnated in human life, but it assumes the form of a *whole humanity* rather than of authority' (Berdyaev 1946: 167). The mystery of the Divine–human nature of the person, the

'Christology of man', becomes finally fully manifest when God is experienced in the Spirit as the immanent–transcendent source of the creative unfoldment of the person. There is a true *coniunctio oppositorum* of the divine and the human taking place here in which human imperfection and chaos becomes the veritable prima materia of creativity.

Berdyaev is obviously not, like so many today, opting for what Neumann calls a 'pleromatic mysticism', i.e. one which seeks a monistic identification with the Divine and a dissolution of personal identity.

> It is not by discarding the principle of personality that the absolutely Divine One can be attained, but rather by exploring the spiritual depths of the personality which is antinomically united to the One . . . The purified, liberated spirituality is a subjectification – a passage into the sphere of pure existence.
>
> (Berdyaev 1946: 177)

One might argue that, in this 'passage', the two dimensions of 'depth psychology' and 'depth theology' become linked within existential experience.

The ethics of creativeness appropriate to this kind of spiritual/existential experience is sharply distinguished from the socially determined ethics of the law by the fact that 'every moral task is for it absolutely individual and creative' (Berdyaev 1945a: 132). We have to bring to bear a sort of creative geniality on the life problems with which we are confronted. We have to seek out a unique, individual solution that leads us to the greatest possible degree of wholeness and fullness of life:

> One ought always to act individually and solve every moral problem for oneself, showing creativeness in one's moral activity, and not for a single moment behave as a moral automaton. A man ought to make moral inventions with regard to the problems that life sets him.
>
> (ibid.)

We have heard Berdyaev say something similar already about the ethics of redemption. On the other hand, we can easily see how the emphasis on the immanently experienced Divine in 'the spiritual depths of the personality' leads quite naturally to an ethical conception that shares many significant similarities with the ethical implications of Jung's psychology of the individuation process. Berdyaev, like Jung, proposes a movement from the *unio mentalis*, in which the soul is liberated from the 'flesh' and united to the spirit, towards a fully embodied, blood-red spirituality which does not shy away from being tainted by passion and imperfection (see Jung 1955/1956: paras 669ff.).

Berdyaev holds up the ideal of the genius and of following and unfolding the quality of genius inherent in the person as a very specific alternative to the vocation of sanctity. This 'daimonic' quality of genius is quite well captured in the image of the winged youth of Philaleta's alchemical allegory, which Jung interprets in *Mysterium Coniunctionis* (Jung 1955/1956: para. 189ff.). This 'shy and delicate youth stands for everything that is winged in the psyche and would like to sprout wings' (ibid.: para. 197). The ethics of creativeness is imbued with this puer-spirit of exuberant enthusiasm which needs to become real through the 'consummation of the hierosgamos' of opposites, 'the "earthing" of the spirit and the spiritualization of the earth, the union of opposites and reconciliation of the divided' (ibid.: para. 207).

Not everybody may be called to be a saint in the traditional sense, to realize the ideal of perfection, but we may instead have a calling to some form of creative enrichment of life. This always means overcoming 'the world' in the Gospel sense, i.e. of the sphere of objectification. But it is a different way of overcoming the world, a different kind of asceticism, from that of the Saint. What Berdyaev develops may be seen as a 'spirituality of individuation', maybe a template for what Simone Weil called a 'new holiness'[4], which is more human and much more involved with the world. Creativity is not concerned with perfection but with wholeness, in the sense of 'fullness of life', including life's chaos and imperfections, which are the soil of creativity: 'Creativeness is bound up with imperfection and perfection may be unfavourable to it' (Berdyaev 1945a: 131). To follow one's creative calling 'is another kind of sainthood . . . Life cannot be completely dissolved in sainthood without residue . . . In the dark womb of life there ever remains some rebellious and God-resisting blood and the pulse of free, creative instinct' (Berdyaev 1962: 161).

The ethics of creativeness does not require a striving for personal perfection, but for a creative transformation of the world. 'The ethics of creativeness springs from personality but is concerned with the world, while the ethics of law springs from the world and society but is concerned with the personality' (Berdyaev 1945a: 133). Striving for personal perfection may be a religious striving to 'save one's soul', or it may be a striving for 'self-realization'. Neither of these is what the ethics of creativeness is about. Its 'alchemical' approach to the inner dynamics of the psyche is in the service of an alchemical approach to the world. It seeks the transmutation of leaden, objectified being into the gold of diaphanous creation. Creative work thus implies a specific form of selflessness.

> Creative genius is not concerned with salvation or perdition . . . Creative activity always involves sacrifice. It means self-transcendence, overstepping the confines of one's limited personal being . . . In so far as a man is self-centred he cannot create anything, he cannot abandon himself to inspiration and imagine a better world.
>
> (Berdyaev 1945a: 130)

If the ethics of creativeness promotes 'wholeness', it is of the kind which Jung has in mind when he said that we often do not overcome, but rather outgrow our problems (see Jung 1929: para. 17). We outgrow them to the extent that we are able to liberate the quality of genius latent within our personalities and follow our unique creative calling, however insignificant it may appear to the eyes of the world. The following of one's unique calling, inasmuch as it is really authentic, implies a self-transcendence towards the world. The individual is destined to overcome ever afresh the objectified condition of the world because 'the real carrier of life is the individual' (Jung 1955/1956: para. 194). From this act of love flows genuine healing, the overcoming of individualism and the realization of personality, which are inseparable from universal communion.

In its youthful will to creative engagement with the world, the ethics of creativeness is characterized by a quite 'unholy' quality of rebellion against the paternal order of social norms and laws. It does not aspire towards adaptation, not even in the sense of the traditional ethics of redemption. It is imbued by the realization that 'collective ideals are not by a long way the breath of life which a man needs in order to live' (ibid.: para. 198). By seeking to imagine and create a better world, the ethics of creativity is inevitably imbued with a refusal to conservatively accept the status quo. While the ethics of creativity is 'the highest and most mature form of moral consciousness . . . at the same time it is the morality of eternal youth. Creativeness is the youth of the soul and its power is bound up with the soul's virginity' (Berdyaev 1945a: 141). The virginity of soul results from a *coniunctio oppositorum* and gives access to the 'central water', the 'fountain of the soul or the fount of wisdom from which the inner life wells up' (Jung 1955/1956: para. 200).

Creativeness is, by its very nature, opposed to sclerotic conventional falsity, lies and hypocrisy, for which the ethics of the law is a breeding ground. This conventional falsity, in Christianity in particular, has often invaded even the deepest and most intimate reaches of people's spiritual life. The religious life is full of an 'inner, hidden falsity, falsity to oneself and to God which eludes detection and comes to be regarded as virtue' (Berdyaev 1945a: 161). The cultivation of the virtue of uncompromising honesty directed against such hypocrisy is arguably one of the key contributions of depth psychology to a renewal of spirituality.

The youthful rebellion of the ethics of creativeness against the falsity and hypocrisy that permeate the traditional patriarchal order therefore has a noble origin in a higher level of moral maturity:

> From the spiritual depths of human nature a protest is raised in the name of pure truth and reality against conventional falsity . . . There arises a longing for ontological truthfulness, a desire to break through to freedom and purity of judgement – to what I should call *original and virginal conscience.*
>
> (ibid.: 163)

We can see here a positive side of the Oedipal myth, of the youth who rebels against and kills the 'father', i.e. the patriarchal order, which has degenerated into falsity and hypocrisy (see Neumann 1969: 122).

The renewal of the father in the son is also a central alchemical motif. Just as in alchemy the *imaginatio vera* plays a central role, so too in the ethics of creativeness. To put 'infinite creative energy in place of commands, prohibitions and taboos' (Berdyaev 1945a: 145) is a labour of the creative imagination. The ethics of creativeness, which seeks the 'realization of creative energy' (ibid.: 144), opposes 'to the "law" of the present life "the image" of the higher one' (ibid.: 143).

Imagination is needed to envision a better world and provide an individually unique solution to moral problems in the service of expressing the quality of genius inherent in the person. It is needed to realize the fullness of life, and 'love is life-in-itself', which 'is to be found only in the firsthand and free moral acts and judgements' (ibid.: 149). What this love really seeks is a maximum of aliveness expressing itself through beauty. Beauty, not 'the good', is the ideal of the ethics of creativeness. 'Beauty means a transfigured creation, the good means creation fettered by law which denounces sin' (ibid.: 144).

We can see how, in the ethics of creativeness to which 'imagination is of fundamental importance' (ibid.: 142), beauty is, just as it is for Schiller, the third term that resolves the inner divisions of the person. The realization of beauty is not to be understood as a final end, however, but as a quality within creative activity itself. If beauty or the good are conceived as ends in themselves, they become abstract norms which constrain life. Therefore 'the good must be conceived in terms of energy and not of purpose' (ibid.: 144). The expression of the good has above all to be beautiful, and imbued with creative imagination. 'Moral life must be determined not by a purpose or a norm but by imagery and the exercise of creative activity. Beauty is the image of creative energy radiating over the whole world and transforming it' (ibid.). A beautiful action expresses in one way or another the quality of wholeness, aliveness and fullness of life. It demonstrates that 'human nature is rooted in infinity and has access to boundless energy' (ibid.: 151).

Creative energy is rooted in the dark unconscious, and reaches up into the superconscious. In transmuting what is dark and chaotic into an image of beauty it overcomes the inner divisions within the person. In the language of Jung's psychology we could say that the ethics of creativeness is based on a progressive unfoldment of the transcendent function. Turning now to Jung, we will want to explore to what extent his 'ethics of individuation' can be seen as complementary to Berdyaev's ethics of creativeness, which seeks to overcome the inner divisions Christianity opened in the psyche in a way 'which continues and completes the spiritual work of redemption' (ibid.: 79).

Jung's ethics of individuation

In his interpretation of Philalethe's alchemical allegory Jung shows how the winged youth needs to face his dark opposite to reach the living fountain of the soul. 'Once the malignity is tempered, sinfulness and its evil consequences are mitigated too, and that which has wings can embrace the earth' (Jung 1955/1956: para. 207). Jung's 'ethics of individuation' may in a similar way help to 'earth' Berdyaev's existential perspective of a dynamic ethics of creativity with its unmistakable puer qualities. While Berydaev offers us an image of a new *spirituality* of individuation, Jung's *psychological* thinking lets us enter into the stark reality of the battle of opposites as it is experienced within the individuating psyche. True, creativeness may be 'in the Holy Spirit' (Berdyaev 1945a: 131) but the dove of the spirit, as Jung points out, is also 'the exact counterpart to the malignity of the thief' and together 'they represent the attack, first from one side and then from the other, of a dualistic being on the more restricted consciousness of man' (Jung 1955/1956: para. 205).

Jung's understanding of conscience and the 'voice' involves the role of the transcendent function, to be understood in a broad sense as a factor that also operates in ethical creativity and that makes possible an ethics of integrity. We have seen that Berdyaev's ethics of creativeness is an erotic ethics. Much of what he says about the healing of inner divisions shows the importance of the archetype of the *coniunctio* to his ethics, and so I want to reflect on this aspect of Jung's psychology. A final theme of this part of the chapter will be Jung's psychological approach to the problem of evil. Both Jung and Berdyaev present us with what we might call an 'alchemical' as opposed to a normative understanding of ethics and the problem of evil, but while Jung interprets alchemy as a potential precursor to his own 'post-Christian' (as well as post-religious) psychology, Berdyaev's ethics is more resonant with the specifically Christian interpretation of alchemy which characterizes the tradition of Christian theosophy.[5]

A psychological view of conscience

We have seen that, for Berdyaev, conscience is so closely related to the person that he could even speak of the person 'being a conscience' (Berdyaev 1938: 163). Can we detect a similarly close connection between Jung's understanding of personality and his view of conscience? The following statement of Jung in his essay *The Development of Personality* would suggest this: '[t]rue personality is always a vocation and puts its trust in it as in God' (Jung 1934: para. 300). Jung closely links the experience of being addressed by a 'voice' with true personality.[6] The individuating personality follows its own law and is, by that very fact, set apart from the collective.

But is Jung really talking about the same thing? To answer this question we need to understand how Jung's understanding of conscience relates to this concept of the 'voice'. For Neumann conscience is the internalized voice of the patriarchal values of the collective, the Freudian superego[7], to which he opposes the 'voice'. Jung's own views on this subject, although similar, are nevertheless more complex. If conscience were really explainable as the superego, which Jung interprets as 'a conscious acquisition and an equally conscious possession' (Jung 1958b: para. 830), its numinous force could not be explained, nor the fact that it seems, at times, to operate unconsciously. The phenomenon of conscience becomes for Jung a demonstration of the insufficiency of the Freudian theory, which in his view postulates 'the absolute dependence of unconscious contents on consciousness' (ibid.: para. 831). Even Freud himself had to allude to the existence of 'archaic vestiges' in the superego, and to its character as 'an almost unconscious factor' (ibid.: para. 830) in order to accommodate the actual phenomenology of conscience. Conscience is a psychological phenomenon that testifies to the objective reality of the psyche.

The phenomenon of conscience in itself 'does not coincide with the moral code, but is anterior to it' (ibid.: para. 840). It is 'a manifestation of *mana*, of the "extraordinarily powerful" ' (ibid.: para. 845). Genuine conscience is thus 'a collision of consciousness with a numinous archetype' (ibid.: para. 854), a quintessentially psychological experience. Conscience for Jung is not, like for Berdyaev, a spiritual intuition but rather an overpowering experience of the numinous: the world of the ego collides with the archetype.

Given this phenomenology of conscience, understanding it as the *vox Dei* is, in Jung's view, psychologically correct because it represents an acknowledgement of the psychological fact that conscience is 'in itself, an autonomous psychological factor' (ibid.: para. 842). The numinous archetype with which consciousness collides in the experience of conscience is the God-image (i.e. the Self) in the depth of the psyche. Given Jung's psychological interpretation of the God-image we can see how this would make for a significant transformation of traditional consciousness-oriented ethical perspectives. Jung's God is, after all, not unambiguously good but also dark and terrifying.

Including darkness means, first of all, including the reality of the unconscious dimensions of the psyche into our conception of ethics. This adds an entirely new dimension of psychological consciousness to ethics. According to M. Stein, one of the important discoveries of analytical psychology was that conscience 'can also speak for the so-called "inner world" of complexes and archetypes' (Stein 1993: 7), to which he opposes the conventional view of conscience as 'an internal spokesperson for social values'. In his book *Solar Conscience, Lunar Conscience*, Stein develops Jung's theory of conscience further, by proposing that conscience as an archetypal reality contains a polarity. Conscience 'has a bipolar structure, with Sol on the one side and Luna on the other. On each side there is a differentiation of levels from primitive to refined' (Stein 1993: 21). The solar aspect equates to the patriarchal superego, consisting of the introjected norms and values of society, whereas the lunar aspect is essentially matriarchal and speaks for the values of wholeness, order and harmony in the realm of nature itself: ‘empathy, reaching out to put the neglected and despised elements of life on their feet, keeping the cosmos whole – these are the movements and gestures of lunar conscience’ (ibid.: 106). Lunar conscience, in its ultimate outreach, ‘speaks for the *unus mundus*’ (ibid.: 112). In its primitive aspect, however, lunar conscience may manifest itself in, for example, compulsions and borderline symptoms, and thus can be as destructive as solar conscience when it manifests itself as the sadistic superego. Lunar conscience, which speaks for the inner world, is clearly what Jung is most interested in and has primarily in mind when he speaks of the inner voice. It is the voice of instinctive, feminine wisdom that is close to the living rhythm of nature and is less likely to get stuck in rigidly petrified absolutes.

In its solar aspect conscience is closely tied up with the internalized moral code, and as such ‘is a psychic reaction which one can call *moral* because it always appears when the conscious mind leaves the path of custom, of the *mores*, or suddenly recollects it’ (Jung 1958b: para. 855). There are cases where the unconscious supports, and even endeavours to promote, this reaction. But the inner voice itself is, for Jung, nevertheless more of an objective voice of (psychic) nature. The moral code is a set of value judgements ‘grounded on rational feeling’ (ibid.: para. 825), which force themselves upon the individual with a compelling force rooted in the ‘primitive fear of anything unusual’ (ibid.: para. 855). Inasmuch as this internalized morality of the collective ‘law’ is only very partially a result of individual reflection, ‘it may be “moral” but can raise no claim to being *ethical*’ (ibid.).

Conscience thus has two layers, ‘the lower one comprising a particular psychic event, while the upper one is a kind of superstructure representing positive or negative judgements of the subject’ (ibid.: para. 825). The moral reaction happens in the ‘upper layer’, in the solar, patriarchal conscience, but the ‘psychic event’ that takes place in the deeper layer of lunar conscience is essentially the experience of the inner voice. At this deeper level conscience ‘commands the individual to obey his inner voice even at the risk of going astray’ (ibid.: para. 841).

To follow this command may mean to be led into conflicts of duty, and at this point a moral reaction based on the fear of leaving the collectively approved path may set in. The individual may nevertheless choose to endure this inner conflict and to engage with it through reflection and conscious scrutiny. In this case, ‘if one is sufficiently conscientious [and] the conflict is endured to the end . . . a creative solution emerges which is produced by the constellated archetype and possesses that compelling authority not unjustly characterized as the voice of God’ (ibid.: para. 856). Only then does conscience become manifest in its individually creative, and thus ethical, aspect.

It is therefore not just a matter of blindly following the inner voice, but rather of attempting the realization of an inner *coniunctio* of the solar and lunar aspects of conscience (Stein 1993: 112ff.). Through this *coniunctio* the higher, ethical and creatively individual aspect of conscience becomes manifest. In this perspective the 'new ethics' does not simply replace the superego or solar conscience with the 'voice', but tempers, refines and integrates it with its complementary opposite. The ethically creative task consists of this *coniunctio*, which requires conscious reflection.

The 'voice' itself is ambivalent. The 'inner voice' can be right as well as wrong, and both of these forms 'stem from the same source, and . . . have approximately the same power of conviction' (Jung 1958b: para. 846). Whereas for Berdyaev the false conscience is a distortion of pure conscience, for Jung the deeper layer of conscience, the 'voice' itself, is ambivalent because as *vox Dei* it implies an encounter with the ambivalent God-image. The moral code is, on this count, a protective device against the perils of the inner voice, but, on the other hand, the hero will never gain the treasure if he does not face the dragon in the dangerous realms beyond the safe haven of collective morality.

Berdyaev's 'pure conscience' is not the same as Jung's 'voice'. But it can perhaps be understood as the *result* of the inner *coniunctio* of the initially separate, and even opposed and hostile, solar–patriarchal and lunar–matriarchal aspects of conscience. This inner *coniunctio* is the fruit of the operation of the transcendent function, which gets activated in the attempt at a creative resolution of conflicts of duty. Jung, we could say, describes the psychological process that leads to the creative 'virginal acts' of conscience which Berdyaev demands. This process is inseparable from a confrontation with the shadow, without which we end up in some form of moral rigorism and fanaticism:

> To confront a person with his shadow is to show him his own light. Once one has experienced a few times what it is like to stand judgingly between the opposites, one begins to understand what is meant by the self. Anyone who perceives his shadow and his light simultaneously sees himself from two sides and gets in the middle.
>
> (Jung 1959a: para. 872)

The path of true individuality is a 'middle path' between the opposites, which are recognized as aspects of the transpersonal Self. The 'voice' as the instinct of wholeness therefore often speaks out for the neglected content, and thus appears to take the side of the shadow, the 'primitive' side of the personality, which the ego may be likely to ignore. Shadow and light both belong to the wholeness of the personality.

The 'middle', in our ethical context, is also aptly symbolized by the image of the tree, which needs to have strong dark roots to grow. In this sense,

> That we are bound to the earth does not mean we cannot grow; on the contrary it is the *sine qua non* of growth . . . The question of where we are going is of course extremely important; but equally important, it seems to me, is the question *who* is going where. The who implies a 'whence' . . . The difficulty lies in striking the dead centre . . . For this an awareness of the two sides of man's personality is essential, of their respective aims and origins.
>
> (Jung 1944: para. 148)

The type of 'conscious reflection' which Jung posits as a precondition for an ethically mature consciousness, and which is capable of dealing with such complexities and ambiguities instead of being 'black and white', is not just that of rational discourse; rather, it primarily stems from an activation of the transcendent function. Here is the source of ethical creativity in Jung's sense.

The transcendent function, Hermes and liminality

The awakening of creative individuality is preceded by an experience of liminality. The consciousness of the average man remains undisturbed by upsetting moral conflicts as long as collective solutions still work for him. The way that a conscious engagement with individual conflicts of duty and one's own shadow relate to this level of conventional morality is analogous to the way that modern physics relates to Newtonian physics (see Jung 1959a: para. 871). Conventional ethics is for Jung, just like for Berdyaev, the 'Newtonian' level of the collective ethics of the law. It is only when the consciousness of personality begins to dawn that the inner divisions which cannot be resolved on a collective level become a real problem for the individual. At this point the Newtonian certainties of the rational mind become insufficient. Up until then, the problem was resolved primarily through the projection of the shadow onto collective entities with a different and therefore potentially threatening value system.

The average man, once he has the misfortune of being pushed beyond the safe boundaries of collective morality, enters into a condition of liminality. According to the anthropologist Victor Turner, the entry into liminality is connected to the experience of opposites. Individuals find themselves in a place of 'invisibility' due to the transition from the old order to a new one. 'They are no longer classified and not yet classified' (Turner 1987: 7). In traditional societies, liminality is ritualized as initiation, a death–rebirth mystery:

> The essential feature of these [liminal] symbolizations is that the neophytes are neither living nor dead from one aspect, and both living and dead from another. Their condition is one of *ambiguity and paradox* . . . a confusion of all customary categories. Jacob Boehme . . . liked to say that

> 'in Yea and Nay all things consist'. Liminality may perhaps be regarded as the Nay to all positive structural assertions, but as in some sense the source of them all, and, more than that, a realm of pure possibility whence novel configurations of ideas and relations may arise.
>
> (ibid.)

J. A. Hall comments: 'What Turner's concept of social *liminality* does for the status in a society, Jung's psychological concept of the *transcendent function* does for the movement of the person through the life process of individuation' (Hall 1991: 34).

Hermes is the god of liminality and of transitions such as midlife (Stein 1983), and as *Hermes–Mercurius* he is the *psychopomp*, the guide of the soul which is hidden in the dark presence of the shadow (Neumann 1969). Whereas Christianity in its collective form advises the suppression of the shadow, the 'hermetic attitude' advocates a more paradoxical stance: to combine the workings of the solar and lunar consciences. Thus it asserts: 'Together Mercurius and Christ symbolize the full self, and both have parts within the workings of conscience' (Stein 1993: 21). Here we have the psychological counterpart of Berdyaev's account of the dialectics of freedom, which find their resolution in Christ, the bringer of freedom. Through Christ, the irrational, tricksterish freedom of Mercurius in the shadows can become transformed.

In liminality, fixities disappear and everything is in flux. This aspect of fluidity is fundamental to Jung's understanding of ethics. Ethics becomes mercurial and situationist, which does not mean arbitrary. The true ethical imperative for Jung is to remain true to the natural flow of psychic energy and its transformations, and therefore there is simply no one single position that can be made into an absolute. It is the Tao, the (irrational or rather suprarational) *Logos* of psychic transformations which constitutes the ultimate, purely innate norm: 'Personality is Tao' (Jung 1934: para. 323). This norm is as fluid and many shaped as mercury. Hermes is the guide of souls but also a thief and a trickster who likes to pull the rug from under our feet.

J. Beebe comments on this understanding of Tao as follows:

> The Tao is a flow of life that does not stop for particular constellations. Rather it moves through them. The archetypes were [for Jung] not ends in themselves but means of entering the stream of Tao. For Jung, Tao was the ground of integrity.
>
> (Beebe 1992: 28)

We are reminded of Berdyaev's understanding of the distorting effect of fanaticism and his demand for a dynamic ethics. Psychologically fanaticism implies possession by a single archetype to the detriment of the whole, the wisdom-filled dynamic of life, the Tao. In the ethical sphere, the transcendent function serves the 'hermetic' task of finding one's own unique 'middle way'. The path of individuation is, Jung says, a '*longissima via*, not straight, but snakelike, a path that unites the opposites in the manner of the guiding *caduceus*' (Jung 1944: para. 6), the staff of Hermes. Certainly, this *logissima via* includes the experience of evil, which Berdyaev sees as being inseparably bound up with human freedom.

Shadow and integrity

We have seen that for Jung, the original experience of conscience as a psychic event is an encounter with the paradoxical God-image. 'There is scarcely any other psychic phenomenon that shows the polarity of the psyche in a clearer light than conscience' (Jung 1958b: para. 844). The experience of conscience, when it reaches ethical maturity, is the experience of standing 'judgingly between the opposites' and perceiving one's 'shadow and light simultaneously' (ibid.: para. 872).

Whereas collective morality resolves the issue by resorting to what is collectively accepted as 'good', in any concrete, individual situation 'good at the wrong moment in the wrong place may be the worst thing possible' (Jung 1959a: para. 866). The decision has to be both an individual and an ethically creative one that promotes the real integrity and wholeness of the particular person. A therapist taking the unique, personal, psychological situation of this individual into account may be forced to say: 'I see very clearly: this is evil, but the paradox is that just for this person in this particular stage of development it may be good' (ibid.). Fixed moral certainties have to give way to an intuitive wisdom attuned to the flow of life. The dynamics of this flow are defined by polarities.

What is allowed to have a say in such an instance is the voice of the lunar conscience, which presses for the dangerous 'alchemical' undertaking which was 'the heretical aim of alchemy . . . not simply to endure the shadow and accept him in a passive way but to actively seek him out and redeem him in the *opus magnum*' (Neumann 1969: 145). But this undertaking, which seeks to transform the deadly mercurial serpent into the *medicina catholica*, requires a high moral stance.

In order to find the 'middle' way, which is the path of one's own unique calling, an attitude which hears the voice of the neglected, inferior, rejected content has to be combined with the capacity to endure the affects of existential guilt, anxiety and shame.[8]

On this path of individuation, upon which the call of conscience to follow the inner voice is heeded, and the individual therefore ventures beyond conventional morality into the uncharted territory of individual ethical decisions, guided by the moral imagination of the transcendent function, a development is set in motion which 'includes Christ in the realm of immediate inner experience and makes him appear as the figure of the total man' (Jung 1951:

para. 122). The Christ-life becomes the symbol of 'the only meaningful life, that is, of a life that strives for the individual realization – absolute and unconditional – of its own particular law' (Jung 1934: para. 310).

Jung's notion of wholeness, which presupposes the process of facing and integrating the shadow, is far from offering easy, lukewarm compromises. His recognition of Christ crucified between the two thieves as being one of the most perfect symbols of the path of individuation which 'leads to a fundamental conflict, to a real suspension between the opposites . . . and to an approximate state of wholeness that *lacks perfection*' (Jung 1951: para. 123, emphasis mine) makes this evident. It is precisely the experience of failure in striving for perfection, of lack, of unredeemed nature and imperfection that is so fundamental to the Christian spiritual practice of *metanoia*, which leads to an experience of wholeness. But it only does so if the striving is genuine. The lack of perfection which is painfully experienced in the dark lacunae of the psyche is the 'dungheap' in which the *lapis* is to be found (*in stercore invenitur*).

Psychologically, this dark place of imperfection is the inferior function, which 'drags with it' the whole unconscious. Lunar conscience, which speaks for wholeness, is 'the voice of nature', of matriarchal wisdom. Because it speaks for wholeness, it speaks for giving a place to the inferior function, which we experience as the source of everything that is inferior and despicable in us. 'What the inner voice whispers to us is generally something negative, if not actually evil' (Jung 1934: para. 319). But if we struggle with it and assimilate what it has to say, that is, if we endure the inner conflict and suffer the suspension between the pairs of opposites

> we realize that evil was, after all, only the semblance of evil, but really a bringer of illumination. In fact, the inner voice is a 'Lucifer' in the strictest and most unequivocal sense of the word, and it faces people with ultimate moral decisions without which they can never achieve full consciousness and become personalities.
>
> (ibid.)

Thus it is only the intimate and personal inner ethical struggle that can 'crucify the serpent' (see Jung 1944: para. 517) and allow us to gain the *medicina catholica*. The inner voice is both good and 'evil'; it is mercurial, and Mercurius is 'the devil, a redeeming psychopomp, an evasive trickster, and God's reflection in physical nature' (Jung 1943/1948: para. 284).

The coniunctio and the transmutation of passion

I have already referred to J. Beebe's notion of integrity. Beebe affirms that, in his work 'first on the dynamics of the dual mother and then on the anima's role in supporting the unification of personality, Jung found a system of integrity well beyond anything western culture had previously imagined'

(Beebe 1992: 87). Jung offers 'a feminine image of the integrity of personality, appropriately carried by his feminine name for personality, psyche' (ibid.: 86). The Tao, to which I have repeatedly referred, is understood by Beebe to be 'the ground of integrity', but integrity itself is, according to Beebe, 'a developed sensitivity to the needs of the whole . . . brought by psychological consciousness to a pre-existing archetype of completeness' (ibid.: 125). This psychological notion of a pre-existing archetype of wholeness corresponds in some respects to Berdyaev's notion of personality as God's idea of man, his *sophianic* image, which integrates body and soul. In the *Aurora consurgens* the Sophia is shown not as descending from above but as needing to be redeemed from its immersion in matter, i.e. the unconscious. Like the virgin guarded by the dragon she has to be liberated. There is not only a 'heavenly' Sophia, but also an 'underworld Sophia' (see Sardello 1995, Ch. 3) but both are nevertheless somehow deeply linked.

An ethics that is oriented towards the feminine image of the integrity of the personality can therefore express a new concept of virtue, replacing the older one, which we are often inclined to regard as representing a violation of wholeness and natural spontaneity. Thus Jung says that the 'refining of the *prima materia*, the unconscious content' demands from the patient

> a putting forth of his best powers . . . The deep meaning of the Christian virtues, especially the greatest among these, will become clear even to the unbeliever; for there are times when he needs them all if he is to rescue consciousness, and his very life, from this pocket of chaos, whose final subjugation, without violence, is no ordinary task.
>
> (Jung 1946: para. 385)

Virtue is seen here in the service of the subjugation *without violence* of the pockets of chaos in us instead of in the service of a violent, even cruel rejection of everything inferior in the name of an abstract norm. This is an erotic ethics instead of a one-sidedly logos-driven, normative ethics, and as such it depends on the anima's role in supporting the unification of the personality. It is easy to discern the parallel to Berdyaev's ethics of creativeness.

For an ethics that has wholeness instead of perfection as its orienting value, the subjugation of the chaotic, inferior aspects of the personality without violence means first of all a painful descent into realism. One has to take up one's imperfections as part of one's wholeness, and this implies a painful experience of limits. One has to learn the humility that is born of truthful self-knowledge. One is confronted with the reality of oneself, 'no longer the earlier ego with its make-believes and artificial contrivances, but another "objective" ego which for this reason is better called the "self" ' (ibid.: para. 400). In place of a 'selection of suitable fictions' we have to face up to 'a string of hard facts, which together make up the cross we all have to carry or the fate we ourselves are' (ibid.).

But even if the personal unconscious is integrated to the extent that we are led to a sober realism about ourselves, we find that the unconscious has still an autonomous life of its own which cannot be integrated in the same way. Instead, the task now becomes to 'bring the conscious and the unconscious into responsible relationship' (Jung in Neumann 1969: 15). This relationship requires a drastic departure from the 'Newtonian' certainties of consciousness, by consciously engaging with the internal 'other'. The development of ethical responsibility thus becomes a process of 'soul-making'. Only if this inner relationship and union with the 'other' happens is it possible to 'subjugate the pockets of chaos in us without violence'.

This process is symbolized by the *Rosarium* pictures – representing the *coniunctio* of *sol* and *luna*, from which the *filius philosophorum* is born – which Jung interprets in *The Psychology of the Transference*. Men and women suffer from inner dividedness due to a one-sided identification with a masculine/animus or a feminine/anima style of consciousness. We are therefore 'at cross purposes with ourselves', a fact that is symbolized by the Rosarium as king and queen, holding crossed branches: they 'are themselves man's cross in the form of the anima and woman's cross in the form of the animus' (Jung 1946: para. 470).

According to Edinger the 'anima and animus are the personifications of passionate desires because they are the gateway to the unconscious' (Edinger 1994: 49). In other words, we are meeting the other in us whenever we are out of control, or gripped by irrational moods or opinions, passionate desires or autonomous contents of the unconscious. The archetype of the *coniunctio* opens up a different method of dealing with 'passions' to the ascetic one.

In *The Psychology of the Transference*, Jung emphasizes the importance of relationships in the process of individuation. The phenomenon of transference has implications that extend far beyond the analytic encounter, and which apply to all human relationships. 'The unrelated human being lacks wholeness, for he can achieve wholeness only through the soul, and the soul cannot exist without its other side, which is always found in a "You" ' (Jung 1946: para. 454). The 'other side' of the soul is the anima (in the case of man) and the animus (in the case of woman), and therefore the issue of greatest importance here is how the sexual relationship deepens into a psychological relationship.

What is sought in a sexual relationship is union with the inner other, the anima/animus, so as to reach wholeness. This inner other is experienced in projection. The *coniunctio* thus implies a descent into the unconscious, leading to a death-experience. Edinger calls this level of *coniunctio* the 'lesser *coniunctio*', which implies an insufficient separation of the opposites and 'occurs whenever the ego identifies with contents emerging from the unconscious' (Edinger 1985: 215). In other words, we are usually drawn into the profound entanglements of a relationship by factors of which we are largely unconscious: primarily, the anima/animus and our union with the other really amounts to 'incest', psychologically speaking, because our desire and love are not really directed towards the other person, but towards what we project onto them.

The death-experience is a *mortificatio*: the soul leaves the body of the relationship, and only the ashes of disillusionment remain. In order for the soul to return what needs to happen is that the 'body' now becomes purified. The purification of the black ashes until they become 'the white, moonlike (purified) body' (Jung 1946: para. 495) happens, psychologically speaking, through a process analogous to 'numerous distillations'. As in alchemy, 'in psychology too . . . [purification] comes from an equally thorough separation of the ordinary ego-personality from all inflationary admixtures of unconscious material' (ibid.: para. 503). This long and painstaking process leads to a gradual withdrawing of projections that depends upon 'painstaking self-examination and self-education' (ibid.) in the 'vessel' of the relationship, because 'a radical understanding of this kind is impossible without a human partner' (ibid.). This purification leads eventually to a 'return of the soul' into the purified 'body', i.e. to a mature psychological relationship in which two whole human beings relate to each other as persons. Berdyaev, as we have seen, understood 'virginity' to be the integrity of the person. Love and passionate desire become an expression of the *whole* person in relation to another whole person.

Whereas the lesser *coniunctio* derives from love as concupiscence, the greater *coniunctio* is both generated by and generates this transpersonal love.

> It has been truly said that object love is the extraverted aspect of individuation. Object love is *objective* love, a love purged of personal desirousness, not one side of a pair of opposites, but rather beyond opposites. This transpersonal love is at the root of all group and social loyalties . . . the extraverted aspect of the *coniunctio* promotes social interest and the unity of the human race; the introverted aspect promotes connection with the Self and unity of the individual psyche.
>
> (Edinger 1985: 223)

The *coniunctio* therefore both generates and is generated by transmuted passion: desire that is not simply denied, but which is transformed in the vessel of relationship. This pattern, derived from the *Rosarium* pictures, works itself out in all types of transference relationships. Let us remind ourselves here that Berdyaev's ethics of creativeness is fundamentally an ethics of the 'gracious regenerating energy' of love that flows out to the world, seeking to creatively transform it.

The *coniunctio* leads to the birth of the Self, which is 'the total, timeless man and as such corresponds to the original, spherical, bisexual being who stands for the mutual integration of conscious and unconscious' (Jung 1946: para. 531). The relationship of the ego to the Self is paradoxical, because while on the one hand, the Self gives birth to the ego as the 'body' of consciousness, on the other hand, the ego in turn gives birth to the Self through its conscious relationship to the unconscious.

The result is the birth of the Self as 'a new personality', which is 'not a third thing midway between conscious and unconscious . . . [but] both together' and which therefore 'transcends consciousness' (Jung 1946: para. 474). The *coniunctio*-experience leading to such a new consciousness can occur on a range of different levels. Berdyaev's designation of the spiritual core of the person as the superconscious or the androgynous image of God in man has the spiritual perspective of Boehme's theosophy as a basis. Jung's hesitancy about employing the term 'superconscious' stems from his less elevated psychological realism: 'The united personality will never quite lose the painful sense of innate discord. . . . The goal is important only as an idea; the essential thing is the *opus* which leads to the goal: *that* is the goal of a lifetime' (Jung 1946: para. 400).

Of course, this is equally true for the 'spiritual level'. But still, from Jung's psychological perspective, ambiguities, inner disunion, and tensions between dark and light take on a particular character due to their basis in the 'alchemical–psychological myth' of the 'unconscious God' coming to consciousness in man. The 'alchemical Sophia' does not descend from above, but has to be freed from its immersion in the darkness of the bowels of the earth. This brings us to the area in which, for all their convergences and complementarities, a sharp contrast between Jung's and Berdyaev's ethical positions makes itself felt.

The problem of evil in the ethics of individuation

Although I have discussed the 'integration of the shadow' in Jung's psychology from a certain perspective, I have left out the most contentious issue. To lead into this I will use a quote from Neumann, who attempted to formulate the ethical consequences of Jung's psychology:

> When evil works unconsciously and emits its radioactivity underground, it possesses the deadly efficiency of an epidemic; on the other hand, *evil done consciously by the ego* and accepted as its own personal responsibility does not infect the environment, but is encountered by the ego as its own problem and as a content to be incorporated into life and the integration of personality like any other psychic content.
>
> (Neumann 1969: 104, emphasis mine)

Clearly, the ethical conceptions of both Jung and Berdyaev are equally concerned with neutralizing the toxic effect of the split-off shadow to which Neumann refers here. We need, as Simone Weil put it, a 'new saintliness' as urgently as 'a plague-stricken town needs doctors' (quoted in Perrin and Thebon 2003: 100ff.)[9]. More often than not the plague comes from the 'good and pious' ones who take the moral high ground. But what mainly interests us is this specific formulation of Neumann: 'evil done consciously by the ego', because in its provocative bluntness it puts the ethical issues associated with the integration of the shadow into sharp relief. It is a formulation which reflects Jung's own position well.

We may find it comparatively easy to accept that the material or chthonic aspects of the psyche needs to be integrated for us to become whole, because it makes sense to say that they also contain some latent good. But Neumann's notion of an integration of *evil itself* is a different matter altogether.

If one understands integration and wholeness to be a condition that comes about by supplying a lack, i.e. by connecting the conscious ego to qualities that are contained in the shadow in order to develop a more 'rounded' and whole personality, then it is difficult to see how there could be anything useful in the integration of evil. Is not evil by its very nature a force of disintegration, a force destructive to wholeness and integrity? One might very well speak of an integration of 'light' and 'darkness', i.e. of the conscious and the unconscious, as constitutive of wholeness. But in this context 'darkness' cannot be equated with 'evil', even though, under certain conditions, it may appear this way to a one-sided consciousness. But in that case what *appears* to the conscious ego to be 'evil' is in reality the claim of wholeness which the lunar conscience makes upon it, i.e. a neglected good that claims attention. Up until now we have considered Jung's statements only from this angle.

In the words of Victor White:

> Evil or badness cannot possibly be something that can be added to something else and so bring about greater completeness. Goodness and completeness are in fact synonymous, and evil or badness can never be an addition to, for it is by definition an abstraction from that completeness. Only the crudest kind of picture-thinking can make it a 'part' or a 'side' of God.
>
> (White 1960a: 153)

On these grounds, Neumann's formulation that 'evil done consciously by the ego' is ethically desirable becomes incomprehensible. The underlying presupposition is that evil is a part of God, and not, as White states (in line with the whole of Christian theological tradition), that evil is a *privatio boni*, and therefore never an addition to, but by definition an abstraction from, wholeness and completeness. In this *privatio boni* view, the essential nature of evil, once unmasked, is its entirely parasitical character, its uncreative emptiness, impotence, boredom and banality.

We have seen that for Berdyaev evil has in essence a phantasmagorical character. It gains reality as a manifestation of irrational freedom. But this parasitical reality of evil is that of a lie. While it is a formidable reality because irrational freedom is at the foundation of all existence, it is nevertheless ultimately doomed to dissolve into its own nothingness. Berdyaev's notion of a 'transformation of evil' therefore seems to be as incompatible with the notion of an 'integration of evil' as White's, insofar as such a notion of integration presupposes that evil is somehow an inalienable part of human wholeness, as it is of the God-image. For Berdyaev, whatever belongs to the sophianic image in man can have nothing to do with evil, which is a quintessentially antisophianic force.

But for Jung, our inability to conceive of such a *coincidentia oppositorum* between good and evil is due only 'to the great psychological difficulties of antinomian thinking which continually . . . [comes] up against the demand for the logical consistency of the metaphysical figures, and for their emotional absoluteness. The *bonum superexcedens* of God allows no integration of evil' (Jung 1955/1956: para. 124). When Jung wrote these words, in *Mysterium Coniunctionis*, he may very well have had his discussions about the *privatio boni* with White in mind. Throughout these discussions Jung did, on the one hand, welcome White as his theological ally and even mentor. But, on the other hand, he also saw himself to be acting as a therapist for White (and, by implication, as a therapist for the traditional Christian attitude represented by White) as becomes evident in a letter he wrote to Catherine Ginsberg shortly after White's death:

> I was at the end of my resources and had to leave him *nolens volens* to the decrees of his fate. I saw that his arguments were valid for him and allowed him no other development. I accepted this in silence, for one can only respect such reasons even though one is convinced that – had the circumstances been favourable – one might yet have reached out beyond them. In such cases I usually tell my patients: here only fate can decide. For me it is, every time, a matter of life and death, where only the person concerned speaks the last word. For it depends entirely on him and his decision what will happen. Knowing how much would depend on whether Father White could understand my arguments or not, I still tried to point out the difficulties in my second last letter to him.
>
> (Lammers and Cunningham 2007: 303)

Obviously Jung felt that White's early death could have been avoided if White had taken up his interventions favourably, and so been able to free himself from the demand for logical consistency that the metaphysical figure of his Christian God imposed on him. For Jung, this demand for logical consistency conflicts with psychological reality. It is an epistemological strait-jacket that has to be shaken off. White's failure to do so resulted in a tragic psychological impasse which manifested itself in a literal premature death, instead of the favourable outcome desired by Jung: the psychological death of the 'old King', White's dominant Christian orientation.

The dispute between White and Jung has its roots in divergent philosophical positions. White is a Thomist, firmly rooted in the classical pre-Kantian metaphysical tradition, whereas Jung is a resolutely post-metaphysical Kantian and nominalist (or 'conceptualist'). 'Being' as a metaphysical concept – and with it, the whole framework of the doctrine of *privatio boni* – is meaningless to Jung. He is, as he so often emphasizes, only concerned with what is empirically given. All of this belongs to the world of consciousness, inasmuch as it is given at all, and beyond this is the impenetrable sphere of the unconscious, which can nevertheless be studied by its manifestations in dreams, visions, symptoms etc. From this point of view, what counts is not the logical consistency of metaphysical speculation, but the psychological accuracy of phenomenological description.

The description of God as *summum bonum* is for Jung psychologically incorrect because it contradicts the actual phenomenology of the Self, the invariable archetypal structure of human wholeness. And for this very reason Jung believes that it could become harmful for someone who is destined, like White, for the path of individuation. The Gnostics who talked of the *agnosia* of God were, in Jung's view, much more correct; 'Psychologically . . . the idea of God's *agnosia*, or of the *anennoetos theos*, is of the utmost importance, because it identifies the Deity with the numinosity of the unconscious' (Jung 1951: para. 303). Why this identification should be psychologically so important to Jung's mind is amply demonstrated by the position he took up in relation to White. He saw in White the struggle between the unconscious drive for a greater wholeness and the conscious dominance of the Christian God-image, which prevented such greater wholeness and thus drove him into an impasse, which resulted in his fateful death.

So what exactly does Jung mean when he talks of the 'integration of evil' in this context? The centrally important term appears to be 'consciousness'. Jung wished that the apocryphal saying of Jesus, 'Man, if thou knowest what thou doest, thou art blessed, but if thou knowest not, thou art accursed and a transgressor of the law', were still in the Gospels, because it 'might well be the motto for a new morality' (Jung 1942/1948: para. 291). To be conscious of evil means to distinguish oneself from it, just as to be conscious of good means to distinguish oneself from it, and so one 'comes to stand' in the middle, not identified with either one or the other.

To understand this better, it may be helpful to go back to an early piece of writing by Jung, which was never intended for publication, entitled the *Seven Sermons to the Dead* (see Segal 1992). This piece of writing, which is couched in Gnostic language, is one of the fruits of Jung's 'confrontation with the unconscious', which gave him, according to his own admission, the raw material for all his later work[10]. The *septem sermones* formulate 'what might have been said by Philemon' (Jung 1995: 215), an autonomous figure of the unconscious who, to Jung, 'psychologically . . . represented superior insight' (Jung 1995: 208). The sermons represent, so Jung suggested, 'a kind of prelude to what I had to communicate to the world about the unconscious: a kind of pattern of order and interpretation of its general contents' (Jung 1995: 217). While Jung discards traditional metaphysics, I have tried to show that he implicitly does endorse a 'metaphysics of the unconscious', a self-expression of the archetypal psyche, of which the *sermons* represent a seed-form.

The *Seven Sermons* are not simply a recasting of Gnostic ideas but an expression of what Jung seems to have seen as his own authentic *psychological* gnosis. He could feel that it was the 'unconscious' revealing itself through his experiences, and he could claim that he subsequently made tremendous scientific efforts to objectively validate this raw material, by employing it as a useful ordering scheme for the formulation of his hypotheses. In Jung's view, this makes for a mode of description and a methodology for the formulation of hypotheses that remains faithful to the psyche's phenomenology. Metaphysics remains closely linked to the actual phenomenology of psychic processes. It does not move in the element of rational logic but in the 'soul's logical life' (Giegerich 2001), which is inherent to actual phenomenologically given psychic processes. The mode of speculative thought operative within Jung's psychology remains dreamlike, ambiguous, it happens by itself, almost mediumistically; only the phenomenologically observing scientific mind is fully alert.

But it is this way of proceeding that arguably becomes highly problematic in the ethical (not to mention 'theological') sphere, because the spiritual appears here only within the psychic. Jung tries to overcome the ethical dualism that is characteristic of the mental structure of consciousness, but this breaking out of the rational 'father world' appears, according to Jean Gebser,[11]

> in an ambivalent expression congruent to the psychic, as the 'beyond the dualism' is reached through a conscious return into the polarity, while the rational interpretation seeks to break through, so to speak, not backwards, but forwards, not into the mythical two-dimensional, but into the four-dimensional. This attempt at breaking out stands in a twilight of maximal ambivalence which is characteristic for the psychic. The fact that Jung as psychologist remains above all caught up in the psychic, brings with it that specifically here [i.e. in relation to the Quaternity] the characteristic weakness of his discipline becomes especially apparent: the absence of the spiritual.
>
> (Gebser 2003: 536, trans.)

Gebser very aptly makes the same point that I have tried to make throughout these pages. In many cases Berdyaev appears to fill in the gaps left in Jung's perspective and this becomes relevant where the ethical and religious implications of his psychology become an issue.

This ambivalent character of Jung's psychological statements, which nevertheless press for wholeness and an overcoming of the inner division characteristic of mental consciousness, needs to be taken into account. Jung commits his own characteristic *petitio principii* in relation to the *privatio boni* doctrine. He is not really willing to take into account the philosophical context of the argument, but recasts it 'a priori' within his 'Kantian', 'psychological–gnostic' context. One therefore cannot but agree with Gebser when he writes:

> The danger exists that all this [Jung's Quaternity and by extension, his ethical position] is taken as too binding, too determining, but this should, because of the psychic constellation and its psychological interpretation, never be the case, because everything psychological is, from a rational point of view, largely non-binding (*unverbindlich*).
>
> (Gebser 2003: 534, trans.)

With this necessary and important caveat in mind, we will now turn to Jung's psychological position on the integration of evil. The Gnostic *annoetos theos* appears in Jung's *Seven Sermons to the Dead* as the *pleroma*, a notion that has its actual source in the *gnosis* of Basilides (see Quispel in Segal 1992: 225). *Pleroma*, which is similar to Boehme's *Ungrund*, is, for Jung, a poetic, Gnostic term for the unconscious in its unknowable aspect (Segal 1992: 35ff.). The *pleroma* is at the same time nothingness and fullness: it is infinite. 'A thing that is infinite and eternal hath no qualities, since it hath all qualities' (Segal 1992: 182). The qualities of the *pleroma* form balanced pairs of opposites which cancel each other out and thus remain 'unmanifest', i.e. unconscious. They become distinguished in *creatura*, which is characterized as 'distinctiveness'. 'Distinctiveness is *creatura*. It is distinct. Distinctiveness is its essence, and therefore it distinguishes' (Segal 1992: 183). This natural striving of the creature for distinctiveness is called the *principium individuationis*. Distinctiveness and consciousness are mutually interchangeable here, while the *principium individuationis* equates closely to the ego as the centre of consciousness. Consciousness distinguishes between the pairs of opposites within the *pleroma*, and in this way the qualities become manifest.

This has a twofold effect. As qualities become manifest they become distinct and separate, and thus effective; they are no longer balanced and void as they are in the *pleroma* 'but are effective. Thus we are victims of the pairs of opposites. The *pleroma* is rent in us' (Segal 1992: 184). Thus, consciousness, by distinguishing between the opposites, disturbs the balance of the unconscious, and we become victims to the pairs of opposites.

Good and evil are the most potent of these opposites, and, as primal distinctions of the *pleroma*, they appear as God and devil. They are distinguished by 'the qualities of fullness and emptiness, generation and destruction' (Segal 1992: 186) and, due to their closeness to the *pleroma*, are characterized by the most intense numinosity or by a supreme 'effectiveness': 'EFFECTIVENESS is common to them both. Effectiveness joineth them. Effectiveness, therefore standeth above both; is a god above god, since in its effect it uniteth fullness and emptiness' (ibid.). 'Effectiveness' is Jung's *psychological*–epistemological *ens realissimum*. Effectiveness and numinosity are interchangeable terms. Beyond this, we are faced with the unknowable *pleroma*.

The problem with consciousness is that while it is still weak, it gets caught up in the opposites. The ego strives for the good and tries to avoid evil, and by so doing it implicitly ascribes these qualities to itself instead of to the *pleroma*/unconscious. But

> these qualities belong to the *pleroma*, and only in the name and sign of distinctiveness can and must we possess or live them. We must distinguish ourselves from these qualities. In the *pleroma* they are balanced and void; in us not. Being distinguished from them delivereth us.
>
> (Jung in Segal 1992: 184)

Here, then, we find, couched in mythical–Gnostic language, the raw material for Jung's psychological position. It elucidates for us the meaning of the demand for the 'integration of evil'. To integrate evil means to become conscious of it as a numinous factor within the unconscious, a factor of equal potency to the good. By becoming conscious of it one can distinguish oneself from it, so that evil is not acted out, but consciously taken up as one's cross. To do so, one has to move from the initial 'projective' mode of the operation of consciousness (involving the differentiation between the opposites) to the 'integrative' mode of the operation of consciousness, as it becomes manifest through the transcendent function. To individuate means to realize one's own unique distinctiveness, which, as consciousness, is the very factor that delivers us from being taken over by the opposites. Individual uniqueness that results from the individuating activity of the transcendent function is the *tertium datur*.

Even after having said all this, Neumann's formulation ('evil done consciously by the ego') still remains problematic. Either it has to be regarded as unacceptable on ethical grounds, or we are actually dealing with two different meanings of evil here. Ann Lammers talks in this context of the 'evil of myth' and 'historical evil' as a necessary distinction that Jung himself never makes, but which is indispensable if we are to understand his writings on this subject (Lammers 1994: 180ff.). This distinction is very helpful.

The evil of myth is archetypal, and relates to the pre-rational, imaginal level of mythic consciousness. This is the level on which the 'metaphysics of the unconscious' of the *sermons* operates. On this level, 'evil and good are in some mysterious sense left hand and right hand . . . they are eternally balanced like left and right' (Lammers 1994: 180). Historical evil is a wholly different matter, and the only reaction to it can be outrage, a reaction which Jung frequently displays. On this basis, Lammers asserts that 'what constitutes "the fourth" for Jung may be mythic evil; it may be the *consciousness* of historical evil. But it cannot be the evil of history itself' (Lammers 1994: 182). This also must apply to Neumann's otherwise totally unacceptable ethical demand. Neumann's formulation served us here only as a means to epitomize the possible misunderstandings and dangerous ambiguities of the ethical consequences of Jung's psychology.

The 'Satan' that Jung places into his 'Quaternity', precisely because it is integrated into this structure of wholeness, no longer has the characteristics of the Christian devil, but possesses the mythical qualities of the dark side displayed by the alchemical *Mercurius*. Although *Mercurius* 'is indeed the dark, chthonic half' he is nevertheless not 'simply evil as such, for he is called "good *and* evil" or a "system of the higher powers in the lower" ' (Jung 1943/1948: para. 271). And so the opposition good–evil appears psychologically–mythologically in Jung, not metaphysically. In his psychology of individuation, Jung posits, like Berdyaev, that 'the sabbath is for man and not man for the sabbath', i.e. the unique individuality, the essential core of the person, is superior to the general law, and this uniqueness has to be consciously realized on the difficult 'middle path'. By travelling along this path the ego gradually, as consciousness increases, becomes the carrier of the opposites. By focusing *exclusively* on this psychological dimension, Jung arrived at his 'psychological–Gnostic' view of evil.

J. Gebser sees in Boehme one of the seers who have seen into the polarity fundamental to the psyche. The psyche is, as the Tao-symbol expresses it, fundamentally characterized by a polarity encompassed in a unity. In it, darkness and light are one. But Gebser goes on to say:

> I am of the opinion that the unity of the soul represents *not* the spiritual, but merely a fundamental condition of the *noema*, i.e. of spiritual insight. As long as we are thrown back and forth by the contradictions of the soul, there can be no question of a conscious *noema*.
>
> (Gebser 1999b: 68, trans.)

This necessity for psychological integration constitutes Jung's exclusive focus. But we might say that in Boehme and in Berdyaev (who developed Boehme more philosophically) a breakthrough to spiritual insight happens, which opens the 'closed circle of psychologism' while allowing us to retain what is valuable in Jung's psychological insights. True, the psychological integration, which Jung's psychology seeks to foster, is a fundamental condition of spiritual insight. But from Berdyaev's and Boehme's perspective it ought not to be allowed to swallow up the spiritual dimension. For Boehme, the alchemical process leads not to a complexio oppositorum of good and evil but rather to a *separation* of good and evil:

> Let us not read Boehme as dreaming of an 'integration' which would make the sum of light and shadow. Sophia is not the monstrous hermaphrodite

> in which the opposites are reunited. The totality which it represents is not the reunion of day and night. The plenitude of the eternal virgin does not appear before the light and the shadows are definitely separated. This separation is the final aim of the *great work*.
>
> (Deghaye 1985: 290, trans.)

After the soul has passed through the trials of freedom it reunites itself to its eternal image in God, while the dark shadows born from the deranged imagination of irrational freedom return to the nothingness from which they rose. This is the passage to superconsciousness, possible only by divine grace, which for Berdyaev takes the form of the creative struggle for a *universal apocathastasis* because 'everyone is responsible for everyone else'[12].

Chapter 8

Conclusion: Moving beyond the pre/trans fallacy

The argument I have presented in this book hinges on the fundamental thesis that Jung's psychology of individuation is driven to engage profoundly with philosophical and theological issues because it has as its central theme the mystery of the person. At the heart of the human person lies a spiritual dimension which cannot be entirely encompassed by depth psychology but transcends its limits. The reason for this is that the category of the person is, in the last analysis, a religious (or spiritual) one. Jung's psychology is therefore constantly pushed beyond the limits of psychology as such. This movement beyond the limits of psychology takes in Jung's thought the form of the creation of a psychological myth. By taking on this mythopoeic character, his psychology ends up 'sublating' philosophy and theology. To Jung's mind we live in a time when 'we are coming to something which Nietzsche foresaw – the rise of psychology in its own right, so much so that it is even threatening to swallow philosophy' (Jung 1931: para. 659) and, we may add, theology. Jung's psychological myth, which takes shape before this background, takes the conceptual form of his Kant-based psychological idealism.

This is where the relevance of Berdyaev's philosophy lies for an interpretation of Jung. Berdyaev's existential thought, precisely because it affirms that '[k]nowledge *is* spiritual life and a part of the reality which is being known' (Berdyaev 1945a: 9) remains close to the psychological position of Jung while at the same time opening the possibility for a differentiation of the spiritual and the psychological dimensions. From this perspective, which Berdyaev's thought opens out, I have tried to offer a critical assessment of Jung's psychology and its tendency towards establishing itself as a new 'psychological religion', which persists as long as such a differentiation does not happen.

The argument for differentiating psychological and spiritual experience as two inseparable dimensions of existential experience that I have made hinges on Berdyaev's trichotomic understanding of the person as a union of body, soul and spirit. We have seen that, for Berdyaev, the person in its essence is a personal spirit which realizes itself as a person by shaping the psychosomatic unity of body and soul according to its unique *Gestalt*, which is, as the *imago*

Dei in man, a pre-existent whole. It is noteworthy what Jung has to say about this (platonic) trichotomic understanding:

> Into this ancient trichotomy, the elevation of the spirit to a divinity has introduced a certain *disorder*, thus *disturbing the equilibrium*. A further complication was caused by the identification of the pneumatic divinity with the *summum bonum*, which forcibly led to matter slipping into the vicinity of the *malum*. These theological entanglements must be avoided in my opinion, *and the psyche must be given a middle or superior position*.
>
> (Meier 2001: 126, emphasis mine)

Much of this book has revolved around exploring the implications of this difference in emphasis between Jung and Berdyaev: whereas the 'existential point of gravity' for Berdyaev is in the spirit, for Jung it is in the psyche. Berdyaev's focus on the spirit means an openness to the trans-psychic while Jung's focus on the psyche is coupled with the establishment of an 'epistemological barrier' against the spiritual. It appears to me that this choice of locating the 'point of gravity' in the psyche is not necessitated by psychology as such. In principle it could just as well be considered purely as a methodological principle for psychology rather than a fundamental 'philosophical' thesis. In Jung's case, though, it *does* constitute an existential–philosophical position-taking, even if it is one that is motivated by therapeutic considerations. It therefore can be challenged on existential–philosophical grounds. Jung's position carries an ambiguity with it. While he denies that analytical psychology is itself a *Weltanschauung* and claims that it can only potentially contribute to the formation of one, his psychology operates somewhat like a Trojan horse which carries with it huge philosophical and religious claims and implications under the humble guise of 'empirical science'. Formulated more positively one can say that Jung's psychology is so imbued by a 'religious' devotion to soul that it becomes something different to what is understood by the term science at present.

I have called this 'existential–philosophical' decision that Jung the psychologist–philosopher makes 'psychological reduction', corresponding to what I have termed 'anthropological reduction' in Berdyaev. Just as this leads for Berdyaev to an existential focus that establishes the human person as the source of his philosophy, so for Jung it is the soul that becomes central. The conception of a 'total personality', the Self, becomes for him the organizing principle for his holistically oriented psychology. I placed these existential–philosophical positions within the wider context of the decline of the 'old metaphysics' and the rise of modern philosophical anthropology.

Along these lines I attempted to interpret the use that Jung and Berdyaev made of Kant's philosophy. For Jung, Kant's epistemology becomes the foundation stone for his exclusive focus on psychological experience and for the affirmation of its absolute priority, which allows him to extend the range of psychology beyond all boundaries. For Berdyaev, Kant's philosophy becomes the foundation for his existential metaphysics, which bases itself on spiritual experience and seeks to move beyond the boundaries of an objectifying rationalistic consciousness.

Connected with this are the differences between Jung's and Berdyaev's understanding of the unconscious. Berdyaev repeatedly emphasizes the need to distinguish a superconscious and a subconscious within the unconscious, and designates the dimension of the superconscious as that of the spirit. 'Spirit is not the same thing as consciousness, but consciousness is formed through spirit and through it, again, reaches superconsciousness' (Berdyaev 1946: 35). The awakening of the personal spirit implies an active-creative transcension of the boundaries of objectified consciousness into the existential dimension of the *noumenon*, of freedom, deemed inaccessible by Kant. This breakthrough is a matter of experience, not of abstract academic debate. For Berdyaev it happened in the form of an illumination that shattered the very foundations of his being.

Jung on the other hand, like Kant, does not allow for such a possibility. His understanding of the unconscious as also containing a 'superconscious' has a different meaning, which is critically assessed by Ken Wilber in his notion of the Pre/trans fallacy. According to Wilber, this fallacy occurs because

> Since the *pre*rational and the *trans*rational are both, in their own ways, *non*rational, then they appear quite similar or even identical. . . . Once this confusion occurs . . . then one of two things inevitably happens: the transrational realms are *reduced* to prepersonal status, or the prerational realms are *elevated* to transrational glory.
>
> (Wilber 1996: 199)

In Jung the superconscious is truly unconscious, i.e. 'prerational': it is confounded with the archaic and numinous, which attain the status of what is quintessentially religious.[1] It is nevertheless not really false reasoning that leads to this confusion in Jung's case but rather his deep conviction that the psyche must be given the superior position over the spirit. This leads him to reject a 'superconscious' in Berdyaev's meaning of the term. This is, one could say, Jung's fundamental existential stance – one may even say, his religious passion.

In contradistinction to Jung's existential stance Berdyaev affirms that a 'pneumatology' has to be conceived which complements the psychological viewpoint in order to really understand the human person. It adds a necessary 'fourth dimension' to the otherwise naturalistic–objectifying perspective:

> The 'Euclidian rationality' is limited within three dimensions. But the meaning of the divine world can only be known if one enters into the

> fourth dimension. Freedom is a truth of the fourth dimension; within three-dimensionality it remains inaccessible.
>
> (Berdyaev 1925: 71, trans.)

Jung, from his empirical–phenomenological point of view, can only suggest the hypothesis of the objective reality of the archetypal psyche, which, among other things, also produces such ideas as that of a 'divine world' as a 'psychological fact' quite independently of its ontological status. In this respect Jung consistently sees himself obliged to practise 'phenomenological *epoche*'. This *epoche* gives exclusive priority to the psychological *intentio obliqua* and does not allow for an *intentio recta* which would presuppose a 'space of truth' beyond the psychological in which the question 'is this really so?' would make sense. Psychological reality is just so and the question of truth remains 'bracketed'. This 'space of truth' is, in Berdyaev's perspective, the 'fourth dimension' of freedom, of the spirit. The human spirit cannot obliterate the question of existential truth without obliterating its awareness of itself. Nature is just so, while the reference to truth brings in the dimension of values in such a way that one cannot rest content with natural processes which are 'just so'.

From the viewpoint of the psyche *qua* nature the principle of polarity assumes precedence over the existential viewpoint, which places psychological processes within the context of the 'fourth dimension' of freedom. Therefore Jung asserts that

> [t]he 'way' is not an upward going straight line f.i. from Earth to Heaven or from matter to Spirit, but rather a *circumambulatio* of and an approximation to the *Centrum*. We are not liberated by leaving something behind, but only by fulfilling our task as *mixta composita* i.e. human beings between the opposites. . . . Materialism denies God, and spiritualism denies creation, i.e. the will of God in Christian terminology. 'Homo Sapiens' has to envisage both. That was the great discovery of 'Mater Alchimia'.
>
> (Jung 1976: 396)

We can now see how this 'alchemical–psychological view' of Jung is founded on his epistemological premises, which are in turn motivated by his positing of the psyche, not the spirit, as the 'existential point of gravity' for modern man, who has to find a solution to the historical conflict between medieval spiritualism and modern materialism. However deeply Jung was engaged with the 'Christian archetype', due to its great importance for the understanding of the 'secret of personality', in the end it is not the (to his mind) 'medieval' Christian spirituality that he seeks to renew. Rather, the new religious attitude for modern man is, for him, the one deriving from psychological consciousness, which was 'unconsciously prefigured and anticipated in alchemy, which showed clear signs of becoming a religion of the Holy Ghost and the *Sapientia Dei*' (Jung 1955/1956: para. 531). In his interpretation of Christian revelation we see him consistently attempting to recast Christian images and symbols in terms of his fundamental insight of the *mysterium coniunctionis*, which, in relation to personality, he expresses when saying that 'Personality is Tao' (Jung 1934: para. 323).

We have also observed certain alchemical motifs in Berdyaev, and I pointed out in my introduction that J. Trinick places Berdyaev in the context of the line of development of the *mysterium coniunctionis* which begins in alchemy and culminates, in Trinick's view, with Jung's final book, *Mysterium Coniunctionis*. Berdyaev's thought cannot be cast as the medieval sort of spiritualism Jung has in mind but develops the *mysterium coniunctionis* in its own way, which is in line with the tradition of the Christian interpretation of alchemy, Christian Theosophy as we find it in Boehme, Kunrath and Dorn. Berdyaev's personalism does not set up a dualism of spirit and matter but posits a transformation of soul and body into the divine likeness through the personal and personalizing spirit. The human person is a unity of body, soul and spirit and this unity we could say is, on the psychological level, the sought for *lapis* of the alchemists.

In another letter to J. Trinick Jung unmistakably clarifies his position on a Christian interpretation of alchemy and therefore, by implication, also on a Christian 'religion of the Holy Ghost and the *Sapientia Dei*', of which we find elements in Russian Sophiology and in Berdyaev. It is clear, he writes to Trinick, that 'you naturally prefer a so-called Christian interpretation of alchemistical thought, understanding it *as an attempt at a spiritualization of chthonic forces*' (Jung 1976: 400ff., emphasis mine). This is also how I have interpreted Berdyaev's 'alchemical' ethics of creativity, which attempts a transformation of the chthonic elements instead of their rejection. Jung concedes that such an interpretation is 'certainly in accord with the general character of medieval alchemy' (ibid.). Since

> historical Christian psychology thinks rather of suppression of evil than of a *complexio boni et mali* . . . alchemy tried the idea of a certain *transformation of evil* with a view to its future integration. In this way it was rather a continuation of Origen's thought that even the devil may be ultimately redeemed, a thought discouraged by the Church.
>
> (ibid.)

This is a thought which Berdyaev passionately defended (albeit not in the way in which it was ascribed to Origen) and which underlies his ethics of creativeness. But Jung thinks that in the end 'alchemy really had a different goal in mind', inasmuch as

> the lapis derives from a synthesis of the opposites, which the dogmatic Christ is definitely not. For these reasons *I cannot agree with the Christian interpretation of the alchemistic procedure*. On the contrary, I see in alchemy the attempt at a *different solution*, namely to bring about the union of the opposites which is lacking in the historical Christian doctrine.
>
> (ibid., emphasis mine)

It is at this point that we seem to meet an irreconcilable difference between Jung and Berdyaev's positions. I discussed this ethical issue (transformation of evil versus integration of evil in the sense of a *complexio boni et mali*) in detail in the last chapter.

Fundamentally, what underlies these different ethical stances is a different understanding of the person: for Berdyaev it is essentially Divine–human, whereas for Jung it is 'Tao', i.e. a *complexio oppositorum* symbolized by the alchemists in the *Lapis*. In both cases dualism is overcome by integrality, but in different ways.

And what underlies these different understandings of the person are different understandings of God. In Berdyaev's case the Trinitarian God of Christian tradition and in Jung's case the 'becoming God' who, initially unconscious comes to consciousness through humanity itself. Jung's God is ultimately an idealistic, Hegelian God and the criticism which V. Soloviev applied to Hegel equally applies to Jung: 'Hegel recognized quite accurately the immanent power of the absolute idea in man and the world, which moves the world process and unfolds itself through it, but he confused without reason this world soul with the absolute itself' (Soloviev 1965: 101, trans.). I have called this immanent world soul in these pages at times the alchemical Sophia.

But are these differences really irreconcilable? On one level they clearly are. From Berdyaev's perspective, Jung's psychological idealism, which leads to an identification of the 'anima mundi' with God, has to be rejected. Inasmuch as it constitutes a quasi-philosophical thesis it has to be criticized on this basis and it also has to be rejected as an illegitimate transgression of the boundaries of psychology. We have heard that for Berdyaev the existential –philosophical critique of the pantheistic position of German idealism which resurfaces in Jung's psychological myth is that it leads at one and the same time to a deification of man (because it is only in man that 'God' becomes conscious) and to a repudiation of man (because the distinctly human, personal element is obliterated and absorbed into the pantheistic world-process as its instrument and medium).

But what happens if we look at Jung's perspectives primarily as psychological interventions while taking his 'psychological myth' with more than a grain of salt? Then things look different. Then we may be able to push open the door that Jung's Kantianism threatens to keep shut. Have we not already suggested a way to reconcile Jung and Berdyaev's perspectives by referring to Gebser's statement that while the unity of soul gained through individuation is not the spiritual, its realization at least to some degree nevertheless constitutes a fundamental precondition for the emergence of the spiritual? This would suggest that by limiting the potential 'totalitarian' claim of Jung's psychology, its complementarity to the kind of spirituality that Berdyaev proposes becomes clearly evident, which returns us to the coniunctio motif so strongly emphasized by Trinick. To address the whole person, not only does psychology need the spiritual, but spirituality needs the sort of psychological refinement Jung's psychology has to offer.

Arie Sborowitz has offered an interpretation of the concept of *teshuva*, the Jewish word for repentance, which aims at precisely such a reconciliation. In the Old Testament this term implies a total turning around of the whole existence of the person, a total change of heart. His thesis is that for modern man *teshuva* has to be conceived in a new way as a complex, two-phased phenomenon, which unites in itself two seemingly irreconcilable, diametrically opposed movements. Sborowitz follows Gebser's diagnosis of modern rational consciousness as gradually having turned from something positive into something destructive from the beginning of the Renaissance onwards. According to Gebser such deteriorations of established structures of consciousness are indicative of imminent mutations. Rational consciousness either turns more and more destructive or mutates into integral consciousness, and this does not happen automatically by a 'process of evolution' but involves a profound psychological–spiritual crisis of present-day humanity.

In this situation the first movement of *teshuva* is one of apparent regression, i.e. of a reconnecting to one's instinctive roots, to soul, to mythical consciousness. It is a going backward that allows a renewed moving forward, a Dionysian descent into the underworld for the sake of renewal. On this level the mythical language in relation to the integration of opposites has its appropriate place.

But once one has reconnected to that place of soul, to one's heart, another movement becomes necessary in which one becomes existentially aware of one's freedom. The renewal has to follow the descent. The *nous* in the heart has to be awakened. This happens through authentic experiences of genuine responsibility and existential guilt: Everybody is responsible for everybody else. Sborowitz interprets Gebser's notion of integral consciousness in terms of an existentially authentic realization of the 'Christ within'. Integral consciousness would then be, as Gebser himself puts it, an 'intensified Christianity' which moves from symbolization to realization in Berdyaev's sense. While Christianity as confessional religion might seem largely dead (at least in the west), the true spirit of Christianity may enter, as Berdyaev assumed, into a new phase of realization:

> The man who becomes reborn . . . enters thereby into an inner communion with the person of Christ . . . By experiencing something of

> this communion, he becomes filled with the specific spirituality which emanates as *agape* from the figure of Jesus. It is *this* which constitutes a new consciousness in him. It is . . . the integral consciousness.
>
> (Sborowitz 1975: 113, trans.)

What is now awakening is love as agape, enabling the capacity for integral consciousness. Sborowitz identifies two aspects of integral consciousness:

- The capacity of vision through personal love leading to transparency
- Freedom and maximal responsibility.

Gebser's conception of vision is that of a capacity for spiritual perception outside what Berdyaev calls the sphere of objectification. Berdyaev's thought as a whole seeks to give expression to this capacity, to a new participatory epistemology. It has nothing at all to do with seeing pictures or mythic imagination, but it nevertheless implies the existence of a synthetic capacity to integrate different levels of consciousness (archaic, magical, mythic, rational). This capacity belongs to what Gebser calls *noema*, the spiritual, as opposed to the rational. The spiritual becomes manifest as an integrative capacity precisely when there is an emerging ability to 'disidentify' from the mental–rational *without* regressing into the pre-rational. It discloses the other and the world in their *diaphanous*, non-objectified nature. Man and world become transparent for the divine. The capacity for vision is creative, transformative. Thus:

> The man of integral consciousness does increasingly no longer experience himself as the ego, which wants to possess and to experience (and adapts itself for precisely that reason), but as a Self which, united to something higher becomes transparent for it, surrenders to it and becomes creative in this surrender.
>
> (Sborowitz 1975: 117)

But the notion of integral consciousness implies that all of this happens consciously and with a maximal awareness of freedom and creative responsibility. This includes the ethical position of Jung's psychology, which stresses the importance of a conscious integration of the shadow.

But as an element of integral consciousness this integration is placed within the broader existential context of the ethics of creativity, in which the person becomes creative in her surrender to the universally creative force of Love. One feels deeper and deeper that 'everyone is responsible for everyone else'. God as the God of wrath, the 'seething lake of fire' is a miasma; it evaporates like the morning mist in the new dawn. Fear of God remains but it is the fear to be separated from love.

Notes

1 Introduction

1 I will be using the terms 'person' and 'personality' interchangeably, even though it would be more correct to use the term 'person' throughout.
2 R. Panikkar's notion of theandrism is very useful in characterizing the open understanding of Christian spirituality which is intended here. Panikkar writes: 'I am not denying that my interpretation of Theandrism is in reality Trinitarian and Christian, but I want to clarify that my interpretation of Theandrism does not inhere principally only in the Christian faith nor is it only shaped by it. Theandrism is present as the final goal towards which the religious consciousness of the whole of humanity aspires, as well as the accurate interpretation of every mystical experience in which religious experience culminates' (Panikkar 1993: 100).
3 See F. Deporteere's book: *Christ in Postmodern Philosophy* (2008).
4 Personal communication.
5 After Joachim of Fiore (1135–1202), a Calabrian abbot who predicted the imminent dawn of the age of the Holy Spirit and was condemned as a heretic by the church but placed into paradise in Dante's *Divine Comedy*.
6 Jean Gebser (1905–1975) was a philosopher of culture who lived and taught for part of his life in Switzerland, including at the the Jung Institute.

2 Berdyaev's life

1 See Hans Jonas' book *Gnosis und Spätantiker Geist* (1934) on the links between Gnosticism and existentialism.
2 'Compared with the animal which always says yes to reality (zum Wirklichsein) . . . man is "the one who can say no", the "ascetic of life", the eternal protestant against all sheer reality (gegen alle blosse Wirklichkeit)' (Scheler 1930: 65, trans.).

3 An introduction to Berdyaev's philosophy

1 The specific nuance of meaning of the term *Weltanschauung* as it is intended here can be traced back to German idealism. There the *Weltanschauung* of the individual was seen as ultimately rooted in a universally human, absolute self-consciousness. Behind this lies the mystical conception of *Zentralschau* ('vision from the centre' i.e. the heart's capacity for intuitive, participatory knowledge) in Boehme, Hahn, Oetinger and the Flemish mystic Johannes van Ruysbroeck (see Benz 1955a and 1955b).

2 Any notion of nationalism has to be absolutely excluded here.
3 Berdyaev's understanding of eschatological Christianity is that of a Christianity of the spirit, which is characterized by a shift from an externalized symbolic expression of spirituality to its full embodiment.
4 Compare this with von Franz:

> As far as we at present can understand the process of individuation, the Self apparently tends to produce such small groups by creating at the same time sharply defined ties of feeling between certain individuals and feelings of relatedness to all people.
>
> (in Jung 1990: 223)

This would be the psychological basis for a 'social projection of personalism'.
5 Arthur Versluis, a scholarly authority in the field, considers Berdyaev as 'without doubt the most important and original theosopher of the twentieth century' (Versluis 2000: 261).
6 For the eastern mind theosophy is less exotic and more easily linked to its theological tradition. Soloviev could talk of the theology of the Greek fathers of the church such as Gregory of Nyssa as a theosophy. If one does not go as far as disregarding 'experience, pure thought . . . tradition and authority' but 'nevertheless considers the inner communion of the human spirit with the absolute as the essential basis, then doctrines emerge which one can, depending on whether the religious or the philosophical element in them takes priority, call mystical theology, mystical philosophy or theosophy' (Soloviev 1965: 344ff., trans.)
7 Tillich emphasizes Berdyaev's self-understanding as a theosopher, insisting that his philosophy cannot really be called a philosophy of religion if this is meant to imply an objective, detached perspective on religion 'outside of any concrete religion'.

> On the other hand, Berdyaev's work is not theology, inasmuch as theology is seen as the traditional explication of ecclesial Dogma. Berdyaev himself calls his type of thought 'theosophy' and means by this a free further development of ecclesial doctrines in the spirit of a speculative metaphysics and mystical intuition. This mode of thought can be seen as the characteristic and most valuable contribution of the Greek Church to the religious thought of the present age. Berdyaev adopted it from the great Russian thinkers of the nineteenth century, above all from his teacher Soloviev.
>
> (Tillich 1971 290ff.)

8 Athanasios, De Incarnat. 54: 25, 192b; see also Ireneus, Adv. Haer. 3, 10, 2: 7, 875: 'ut fieret filius hominis, ad hoc ut et homo fieret filius Dei'.
9 For Schelling's influence on Khomyakov, Kireevsky and Soloviev see Zenkovsky 2003: 185, 210–211, 496.
10 See Note 2, Chapter 1.
11 Nevertheless, this vision for Berdyaev never implied a rupture with the existing, visible Church.
12 'The task of art in its completeness as free theurgy consists . . . in transforming reality and to replace the external relations of the divine, human and natural element, in all and everything by the inner organic unity of these three principles' (Soloviev 1978: 517).
13 Berdyaev criticizes Soloviev for not remaining entirely true to his own insight that 'being', i.e. the fundamental category of all rational thought, is not a subject, but 'a predicate only . . . In reality the subject of philosophy ought not to be being in general but that to whom being belongs, the existent' (Berdyaev 1992: 186).

14 The term 'anthropological reduction' has been used by M. Buber to characterize Feuerbach's thought.
15 See Zenkovsky 2003: 560ff.
16 See J. Hillman's introduction to Carus 1970.

4 Person in Jung and Berdyaev

1 See Scheler 1973: 396ff.
2 See von Franz 1965.
3 Leibnitzian Monads are 'centres which express an infinite circumference' (Mahnke 1937: 17, trans.; see also Jung 1951: para. 340ff. and Jung 1955/1956: paras 36–50).
4 Jung discusses this mandala in *Archetypes and the Collective Unconscious* (1934/1954: para. 543ff.).
5 For the historical development of this archetypal image, see Mahnke (1937) and von Franz (1980b: 60–61): 'On the other hand, yet another historical process in the use of the sphere-image took place: its increasingly psychological interpretation. To be sure, the image is still applied almost conventionally by Fichte to the Godhead, but at the same time it is also widely used to indicate a centrepoint of the personality to be found in the human being, a point Fichte describes as the "productive, creative ego" or the "absolute ego" (in contrast to the usual, empirical ego). The "infinite ego-substance" is again and again constantly taking on the specific form of the accidental ego. The latter, for its part, is always striving to extend itself asymptotically toward that ideal of the absolute ego. Hardenberg (Novalis) understands this Fichtean ideal ego more as an image of God within the individual. How closely these ideas approach to the Jungian concept of Self and ego is quite obvious.'
6 On the tragic as fundamental to Nietzsche, see Pfeffer 1972.
7 See Jung's reference to this same concept in Jung 1955/1956: para. 592.
8 See Jung 1943: para. 165ff.; Jung 1951: Ch. 13, 14; Jung 1955/1956: Ch. 4, 5, 6 (Rex as Anthropos); von Franz 1998: Ch. VI.
9 Scheler writes: 'the person is the concrete and essential unity of being and acts of different essences which in itself . . . precedes all essential act-differences . . . The being of the person is therefore the "foundation" of all essentially different acts' (Scheler 1973: 383). Berdyaev carried this understanding further than Scheler by using it to de-ontologize the person.
10 Compare with Scheler: 'Thus we can say that the person lives into time and executes his acts into time in becoming different. But the person does not live within phenomenal time which is immediately given in the flow of inwardly perceived psychic processes . . . Because the person lives his existence precisely in the experiencing of his possible experiences, it makes no sense to try to grasp the person in past lived experiences' (Scheler 1973: 385ff.).
11 See Jung 1947/1954: paras 421 ff., especially para. 429; cf. Shamdasani 2003: Ch. 1.
12 Hans Trueb reports a conversation with Jung on the subject of the role of the personal in his psychology where Jung stated: 'The personal for me is something so irrational and contingent, that I cannot do anything with it – I cannot help myself in any other way than to remove it from my eyes' (Trueb 1962: 40, trans.).
13 See Jung 1939: para. 527; 1957b: para. 544.
14 Schiller wrote, in a letter to Goethe: 'From simple organisation you ascend step by step to the more complicated ones to finally construct the most complicated of all genetically [not of course to be understood in the modern biological sense!] out of the materials of the whole edifice of nature' (Leisegang 1932: 21, trans.).
15 See also Edinger 1990.

16 See Edinger 1984, and Jung's 'late thoughts' in *Memories, Dreams, Reflections* (1995).
17 On the therapeutic significance of play, see also Winnicott 2001.
18 The term 'nature' is always meant in the Romantic sense in this analysis, as it is derived from Schelling's 'Naturphilosophie'.
19 Jung 1947/1954: para. 352, 356, 369 n35; 1944: para. 397.

5 Esse in anima and the epistemology of the heart

1 'The essence of original participation is that there stands behind the phenomena, and on the other side of them from me, a represented which is of the same nature than me. Whether it is called mana or by the name of many gods and demons, or God the Father, or the spirit world, it is of the same nature than the perceiving self, inasmuch as it is not mechanical or accidental, but psychic and voluntary' (Barfield 1988: 42).
2 See Berdyaev 1938: Ch. 2.
3 The idea is 'a concept made up of notions, which goes beyond the possibility of experience, is an idea or a concept of reason' (Kant 1974: B 377, trans.).

6 Person and God image

1 See the work by Berdyaev's friend S. Bulgakov (2008).
2 See Chapter 3, p. 20.
3 The notion of the 'eye of the spirit' or 'the eye of contemplation' has a long history within Christian spirituality. See also Wilber 1996: 2ff.
4 See Hartshorne 1957.
5 This is an expression used by M.A. Meerson (cf. Meerson 1998).
6 The Trinity, according to dogma, is three hypostases = persons in one ousia, ousia being the Greek word for 'substance'.
7 See L. Schlamm's article The Holy: A Meeting-Point between Analytical Psychology and Religion (in Ryce-Menuhin 1994).
8 Cf. Otto (1924: 170ff.) on Goethe's notion of the daemonic, in which the aspects of the numinous are clearly present: 'Goethe's intuition is not far from Hiob's' (ibid.: 171). On this see also Sborowitz 1975.
9 Otto uses the term numinosum to designate 'the Holy minus its ethical element and . . . minus its rational element' (Otto 1924: 6, trans.). Mysticism, in his view, is 'in its essence everywhere the highest tension and hypertension of the irrational element in religion' (ibid.: 22).
10 Stein rightly points out that the Paracelsian conception of the lumen naturae, which can accomplish the union of light (the spiritual) and darkness (the body, nature, the unconscious), 'contains the key for understanding Jung's own writings on Christian doctrine and tradition, because it states the goal of his psychotherapy: not the separation but the union of the two natures, body and spirit' (Stein 1986: 112).
11 Cf. Jung 1942/1948: para. 268, trans.: 'These formulations [about the Trinity and the Quaternity] can – and even have to for scientific reasons – be reduced to man and his psychology, because they are products of the human spirit which cannot be endowed with metaphysical validity.'
12 Cf. Jung 1951: para. 73ff.
13 Jung continues the sentence in a way which seems to leave a door open: 'though this does not, of course, tell us what else it might be. That lies outside the province of science' (Jung 1938: para. 127). Yet my argument in these pages is that, if this

'what else it might be' is, for epistemological reasons, unknowable not only for psychology but in principle, it becomes irrelevant and what remains are psychological projections and the psyche as their source. Any genuine form of transcendence is excluded.

7 Individuation and the ethics of creativity

1 See for this the study by F. Nucho (Nucho 1966).

2 According to Bachofen these are the haeteric–gyneocratic stage, the matriarchal stage and the patriarchal stage.

3 Similar ideas can also be found in Franz von Baader's 'erotic philosophy' (see Faivre 1994: 201–274).

4 'To-day . . . we must have the saintliness demanded by the present moment, a new saintliness, itself without precedent . . . The world needs saints who have genius, just as a plague-stricken town needs doctors. Where there is a need there is also an obligation' (Letter VI, *Waiting on God*: 45–46, quoted in Perrin and Thibon 2003: 100ff.).

5 Next to Jacob Boehme, Paracelsus, G. Dorn and H. Kunrath can be named here (see Faivre 2000: 6ff.).

6 'The original meaning of "to have a vocation" is "to be addressed by a voice" ' (Jung 1934: para. 301).

7 Freud talks of 'a differentiation within the ego, which may be called the "ego-ideal" or "super-ego" ' (Freud 1961: 28). In his view '[a]s a child grows up, the role of the father is carried on by teachers and others in authority; their injunctions and prohibitions remain powerful in the ego ideal and continue, in the form of conscience, to exercise censorship' (ibid.: 37). See the whole of chapter III: 'The Ego and the Super-Ego' (Freud 1961: 28–39) and also *Totem and Taboo* (Freud 1955: 67–70).

8 J. Beebe, in his book *Integrity in Depth*, makes a powerful case for reclaiming these rejected 'puritan' qualities in a psychologically intelligent way, i.e. as 'symptoms of integrity' (Beebe 1992: 69).

9 'To-day . . . we must have the saintliness demanded by the present moment, a new saintliness, itself without precedent . . . The world needs saints who have genius, just as a plague-stricken town needs doctors. Where there is a need there is also an obligation' (Letter VI, *Waiting on God*: 45–46, quoted in Perrin and Thibon 2003: 100ff.).

10 'I have never lost touch with my initial experiences. All my works, all my creative activity, has come from these initial fantasies and dreams . . . Everything that I accomplished in later life was already contained in them' (Jung 1995: 217).

11 Gebser has developed a model of five different structures of consciousness on the basis of extensive research into various fields of cultural history. These structures all have a different relation to the time–space continuum. The archaic structure is pre-temporal/pre-spacial and is thus 'zero-dimensional'; the magical structure is 'one-dimensional', i.e. space-timeless but already potentially spatio-temporal; the mythical structure is two dimensional, which means that it is spaceless but immersed in cyclical, mythological time; the mental structure is three dimensional; and the integral structure is four dimensional, i.e. time and space-free by integrating all the preceding structures (see Gebser 1978, 2003).

12 See Chances (2001) page 119: 'Dostoevesky's final novel *The Brothers Karamazov* . . . outlines two paths open to people. One is marked by western rational thought, isolation, individualism, egoism and literal or spiritual death. This is the path followed by Ivan Karamazov, who questions the very structure of God's universe

. . . His thought leads to a universe in which "everything is permitted". The other path is followed by his brother, Alesha, who does not rebel against God's order, who accepts the world as it is, who conforms to God's community. His path is marked by unconditional love and by an "everyone is responsible for everyone else" approach to life'.

8 Conclusion: Moving beyond the pre/trans fallacy

1 Not everyone accepts Wilber's criticism of Jung's thought. Michael Washburn for example endorses Jung's 'spiral paradigm' over against Wilber's 'ladder paradigm' (Washburn 1994: xiiff.) but, while accepting Jung's overall conception of the 'non-egoic core', reinterprets it inasmuch as he proposes a conception that understands its influences 'exclusively in a developmental sense. That is, it understands pre and trans as referring to stage-specific manifestations of non egoic potentials not, as typically is the case with Jung, to opposing sides or types of non-egoic potentials' (ibid.).

Bibliography

Arraj, J. (1986) *St John of the Cross and Dr. C.G. Jung*. Chiloquin: Inner Growth Books.

Assagioli, R. (1975) *Psychosynthesis*. Wellingborough: Turnstone Press.

Baader, F. (1987a) *Fermenta Cognitionis*. In Werke, Bd. II. Aalen: Scientia Verlag.

—— (1987b) *Vorlesungen ueber spekulative Dogmatik*. In Werke Bd. VIII, Bd. IX. Aalen: Scientia Verlag.

Bachofen, J. J. (1861) *Das Mutterrecht*. Stuttgart: Verlag Krais & Hoffmann.

Barfield, O. (1988) *Saving the Appearances, A Study in Idolatry*. New Hampshire: Wesleyan University Press.

Beebe, J. (1992) *Integrity in Depth*. Carolyn and Ernest Fay Series in Analytical Psychology II. Texas: A&M University Press.

Behr-Sigel, E. (2004) *Le Lieu du Coer. Initiation a la Spiritualite de l'Eglise Orthodoxe*. Paris: Editions du Cerf.

Benz, E. (1934) *Ecclesia Spiritualis*. Stuttgart: Kohlhammer Verlag.

—— (1955a) *Schelling's theologische Geistesahnen*. In Akademie der Wissenschaften und der Literatur. Geistes- und Sozialwissenschaftliche Klasse. Jahrg. 1955. Nr 1–8. Nr 3., pp 236–306.

—— (1955b) *Schelling*. Zuerich: Rhein-Verlag.

—— (1967) *Evolution and Christian Hope*. London: Victor Gollancz Ltd.

Berdyaev, N. (1925) *Die Weltanschauung Dostovievskijs*. Muenchen: C.H. Beck'sche Verlagsbuchhandlung.

—— (1928) 'The Metaphysical Problems of Freedom'. Internet document. Available at www.berdyaev.com/berdiaev/berd_lib/1928_329.html

—— (1932a) 'Studien ueber Jacob Boehme I: Jacob Boehme's Lehre vom Ungrund und von der Freiheit'. Internet document. Available at www.borisogleb.de/ungrund.html

—— (1932b) 'Studien ueber Jacob Boehme II: Die Lehre ueber Sophia and das Androgyne. J. Boehme und die Russische Sophiologische Stroemung'. Internet document. Available at www.borisogleb.de/boehme7.html

—— (1933) 'The New Middle Ages'. In *The End of our Time*. London: Sheed and Ward.

—— (1934) *Wahrheit und Luege des Kommunismus*. Luzern: Vita Nova Verlag.

—— (1935a) *Freedom and the Spirit*. London: Geoffrey Bles.

—— (1935b) *Das Schicksal des Menschen in unserer Zeit*. Luzern: Vita Nova Verlag.

—— (1936a) *Christentum und Klassenkampf*. Luzern: Vita Nova Verlag.
—— (1936b) 'The Problem of Man'. Internet document. Available at www.berdyaev.com/berdiaev/berd_lib/1936_408.html
—— (1938) *Solitude and Society*. London: Geoffrey Bles.
—— (1943) *Slavery and Freedom*. London: Geoffrey Bles.
—— (1945a) *The Destiny of Man*. London: Geoffrey Bles.
—— (1945b) *The Meaning of History*. London: Geoffrey Bles.
—— (1946) *Spirit and Reality*. London: Geoffrey Bles.
—— (1947) *Von der Wuerde des Christentums und von der Unwuerde der Christen*. Luzern: Vita Nova Verlag.
—— (1949a) *The Divine and the Human*. London: Geoffrey Bles.
—— (1949b) *Towards a New Epoch*. London: Geoffrey Bles.
—— (1950) *Dream and Reality*. London: Geoffrey Bles.
—— (1952) *The Realm of the Spirit and the Realm of the Cesar*. London: Victor Gollancz.
—— (1953a) *Truth and Revelation*. London: Geoffrey Bles.
—— (1953b) *Selbsterkenntnis*. Darmstadt: Holle Verlag. (This is the German version of *Dream and Reality* which I sometimes used where the English translation was incomplete.)
—— (1962) *The Meaning of the Creative Act*. New York: Collier Books.
—— (1976) *The Beginning and the End*. Westport: Greenwood Press (Reprint).
—— (1992) *The Russian Idea*. Hudson, NY: Lindisfarne Press.
—— (1998) Bambauer, K. & G. (eds.) *Wahrheit und Offenbarung*. Waltrop: Hartmut Spenner.
Bishop, P. (1995) *The Dionysian Self: C.G. Jung's Reception of Friedrich Nietzsche*. Berlin: De Gruyter.
—— (2000) *Synchronicity and Intellectual Intuition in Kant, Swedenborg and Jung*. Lampeter: Edwin Mellen Press.
Boehme, J. (1942) *Saemtliche Schriften, Faksimile-Neudruck der Ausgabe von 1730 Dritter Band, IV* [reprint of the 1730 edition, Vol. 3]. Stuttgart: Fr. Frommanns Verlag.
—— (1955/1960) *Saemtliche Schriften, Bd 1–11, Faksimile-Nachdruch der Ausgabe von 1730, neu herausgegeben von Will-Erich-Peuckert*. Stuttgart: Frommann-holzboog Verlag. (Quotations according to the numberings in this edition, which is a reprint of the edition by J.G. Gichtel.)
Bonardel, F. (1984) *Jung et L'Alchimie*. Paris: Cahiers de L'Herne.
—— (1985) *L'Hermetisme*. Paris: Presses Universitaires de France.
Bonner-Richardson, D. (1968) *Berdyaev's Philosophy of History*. The Hague: Martinus Nijhoff.
Brinton, H. (1931) *The Mystic Will. Based on a Study of the Philosophy of Jacob Boehme*. London: G. Allen & Unwin.
Buber, M. (1979) *Ich und Du*. Heidelberg: Verlag Lambert Schneider.
—— (1993) *Nachlese*. Heidelberg: Lambert Schneider Verlag.
—— (1994) *Gottesfinsternis*. Gerlingen: Verlag Lambert Schneider.
—— (2002) *Das Dialogische Prinzip*. Guetersloh: Guetersloher Verlags-Haus.
Bulgakov, S. (1993) *The Wisdom of God*. Hudson, NY: Lindisfarne Press.
—— (1998) *The Orthodox Church*. Crestwood, NY: St Vladimir's Seminary Press.
—— (2008) *The Lamb of God*. Grand Rapids, MI; Cambridge: William B. Eerdmans.

Carus, C.G. (1970) *Psyche: On the Development of the Soul. Pt 1: The Unconscious*. Dallas: Spring Publications.
—— (1975) *Psyche*. Darmstadt: Wissenschaftliche Buchgesellschaft.
Chances, E. (2001) 'The superfluous man in Russian literature. In Cornwell, N. (ed.), *The Routledge Companion to Russian Literature*. London & New York: Routledge (pp. 111–122).
Christou, E. (1976) *The Logos of the Soul*. Dallas: Spring Publications.
Clarke, O. F. (1950) *Introduction to Berdyaev*. London: Geoffrey Bles.
Clement, O. (1991) *Berdiaev, Un philosophe russe en France*. Paris: Desclee de Brouwer.
—— (2000) *On Human Being: A Spiritual Anthropology*. London: New City.
—— (2002) *The Roots of Christian Mysticism*. London: New City.
Corbin, H. (1984) *La Sophia Eternelle*. Paris: Les Cahiers de L'Herne.
Danielou, J. (ed.) (2001) *From Glory to Glory.Texts from Gregory of Nyssa's Mystical Writings*. New York: St Vladimir's Seminary Press.
Davy, M. M. (1991) *Nicolas Berdiaev: l'homme du huitième jour*. Paris: Éditions du Félin.
Deghaye, P. (1985) *La Naissance de Dieu ou la doctrine de Jacob Boehme*. Paris: Albin Michel, Collection Spiritualites Vivantes.
Deporteere, F. (2008) *Christ in Postmodern Philosophy*. London: T&T Clark.
Dietrich, W. (1975a) *Provokation der Person, Bd. 1, Nikolai Berdjajews Leben und Werk*. Berlin: Burckhardthaus Verlag.
—— (1975b) *Provokation der Person, Bd.2*. Berlin: Burckhardthaus Verlag.
—— (1975c) *Provokation der Person, Bd. 3*. Berlin: Burckhardthaus Verlag.
—— (1979) *Provokation der Person, Bd 5*. Berlin: Burckhardthaus Verlag.
Dilthey, W. (1957). In Kluback, W., & Weinbaum M. (eds.), *Dilthey's Philosophy of Existence: Introduction to Weltanschauungslehre*. Westport, CT: Greenwood Press.
Dostoyevsky, F. (1993) *The Brothers Karamazov*. London: Penguin Classics.
Dourley, J. P. (2001) 'Revisioning Incarnation: Jung on the Relativity of God', *Shim-Song Yon-Gu: Journal of the Korean Jung Institute, Vol. 16, No. 1, p.1–29*.
Edinger, E. (1984) *The Creation of Consciousness*. Toronto: Inner City Books.
—— (1985) *Anatomy of the Psyche*. Illinois: Open Court.
—— (1990) *Goethe's Faust. Notes for a Jungian Commentary*. Toronto: Inner City Books.
—— (1992) *Ego and Archetype*. London: Shambhala.
—— (1994) *The Mystery of the Coniunctio*. Toronto: Inner City Books.
—— (1995) *The Mysterium Lectures*. Toronto: Inner City Books.
—— (1996a) *The New God-Image*. Wilmette, IL: Chiron Publications.
—— (1996b) *The Aion Lectures*. Toronto: Inner City Books.
Ellenberger, H. F. (1994) *The Discovery of the Unconscious*. London: Fontana Press.
Epstein, M. N. (1995) *After the Future. The Paradoxes of Postmodernism & Contemporary Russian Culture*. Amherst: The University of Massachusetts Press.
—— & Berry, E. M. (1999) *Transcultural Experiments. Russian and American Models of Creative Communication*. New York: St Martin's Press.
Evdokimov, P. (1970) *Le Christ dans la Pensee Russe*. Paris: Editions du Cerf.
Faivre, A. (1994) *Access to Western Esotericism*. New York: SUNY Press.
—— (2000) *Theosophy, Imagination, Tradition*. New York: SUNY Press.

—— & Needleman, J. (eds.) (1995) *Modern Esoteric Spirituality*. New York: Crossroad.

Feuerbach, L. (1904) *Grundsaetze einer Philosophie der Zukunft* in *Werke, Bd. II. Philosophische Kritiken und Grundsaetze*. Stuttart: Fr. Frommanns Verlag, pp. 245–320.

—— (1956) *Das Wesen des Christentums*. Berlin: Akademie Verlag.

Florensky, P. (2004) *The Pillar and Ground of Truth*. Princeton: Princeton University Press.

Frensch, M. (2000) *Weisheit in Person. Das Dilemma der Philosophie und die Perspektive der Sophiologie*. Schaffhausen: Novalis Verlag.

Freud, S. (1955) *Totem and Taboo*. In *The Standard Edition of the Complete Psychological Works of Sigmund Freud, Vol. XIII*. London: The Hogarth Press.

—— (1960) *The Psychopathology of Everyday Life*. In *The Standard Edition of the Complete Psychological Works of Sigmund Freud, Volume VI*. London: The Hogarth Press.

—— (1961) 'The Ego, the Id and the Super-Ego'. In *The Standard Edition of the Complete Psychological Works of Sigmund Freud, Volume XIX*. London: The Hogarth Press.

Frey-Rohn, L. (1974) *From Freud to Jung*. New York: Putnam.

Gagnebin, L. (1994) *Nicolas Berdiaeff ou de la destination creatrice de l'homme*. Lausanne: L'Age d'Homme.

Gebser, J. (1978) *Ursprung und Gegenwart. Erster Teil*. Schaffhausen: Novalis Verlag.

—— (1999a) *Ursprung und Gegenwart. Kommentarband*. Schaffhausen: Novalis Verlag.

—— (1999b) *Vorlesungen und Reden zu 'Urspung und Gegenwart' V/1*. Schaffhausen: Novalis Verlag.

—— (2003) *Ursprung und Gegenwart. Zweiter Teil*. Schaffhausen: Novalis Verlag.

Giegerich, W. (1998) *Jung's Betrayal of his Truth. The Adoption of Kant-based Empiricism and the Rejection of Hegel's Speculative Thought*. *Harvest* Vol. 44, No 1.

—— (1999) *The Patriarchal Neglect of the Feminine Principle: A Psychological Fallacy in Jungian Theory*. *Harvest* Vol 45, No 1.

—— (2001) *The Soul's Logical Life*. Frankfurt A. M.: Peter Lang

—— (2005) *The Neurosis of Psychology. Primary Papers Towards a Critical Psychology*. New Orleans: Spring Journal Books.

Grunsky, H. (1956) *Jacob Boehme*. Stuttgart: Frommanns Verlag.

Habermas, J. (1958) 'Anthropologie'. In Diemer A. (ed.), *Das Fischer Lexikon: Philosophie*. Frankfurt A.M.: Fischer Buecherei.

Hall, J. A. (1991) 'The watcher at the gate of dawn: The transformation of the self in liminality and by the transcendent function'. In Schwartz-Salant, N., & Stein, M. (eds.), *Liminality and transitional phenomena*. Wilmette IL: Chiron, pp. 33–51.

Hannah, B. & von Franz, M. L. (2004) *Lectures on Jung's Aion*. Wilmette, IL Chiron.

Hartshorne, C. (1957) *Whitehead and Berdyaev: Is there Tragedy in God? The Journal of Religion* Vol. XXXVII, No 2.

Heidegger, M. (1986) *Sein Und Zeit*. Tuebingen: Max Niemeyer Verlag.

—— (1991) *Kant und das Problem der Metaphysik*. Frankfurt A.M.: Vittorio Klostermann.

Helminiak, D. A. (1996) *The Human Core of Spirituality*. New York: SUNY.
—— (1998) *Religion and the Human Sciences. An Approach via Spirituality*. New York: SUNY.
Hierotheos, Metropolitan of Nafpaktos (1994) *Orthodox Psychotherapy*. Levadia: Birth of the Theotokos Monastery.
—— (1999) *The Person in the Orthodox Tradition*. Levadia: Birth of the Theotokos Monastery.
Hillman, J. (1992) *Re-Visioning Psychology*. New York: Harper Perennial.
Homans, P. (1995) *Jung in Context. Modernity and the Making of a Psychology*. Chicago, London: University of Chicago Press.
Hossein Nasr, S. (1989) *Knowledge and the Sacred*. New York: SUNY Press.
Hycner, R. (1993) *Between Person and Person: Toward a Dialogical Gestalt Therapy*. New York: The Gestalt Journal Press.
—— & Jacobs, L. (1995) *The Healing Relationship in Gestalt Therapy. A Dialogic/Self Psychology Approach*. New York: The Gestalt Journal Press.
Jaffé, A. (1971) *The Myth of Meaning*. New York: Penguin Books.
Jakim, B. & Bird, R. (eds.) (1998) *On Spiritual Unity. A Slavophil Reader*. Hudson, NY: Lindisfarne Press.
Jaspers, K. (1985) *Psychologie der Weltanschauungen*. Muenchen: Serie Piper.
Jonas, H. (1934) *Gnosis und spätantiker Geist. Teil I. Die mythologische Gnosis. Mit einer Einleitung Zur Geschichte und Methodologie der Forschung*. Göttingen: Vandenhoeck & Ruprecht.
Jung, C. G.: Unless otherwise stated: *The Collected Works of C. G. Jung* (CW). Sir H. Read, M. Fordham, G. Adler and W. McGuire (eds.). London: Routledge & Kegan Paul (1953–1983).
Jung, C. G. (1902) *On the Psychology and Pathology of So-called Occult Phenomena*. CW 1.
—— (1912) 'New Paths in Psychology'. CW 7.
—— (1914) *Some Crucial Points in Psychoanalysis: A Correspondence Between Dr Jung and Dr Loy*. CW 4.
—— (1916/1917) *Prefaces to 'Collected Papers on Analytical Psychology'*. CW 4.
—— ([1916]1957) *The Transcendent Function*. CW 8.
—— (1921) *Psychological Types*. CW 6.
—— (1926/1946) *Analytical Psychology and Education*. CW 17.
—— (1928/1931) *Analytical Psychology and 'Weltanschauung'*. CW 8.
—— (1928) *The Relationship between the Ego and the Unconscious*. CW 7.
—— (1929) *Commentary on The Secret of the Golden Flower*. CW 13.
—— (1930–1931) *The Stages of Life*. CW 8.
—— (1931) *Basic Postulates of Analytical Psychology*. CW 8.
—— (1934) *The Development of Personality*. CW 17.
—— (1934/1954) *Archetypes and the Collective Unconscious*. CW 9i.
—— (1935a) *Principles of Practical Psychotherapy*. CW 16.
—— (1935b) *The Tavistock Lectures*. CW 18.
—— (1936) *The Concept of the Collective Unconscious*. CW 9i.
—— (1938) *Psychology and Religion*. CW 11.
—— (1939) *On the Psychogenesis of Schizophrenia*. CW 3.
—— (1940/1950) *Concerning Rebirth*. CW 9i.
—— (1942) *Paracelsus as a Spiritual Phenomenon*. CW 13.

—— (1942/1948) *A Psychological Approach to the Dogma of the Trinity*. CW 11.
—— (1943) *On the Psychology of the Unconscious*. CW 7.
—— (1943/1948) *The Spirit Mercurius*. CW 13.
—— (1944) *Psychology and Alchemy*. CW 12.
—— (1945/1948) *The Phenomenology of the Spirit in Fairy Tales*. CW 9i.
—— (1945/1954) *The Philosophical Tree*. CW 13.
—— (1946) *The Psychology of the Transference*. CW 16.
—— (1947/1954) *On the Nature of the Psyche*. CW 8.
—— (1950) *Foreword to the I Ching*. CW 11.
—— (1951) *Aion*. CW 9ii.
—— (1952) *Synchronicity: An Acausal Connecting Principle*. CW 8.
—— (1952/1967) *Answer to Job*. CW 11.
—— (1955) *On the Discourses of the Buddha*. CW 18.
—— (1955/1956) *Mysterium Coniunctionis*. CW 14.
—— (1956a) *Symbols of Transformation*. CW 5.
—— (1956b) *On the Discourses of the Buddha*. CW 18.
—— (1957a) *The Undiscovered Self*. CW 10.
—— (1957b) *Recent Thoughts on Schizophrenia*. CW3.
—— (1958a) *Flying Saucers: A Modern Myth of Things Seen in the Skies*. CW 10.
—— (1958b) *A Psychological View of Conscience*. CW 10.
—— (1959a) *Good and Evil in Analytical Psychology*. CW 10.
—— (1959b) *Introduction to Tony Wolff's 'Studies in Jungian Psychology'*. CW 10.
—— (1973) *Letters Vol 1*. London: Routledge & Kegan Paul, Ltd.
—— (1976) *Letters Vol 2*. London: Routledge & Kegan Paul, Ltd.
—— (1988) *Nietzsche's Zarathustra. Notes of the Seminar given in 1934–39 by C.G. Jung*. Jarrett, J.L. (ed.). Princeton: Princeton University Press.
—— (1990) *Man and His Symbols*. London: Arcana.
—— (1992) *Erinnerungen, Gedanken, Traeume*. Olten: Walter Verlag.
—— (1995) *Memories, Dreams, Reflections*. London: Fontana.
Jung, E. & von Franz, M. L. (1980) *Die Graalslegende in Psychologischer Sicht*. Freiburg I.B.: Walter Verlag.
Kant, I. (1971) *Kritik der Reinen Vernunft*. Hamburg: Felix Meiner Verlag.
—— (1974) *Kritik der Praktischen Vernunft. Grundlegung der Metaphysik der Sitten*. Frankfurt: Suhrkamp. (Quotations according to the original page numberings in the A and B versions of the first and second critiques.)
Kelly, J. N. D. (2003) *Early Christian Doctrines*. London: Continuum.
Kelly, S. (1993) *Individuation and the Absolute*. New York: Paulist Press.
Klein, P. (1976) *Die 'Kreative Freiheit' nach Nikolaj Berdjajew*. Regensburg: Verlag Friedrich Pustet.
Kobusch, T. (1997) *Die Entdeckung der Person: Metaphysik der Freiheit und Modernes Menschenbild*. Darmstadt: Wissenschaftliche Buchgesellschaft.
Koepgen, G. (1978) *Die Gnosis des Christentums*. Trier: Spee Verlag
Koslowsky, P. (1993) *Die Philosophie, Theologie und Gnosis Franz von Baaders*. Wien: Passagen Verlag.
—— (2003) *Philosophien der Offenbarung*. Paderborn: Schoeningh.
Koyre, A. (1929) *La Philosophie de Jacob Boehme*. Paris: Librairie Philosophique J. Vrin.
Kroner, R. (1977a) *Von Kant bis Hegel Vol 1*. Tuebingen: J.C.B. Mohr.

—— (1977b) *Von Kant bis Hegel Vol 2*. Tuebingen: J.C.B. Mohr.

Lammers, A. C. (1994) *In God's Shadow. The Collaboration of Victor White and C. G. Jung*. New York: Paulist Press.

—— & Cunningham, A. (eds.) (2007) *The Jung–White Letters*. London: Routledge.

Larchet, J. C. (2008) *Therapeutique des maladies spirituelles*. Paris: Les editions du cerf.

Lawrie, D. A. (1960) *Rebellious Prophet, A Life of Nicolai Berdyaev*. London: Victor Gollancz Ltd.

Leibnitz, G. W. (1982) *Vernunftprinzipien der Natur und der Gande: Monadologie*. Hamburg: Felix Meiner Verlag.

Leisegang, H. (1932) *Goethe's Denken*. Leipzig: Verlag Felix Meiner.

Lossky, N. O. (1952) *History of Russian Philosophy*. London: Henderson and Spalding.

Lossky, V. (1976) *The Mystical Theology of the Eastern Church*. Crestwood, NY: St Vladimir's Seminary Press.

—— (1978) *Orthodox Theology: An Introduction*. Crestwood, NY: St Valdimir's Seminary Press.

—— (2001) *In the Image and Likeness*. Crestwood, NY: St Vladimir's Seminary Press.

McGinn, B. (1991) *The Foundations of Christian Mysticism*. London: SCM Press.

McLachlan, J. M. (1992) *The Desire to be God, Freedom and the Other in Sartre and Berdyaev*. New York: Peter Lang.

McLean, A. (ed.) (1983) *The Paradoxical Emblems of D. A. Freher*. Edinburgh: Magnum Opus Hermetic Source Works No 16.

—— (ed.) (1991) *The 'Key' of Jacob Boehme. Magnum Opus Hermetic Sourceworks*. Grand Rapids: Phanes Press.

Mahnke, D. (1937) *Unendliche Sphaere und Allmittelpunkt, Beitraege zur Genealogie der mathematischen Mystik*. Deutsche Vierteljahresschrift fuer Literaturwissenschaft und Geistesgeschichte, Bd. 23. Halle: Max Niemeyer Verlag.

Maillard, C. (1993) *Du Plerome a l'Etoile. Les Sept Sermons aux Morts de Carl Gustav Jung*. Nancy: Presses Universitaires de Nancy.

Main, R. (2004) *The Rupture of Time: Synchronicity and Jung's Critique of Modern Culture*. Hove and New York: Brunner-Routledge.

Mantzaridis, G. I. (1984) *The Deification of Man*. Crestwood, NY: St Vladimir's Seminary Press.

Meerson, M. A. (1998) *The Trinity of Love in Modern Russian Theology*. Quincy: Franciscan Press.

Meier, C. A. (ed.) (2001) *The Pauli–Jung Letters*. London: Routledge.

Miller, J. C. (2004) *The Transcendent Function*. New York: SUNY.

Mounier, E. (2004) *Personalism*. Notre Dame, Indiana: University of Notre Dame Press.

Nagy, M. (1991) *Philosophical Issues in the Psychology of C. G. Jung*. New York: SUNY.

Neumann, E. (1954) *The Origins and History of Consciousness*. London: Routledge & Kegan Paul.

—— (1969) *Depth Psychology and a New Ethic*. London: Hodder and Stoughton.

—— (1971) *Amor and Psyche. The Psychic Development of the Feminine*. New York: Princeton University Press.

—— (1989) *Die Grosse Mutter. Eine Phaenomenologie der weiblichen Gestaltungen des Unbewussten*. Olten: Walter Verlag.
—— (2002) *The Child*. London: Karnac.
Nichols, A. (2005) *Wisdom from Above: A Primer in the Theology of Father Sergei Bulgakov*. Leominster: Gracewing.
Nietzsche, F. (1992) *Also sprach Zarathustra*. Stuttgart: Reclam.
Nucho, F. (1966) *Berdyaev's Philosophy: The Existential Paradox of Freedom and Necessity*. New York: Doubleday.
Otto, R. (1924) *Das Heilige*. Stuttgart: Verlag Friedrich Andreas Perthes.
Panikkar, R. (1993) *Trinitaet. Ueber das Zentrum menschlicher Erfahrung*. Kempten: Koesel.
—— (1998) *The Comsotheandric Experience*. New Delhi: Motilal Banarsidass Publishers.
Papadopoulos, R. (ed.) (2006) *The Handbook of Jungian Psychology*. London: Routledge.
—— & Saayman, G. S. (eds.) (1991) *Jung in Modern Perspective*. Bridgeport: Prism Press.
Pappe, H. O. (2006) Philosophical Anthropology. In *The Encyclopedia of Philosophy*. New York & London: Thompson Gale.
Perrin, J. M. & Thibon, G. (2003) *Simone Weil as We Knew Her*. London: Routledge.
Pfeffer, R. (1972) *Nietzsche, Disciple of Dionysos*. Lewisburg: Brucknell University Press.
Porret, E. (1944) *La Philosophie Chretienne en Russie: N. Berdiaeff*. Neuchâtel: Editions de la Baconniere.
Raff, J. (2000) *Jung and the Alchemical Imagination*. York Beach, Maine: Nicholas-Hays, Inc.
—— (2003) *The Wedding of Sophia*. Berwick, Maine: Nicholas-Hays, Inc.
Richardson, D. B. (1968) *Berdyaev's Philosophy of History*. The Hague: Martinus Nijhoff.
Ritter, J. (ed.) (1971–2004) *Historisches Worterbuch der Philosophie, Bd I-XII*. Darmstadt: Wissenschaftliche Buchgesellschaft.
Roessler, R. (1956) *Das Weltbild Nikolai Berdjajews*. Goettingen: Vanderhoek & Ruprecht.
Ryce-Menuhin, J. (1994) *Jung and the Monotheisms*. London, New York: Routledge.
Sakharov, N. V. (2002) *I Love Therefore I Am*. Crestwood, NY: St Vladimir's Seminary Press.
Samuels, A. (1985) *Jung and the Post-Jungians*. London: Routledge
——, Shorter, B. & Plaut F. (1986) *A Critical Dictionary of Jungian Analysis*. London: Routledge.
Sardello, R. (1995) *Love and the Soul: Creating a Future for the Earth*. New York: Harper Perennial.
Sborowitz, A. (1955) *Beziehung und Bestimmung*. Darmstadt: Wissenschaftliche Buchgesellschaft.
—— (1975) *Individuation und Glaube*. Darmstadt: Wissenschaftliche Buchgesellschaft.
—— & Michel, E. (eds.) (1979) *Der Leidende Mensch. Personale Psychotherapie in Anthropologischer Sicht*. Darmstadt: Wissenschaftliche Buchgesellschaft.
Scheler, M. (1930) *Die Stellung des Menschen im Kosmos*. Darmstadt: Otto Reichel Verlag.

—— (1954) *Philosophische Weltanschauung*. Bern: Francke Verlag.

—— (1973) *Formalism in Ethics and Non-Formal Ethics of Values*. Evanston: Northwestern University Press.

Schelling, F. W. J. (1990) *Philosophische Untersuchungen ueber das Wesen der Menschlichen Freiheit und die damit zusammenhaengenden Gegenstaende*. In *Schriften von 1806–1813*. Darmstadt: Wissenschaftliche Buchgesellschaft Darmstadt (cited according to the original page numbering).

Schiller, F. (1991) *Ueber die Aesthetische Erziehung des Menschen*. Stuttgart: Reclam.

Scholem, G. (1974) *Major Trends in Jewish Mysticism*. New York: Schocken Books.

Schulze, B. (1938) *Die Schau der Kirche bei Nikolai Berdiajew*. Rome: Orientalia Christiana Analecta 116.

Scott, W. (ed.) (1993) *Hermetica, the writings attributed to Hermes Trismegistos*. Bath: Solos Press.

Segal, R. A. (1992) *The Gnostic Jung*. London: Routledge.

Segundo, J. L. (1963) *Berdiaeff, Une Reflexion Chretienne sur la Personne*. Paris: Aubier.

Shamdasani, S. (2003) *Jung and the Making of Modern Psychology: The Dream of a Science*. Cambridge: Cambridge University Press.

Soloviev, V. (1965) *Deutsche Gesamtausgabe der Werke Bd. 6*. Muenchen: Erich Wewel Verlag.

—— (1978) *Kritik der Abstrakten Prinzipien, Vorlesungen ueber das Gottmenschentum*. In *Gesamtausgabe Bd. 1*. Muenchen: Erich Wewel Verlag.

—— (1996) *The Crisis of Western Philosophy: Against the Positivists*. Hudson, NY: Lindisfarne Press.

Spader, P. H. (2002) *Scheler's Ethical Personalism*. New York: Fordham University Press.

Spaemann, R. (1998) *Personen, Versuche ueber den Unterschied zwischen 'Etwas und 'Jemand'*. Stuttgart: Klett-Kotta.

Spidlik, T. (1986) *The Spirituality of the Christian East*. Kalamazoo, MI: Cistercian Publications.

—— (2002) *Die Russische Idee. Eine Andere Sicht des Menschen*. Wuerzburg: Verlag 'Der Christliche Osten'.

Staniloe, D. (2003) *Orthodox Spirituality*. South Canaan, PA: St Tikhon's Seminary Press.

Stein, M. (1983) *In Midlife*. Dallas, TX: Spring Publications.

—— (1986) *Jung's Treatment of Christianity*. Wilmette, IL: Chiron Publications.

—— (1993) *Solar Conscience, Lunar Conscience*. Wilmette, IL: Chiron Publications.

Taylor, C. (2005[1975]) *Hegel*. Cambridge: Cambridge University Press.

—— (1992) *The Sources of the Self: The Making of the Modern Identity*. Cambridge: Cambridge University Press.

Teilhard de Chardin, T. (1965) *The Phenomenon of Man*. London: Fontana Books.

Tillich, P. (1971) *Nikolai Berdiajew. Eine Geistesgeschichtliche Wuerdigung*. Gesammelte Werke Band XII. Stuttgart: Evangelisches Verlagswerk.

—— (1978) *Systematic Theology 1–3*. London: SCM Press.

—— (1980) *The Courage to Be*. New Haven & London: Yale University Press.

Trinick, J. (1955–1956) *N. Berdyaev and Human Creativity. The Eastern Churches Quarterly*, Vol. XI, 4.

—— (1957) *New Light on Nicolas Berdyaev. The Eastern Churches Quarterly*, Vol. XII, 2.

—— (1967) *The Fire-Tried Stone*. London: Stuart & Watkins, Ltd.

Trueb, H. (1962) *Heilung aus der Begegnung*. Stuttgart: Ernst Klett Verlag.

Turner, V. (1987) *Betwixt and Between: The liminal period in rites of passage*. In Mahdi, L. C., Foster, S., & Little, M. (eds.), *Betwixt and Between: Patterns of Masculine and Feminine Initiation*. La Salle, Il.: Open Court, pp. 3–19.

Ueberweg, F. (1924) *Grundriss der Geschichte der Philosophie, Vierter Teil*. Berlin: S. Mittler & Sohn.

Vallon, M. A. (1960) *An Apostle of Freedom: Life and Teachings of Nicolas Berdyaev*. London: Vision Press.

Versluis, A. (1994) *Theosophia. Hidden Dimensions of Christianity*. Hudson, NY: Lindisfarne Press.

—— (1999) *Wisdom's Children: A Christian Esoteric Tradition*. New York SUNY Press.

—— (2000) *Wisdom's Book: The Sophia Anthology*. St Paul, MN: Paragon House.

von Franz, M. L. (1965) The Idea of the Macro- and Microcosm in the Light of Jungian Psychology, *Ambix* XIII, 1.

—— (1980a) *Alchemy*. Toronto: Inner City Books.

—— (1980b) *Projection and Recollection in Jungian Psychology*. London: Open Court.

—— (1995) *Aurora Consurgens (Mysterium Coniunctionis, Ergaenzungsband)*. Solothurn: Walter Verlag.

—— (1998) *C. G. Jung, His Myth in Our Time*. Toronto: Inner City Books.

von Hartmann, E. (1923) *Die Philosophie des Unbewussten (1, 2, 3 Teil)* Leipzig: Alfred Kroener Verlag.

Ware, K. (2002) 'How Do We Enter the Heart?'. In Cutsinger, J. S. (ed.), *Paths to the Heart. Sufism and the Christian East*. Bloomington, Indiana: World Wisdom Press, pp. 2–23.

Washburn, M. (1994) *Transpersonal Psychology in Psychoanalytic Perspective*. New York: SUNY Press.

Wehr, G. (1977) *Jacob Boehme in Selbstzeugnissen und Bilddokumenten*. Hamburg: Rowohlt Verlag.

—— (1988) *C. G. Jung. Leben, Werk, Wirkung*. Zuerich: Diogenes Verlag.

—— (1990) *The Mystical Marriage*. Wellingborough: Crucible, Aquarian Press.

White, V. (1955) *Kinds of Opposites*. In *Studien zur Analytischen Psychologie C. G. Jungs*. Zuerich: Rascher Verlag, pp. 141–150.

—— (1960a) *Soul and Psyche*. London: Collins and Harvill Press

—— (1960b) *God and the Unconscious*. London: Fontana Books.

Wilber, K. (1996) *Eye to Eye, The Quest for a New Paradigm, Ch 7: The Pre/Trans Fallacy*. Boston: Shambala.

Winnicott, D. W. (2001) *Playing and Reality*. London: Routledge

Wittgenstein, L. (1958) *Philosophical Investigations*. Oxford: Basil Blackwell.

Yannaras, C. (1991) *Elements of Faith*. Edinburgh: T&T Clarke.

Zenkovsky, V. (2003) *A History of Russian Philosophy*. London: Routledge.

Index

Note: Page references in *italic* refer to figures.